D1320626

HOW ENGLISH BECAME THE GLOBAL LANGUAGE

How English Became the Global Language

David Northrup

palgrave
macmillan

HOW ENGLISH BECAME THE GLOBAL LANGUAGE
Copyright © David Northrup, 2013.

First published in 2013 by
PALGRAVE MACMILLAN®
in the United States—a division of St. Martin's Press LLC,
175 Fifth Avenue, New York, NY 10010.

Where this book is distributed in the UK, Europe and the rest of the world,
this is by Palgrave Macmillan, a division of Macmillan Publishers Limited,
registered in England, company number 785998, of Houndmills,
Basingstoke, Hampshire RG21 6XS.

Palgrave Macmillan is the global academic imprint of the above companies
and has companies and representatives throughout the world.

Palgrave® and Macmillan® are registered trademarks in the United States,
the United Kingdom, Europe and other countries.

ISBN: 978–1–137–30306–6 (paperback)
ISBN: 978–1–137–30305–9 (hardcover)

Library of Congress Cataloging-in-Publication Data

Northrup, David, 1941– author
    How English Became the Global Language / David Northrup.
        pages cm
    Includes index.
    ISBN 978–1–137–30305–9 (alk. paper)—
    ISBN 978–1–137–30306–6 (alk. paper)
        1. English language—Globalization. 2. English language—History.
    3. English language—Foreign countries. 4. English language—Variation.
    I. Title.

PE1073.N67 2013
420.9—dc23   2012038715

A catalogue record of the book is available from the British Library.

Design by Newgen Imaging Systems (P) Ltd., Chennai, India.

First edition: March 2013

10 9 8 7 6 5 4 3 2 1

Contents

Figures and Tables

Figure

Tables

Abbreviations

As is fitting in a work of world history, international abbreviations are used in dates in preference to the abbreviations AD and BC that are common in Western countries.

BCE   Before the Common Era
CE   Of the Common Era

Two much used texts are cited in abbreviated form:

CHEL   *The Cambridge History of the English Language*
OCEL   *The Oxford Companion to the English Language*

Other shortened terms:

EIC   East India Company
INC   Indian National Congress
MNC   multinational corporation
SPCK   Society for the Promotion of Christian Knowledge
SWAPO   Southwest African Peoples Organization
UK   The United Kingdom of Great Britain and
               Northern Ireland
US   The United States of America

Preface and Acknowledgments

History reveals itself most clearly in retrospect. Only now that English has emerged as the first global language is it possible to explain how that happened. As recounted in this book, the expansion of English occurred over two millennia, gaining ground very slowly in the British Isles, at a more rapid pace in North America, and then globally with growing speed in recent decades. Although a few farsighted souls had predicted more than two centuries ago that English would become the global language, no master plan controlled these historical events. The complex and rather improbable story had many separate strands, which this account attempts to untangle.

Similarly, how I came to write that history is a long, improbable tale, which seems coherent only in retrospect. Let me mention three particular experiences that have prodded me to undertake this project. The earliest experience was in the mid 1960s when I spent two years teaching the English language (and teaching other subjects in English) in a new secondary school in rural Nigeria, shortly after the country's independence from Britain. In addition to learning about Africa and teaching English as a Second Language, I was forced to contemplate the global power dynamics involved in postcolonial relations. At a reception in the new parliament building in Lagos, the Nigerian Minister of Education (dressed in Muslim robes) had welcomed my Peace Corps group as "the new missionaries." He explained that, like the Christian missionaries in the colonial period, we volunteers (and our British and Canadian counterparts) were helping to expand Nigeria's school system, but that we differed from the old missionaries who used schools to spread Christianity, in that we had no other agenda we wished to leave behind. I was disconcerted by the comparison to missionaries, which caused me to wonder whether I might be an unsuspecting agent of American cultural imperialism. Such doubts diminished once I met fellow teachers, primarily Nigerians along with an Indian from Kerala and an Irishman. All of us would be teaching in English, the language the new government of Nigeria mandated in all schools beyond the early primary years. My doubts vanished as I got to know my students, very few of whose parents had more than a few years of formal education, and I sensed their eagerness to master a curriculum in English that would be their ticket to personal success and a vital part of Nigerian national unification. It was clear that, whatever American agendas existed, Nigerian aspirations were in control.

Many years later, when a professor of African history at Boston College, I attended a conference on global English where a professor asserted that English was destroying the languages of India. The speaker was herself Indian-born, but her proposition seemed quite improbable to me on the basis my experiences in Nigeria, where the local languages seemed to suffer no loss of vitality as a result of English becoming the national language and the language of education. I resolved to investigate further.

A third experience came from teaching a large course on the history of globalization. Because cultural globalization seemed to provide a more interesting narrative, I paid particular attention to that theme, though English got little attention until the last couple of lectures. Still, teaching that course forced me to expand my knowledge of changes taking place around the world in many aspects of culture.

In giving thanks to those who have aided me in completing this vast and complex project, first mention should go to my students, in Nigeria, Tuskegee Institute, and Boston College. The scholars from whom I have learned so much in the course of this research deserve acknowledgment almost as high on the list. In addition, I must give credit of a different sort to Boston College for generously providing me with two sabbatical leaves so that I could conduct the research. I also want to thank the Boston College Libraries, whose excellent collections, online resources, and interlibrary loans enabled me to pursue countless arcane lines of research.

As the project developed, I was accorded the opportunity to present parts of my research to academic audiences, for whose valuable feedback I am most grateful. Special thanks goes to Felipe Fernandez-Armesto for inviting me to give my first presentation to the Pearson Prentice-Hall Seminar in Global History at Tufts University. I also wish to thank Laura Doyle, professor of English at the University of Massachusetts, Amherst, for organizing my presentation to the faculty there. Finally, I am grateful to the graduate students in the Department of History at Boston College for giving me the chance to try out my ideas on them.

A couple of brave souls even agreed to read some of the manuscript. Special thanks for their comments and kind recommendations go to Professor Patrick Manning of the University of Pittsburgh, Professor Salikoko Mufwene of the University of Chicago, and my old friend John F. Thornton. My wife Nancy Northrup carefully read the entire manuscript and suggested numerous corrections and improvements. I also wish to express my appreciation to my former colleagues Alan Rogers and Kalpana R. Seshadri for their comments on individual chapters. Needless to say, the author is entirely to blame for the flaws that remain.

Chapter 1

Introduction: Disciplines, Perspectives, Debates, and Overview

One cannot travel far these days without being struck by the pervasiveness of English as the world's second language. Signage in the Seoul subway is in English as well as Korean. Along Venice's Grand Canal the vaporetto stops are announced in Italian and English. Announcements in airports everywhere and on planes are routinely in English, and, less obvious to passengers, English is used exclusively for communication between cockpits and control towers. At international meetings English is often the default language or even the only language. In many fields of knowledge publication is primarily in English. Other languages continue to be vital locally, nationally, and regionally, but for the first time in history a single language has become the global lingua franca.

Explaining how English became the first global language is an exercise in world history, not just because it includes most parts of the world but even more because the story of the English language's spread intersects with so many other themes of world history. Before examining the chronology and causation of English's march to globalism, this study will highlight here in this chapter some of the larger themes and controversies linked to global English. Three topics are examined: how a historian's treatment of English differs from other professions' approaches, how the rise of global English has gotten mixed up with debates about the origins of the modern world, and what the story of English has in common with the spread of other languages.

How Different Disciplines Tell the History of English

Accounts of the spread of English differ widely, as do the disciplines their authors come from. On the shelves of a good library there is no shortage of volumes offering histories of English, but even a casual examination of their contents reveals great differences in their approaches and emphases. One of the most familiar approaches is the survey of English literature. Traditionally academic English departments have been less concerned with how common folk spoke than with the development of a literary canon and "good English usage." An introductory literature survey might begin with a nod to the Old English of *Beowulf* and the Middle English of Chaucer's *Canterbury Tales* before settling into the Modern English of Elizabethan and Jacobean drama and the King James Bible. The course is likely to give considerable attention to the subsequent development of poetry, plays, and the novel. Most surveys include examples of American literature, and, of late, it has become common for such courses to include at least a passing nod to literary works written in English by Asian, African, and perhaps Caribbean authors. Even if it acknowledges that literature in English has recently become global, the survey's central emphasis would still be on the development of British and American writers. Nor does the recent tendency to include writers whose voices are more vernacular than literary substantially alter the survey's emphasis on identifying an essentially hierarchical structure of literary achievement, though who deserves to be where in the canon is hotly debated. The many tensions in the traditional survey have led some to prefer national approaches in English and to adopt subnational selection criteria, including gender, that are more inclusive and less judgmental. Of course, such partitioning comes at the expense of a sense of the unity and continuity of a literary tradition.[1]

In contrast, professional linguists are inclined to concentrate on spoken English rather than on proper usage and literature. They analyze regional and class variations within the language, recounting movements overseas and the divergence of the mother tongue into distinct "Englishes." Other scholars of language, whose training may not be exclusively in linguistics, share this emphasis on diversity. For example, a recent collection of studies on English as an International Language (EIL) begins with the observation:

> A major part of the literature concerned with English as a world language is characterized, in dealing with its subject matter, by tensions between opposites—unity vs diversity, monocentrism vs pluricentrism, native speaker vs non-native speaker, description vs perception, centre vs periphery, and so on. The present volume is no exception.[2]

The standard texts on the history of English tend to share this approach. For example, a recent text, *English—One Tongue, Many Voices,* traces the growth, spread, and variations of English, with an emphasis on native speakers in Britain, the United States, and individual British settler colonies. Part of the final chapter examines "world English" and globalization but also gives great attention to the diversity of "Englishes."[3]

Studying the diversity of English has many virtues, but explaining the astonishing linguistic unity that is at the basis of the global spread of English is not well served by the approaches cited above, even in those works attempting to balance the themes of linguistic unity and diversity. Unlike Latin, which evolved into a family of distinct and mutually incomprehensible languages, English has remained a single language even as it has spread throughout the British Isles, across the Atlantic, and around the world. As chapter 2 recounts, this outcome would have surprised some language specialists in the early United States who expected the American language would diverge from British English to the point of mutual incomprehension within a century. Instead of following the pattern exemplified by Latin's divergence into a family of Romance languages, English not only kept great uniformity as it spread but also, in recent years, the differences between British and American English seem to be diminishing. The high degree of literacy among North Americans seems to account for the changes in their spoken language from affecting their familiarity with the ancestral language. The recent convergent trend seems to be partly the result of greater travel and even more because broadcast media have made stay-at-home English speakers on both sides of the Atlantic more familiar with each other's usages and pronunciations. As a result, the variations in the speech of native English speakers today are smaller than they were within the British Isles at the time of Chaucer or Shakespeare.

There is no denying that quite distinct class and regional variations of English exist, such as Cockney or Brooklynese, but these variations are minor in importance and are being eradicated by educators' efforts to teach children standard English. However interesting the variations in English can be, the uniformity and mutual intelligibility of English across its major variations is the far more remarkable phenomenon. The globalization of English has reinforced the trend toward uniformity, countering natural tendencies pulling in the opposite direction. Some fields, such as communication, business, and science, have long used specialized vocabularies to sustain intelligibility in English (a topic discussed in chapter 4). Schools where English is most people's first language attempt to teach a national version; those promoting English as a second language are likely to adopt an international standard.

Another reality is that many native speakers and some nonnative speakers of English are readily able to move between different registers of English. For example, West Indians seeking to communicate outside their own communities would not normally use the Caribbean English Creole they speak at home, since other English speakers could not easily understand them. They might do better using Caribbean English, a more standard version, but a Jamaican trying to publish a scientific paper, close a deal with a South Asian colleague, or speak at the United Nations would most likely use the standard English taught in Jamaican schools, even though only a small proportion of the population of Jamaica or other parts of the Commonwealth Caribbean use it as their normal spoken language.[4]

Global English, as the term is used in this study, therefore, is not the sum of all the different forms of English spoken on Earth. Rather it is the more standardized form of English used for global communication. Variations within global English certainly exist, but they are constrained by the need to be intelligible. A polished Jamaican or Nigerian diplomat addressing the UN General Assembly may have a distinctive accent but not one that others find difficult to understand. Written global English is even more standardized, since pronunciation doesn't affect it, except in novels trying to capture local speech patterns. Who speaks global English? It seems reasonable to say that most native speakers do, even if some of them (as in Jamaica) might have to make a special effort to do so. American, British, Canadian, and Australian English, as used by reasonable well-educated people, are not the same, but they function efficiently as part of global English. Global English, most commonly in its American or British form, is what students throughout the world are struggling to master, even if some are more successful than others. Some champions of vernacular speech will find this an undemocratic definition of global and they will be right. The key point is not that everyone needs to speak English with an Oxford or Ivy-League accent, but that, as a practical matter a global language needs to be fairly standard to be understood. At this stage in the process, there are good historical reasons why British and American usages greatly influence the global standard for intelligibility. That may change, for global English is an ongoing and self-corrective process. Even as the diversity of accents in English grows, the quality of English spoken and written by nonnative speakers is greatly improving.

How would a historian approach the history of English? The answer must be speculative because, to a very large extent, professional historians leave language histories to other specialists, much as they leave art history to art departments, and music history to music departments. As a result, histories of English have been written by people trained in other disciplines.[5] In venturing into a field so neglected by historians, I have naturally learned much from these other disciplines. At the same time, I have found it necessary to reconceptualize their visions, question some of their conclusions, and draw upon a lifetime of professional and personal experience. I have had to venture into many new subjects (such as the history of education, science, and business, as well as of language), while at the same time drawing upon many things I have learned as a peripatetic student of history. As an undergraduate I studied history in the United States and in France. My graduate training started in medieval European history, and then moved on to the new field of African history, which included considerable interdisciplinary training. Because of Africa's connections to the rest of the world, in the course of my teaching and research I was drawn to expand my perspective to include African connections across the Atlantic, with Europe, and in the Indian Ocean. In time, my interest in intercontinental relations led me into another new field, world history. I have written other monographs with international scopes, coauthored a college textbook in world history, and served as president of the World History Association.

I cannot speak for all historians, but this historian brings three perspectives to this topic: global, historical, and objective.

1. This is a world history, both in the scope of its coverage and in its concern with the process of global interaction that underlies the spread of the English language. It is, therefore, part of the larger history of globalization. The study argues that English became the global language quite recently, but it also argues that that improbable outcome has a long and complex history. Globalization involves standardizing some things, whether language, Internet protocols, or credit cards, yet, contrary to what some believe, it is not primarily a process of homogenization but of interaction and exchange.[6]
2. As a professional historian, I feel it necessary to see the spread of English as part of larger historical changes, including the growth and decline of languages, empires, and other interactions. Historians need to do more than relate what happened; we need to explain why things happened. Examining cause and effect includes using comparative histories to highlight patterns and divergences, as well as paying close attention to agency. How English became the first global language is a long and complicated story in which powerful forces from above were met with even more powerful agencies from below.
3. This is a pragmatic study not an ideological one. Its concern is to explain why things happen, not to score points off them. This is neither a celebration of global English and globalization nor a manifesto against their spread. It attempts to balance accounts of English as a first language and as a second language, avoiding the tendency in some circles to give native speakers ownership of the language or to poke fun at others' accents. In examining the role of Western imperialism and hegemonies in globalizing English, this study seeks to avoid both moralizing about these events and underestimating the

abilities of non-Westerners to make informed decisions about their own best interests.

The next section of this chapter situates the history of English's spread in the larger history of language development, expansion, and decline. In becoming the first global language, English has done something unique, but in so doing it has followed many familiar paths. The final section concerns the prominent coterie of intellectuals who denounce both globalization and global English on moral grounds. Even if they had their facts straight, such critics are tilting at windmills, since they neither understand the larger processes nor the personal choices being made by individuals around the world. More fundamentally, globalization and global English are not moral options, they are facts of contemporary life.

An Introduction to Language History

Was there originally a single language? Many ancient traditions supposed so, and for a time scholars attempted to identify it. European scholars in the 1600s suspected that Ge'ez, the ancient language of Ethiopia, or Chinese might be the parent language. Although few historical linguists these days believe that a primal language can be identified, if it ever existed, the story in the Hebrew Bible, that the people of Babel were punished for trying to build a tower to heaven by God creating new languages, captures the fundamental reality that languages have tended to increase in number throughout most of human history. These language changes resulted from small populations spreading across the continents and losing touch with each other rather than because of divine intervention. Over time, due to the natural changes in pronunciation, vocabulary, and syntax that all languages undergo, ancestrally linked languages became mutually unintelligible. The process of language multiplication was sped by the fact that, until recent times, human communities were small and isolated. As recently as five hundred years ago, there were perhaps 80 million humans, 1 percent of the population today. Any distance greater than could be walked in a couple of days was a huge impediment to the regular contacts that sustaining a common tongue necessitates. The continuous spread of small communities of humans to the far corners of the planet thus produced an incomprehensible babble of speech.[7]

Even though disasters, migrations, and other circumstances caused some languages to become extinct, by a thousand years ago, the number of languages in use had grown to ten or fifteen thousand. Despite the many changes since then, the linguistic footprint of the past is still clearly evident in the geographical distribution of languages. The greatest language diversity exists in regions where communities were traditionally small and isolated. Today, half of all living languages are spoken in Africa and the Pacific islands, which together contain only about 13 percent of the world's population. The small island communities of the Pacific region developed the largest ratio of languages to population. Within that region, the greatest concentration of languages (over 800 still surviving) is on the single island of Papua New Guinea, where traditionally most people lived in small communities isolated in deep, narrow valleys. In contrast, regions that have experienced greater political and economic integration display the opposite characteristic. Asia has over 60 percent of the world's population but is home to only a third of the Earth's living languages. Similarly, Europe has 12 percent of the globe's population but just 3 percent of its living languages. In both continents political and cultural amalgamation during the past several centuries has also marginalized many languages or driven them to extinction. This result can also be seen in the Americas, where European colonization, immigration, and national policies have produced a situation where 95 percent of the inhabitants speak a European language as their first language, yet nearly a thousand pre-Columbian languages are still in use.[8]

For most of human history, the multiplication of languages was part of a much larger process of cultural fragmentation and differentiation. In some places the process was countered by the rise of territorial empires, the growth of long-distant trade, and the spread of religions. Overall, however, divergent tendencies were dominant in most parts of the world until about a thousand years ago. Then, forces promoting convergence and consolidation began to overtake the forces for divergence. The expansion of long-distance trade both over land and by sea, the rise of new empires and expansion of old ones, and the spread of Islam and Christianity were forces that united people and promoted the growth of literacy. Although many new languages have evolved during the past millennium, the dominant trends have been the expansion of some languages and the decline or disappearance of others. By one estimate, the number of languages in use in the world fell by half between 1000 and 2000 CE, and by 2050 the number is likely to fall by half again.[9]

Although there have been many specific causes of this phenomenon, there is a remarkable correlation between the decline in spoken languages and the rapid growth of human population. Humans numbered about 400 million in 1000 CE; today there are over 7 billion of us. Both language and population changes have accelerated in the past century and are still accelerating. While there is an understandable tendency to describe the loss of living languages as a decrease in the cultural heritage of humankind and, at least until recently, an understandable tendency to celebrate population increases, since they were associated with falling infant and childhood mortality, improving public health, and rising longevity, the challenge is to understand the intimate connections between the two, to understand that in many ways they are part of a package.

Population growth fed expanding contacts among humans in all regions and corners of the world. Growing commercial and cultural contacts, in turn, reduced isolation and encouraged people to learn languages that were dominant in regional trade or carried cultural prestige. Adding a new language did not automatically delete an old one, but as a practical matter over time some smaller languages lost ground to the rising ones. A notable example of this great convergence in medieval times was spread of the Arabic language in tandem with the spread of Islam and the growth of trade. Arab conquests before 1000 CE had spread Arab rule around the Mediterranean Sea. In the wake of these conquests and the opportunities they created, most people in the Middle East and North Africa chose to adopt Islam and learn the Arabic language. Arabic and Islam were also expanding beyond that heartland in the centuries before 1500, becoming important in the trading cities around the Indian Ocean and in the commercially powerful Sudanic empires below the Sahara. Trade not conquest was the primary agent for spreading Islam and Arabic in these new lands.

A second difference was that below the Sahara and from Iran eastward Arabic did not displace or marginalize other languages to the degree it had done in the Middle East and North Africa. People continued to speak traditional vernaculars, while using Arabic for religious and commercial purposes. The Moroccan scholar Ibn Battuta visited the four corners of the Islamic world in the 1300s, receiving hospitality from fellow Muslims and conversing with them in Arabic. Outside of the Arabized heartland, as Ibn Battuta learned, educated Muslims could still read and understand Arabic, much as educated Christians in medieval Europe learned Latin or Greek. In the empire of Mali south of the Sahara, for example, Ibn Battuta praised the Koranic schools where boys learned to read and recite the entire Koran in Arabic, though they still spoke other languages outside of school.[10]

This layering of languages—local vernaculars, regional trading languages, and languages of learning—was a characteristic feature of most interacting parts of the medieval world. When the young Marco Polo of Venice followed the Silk Road in the 1200s, he seems to have used medieval Persian as far as China. Marco and his older relatives were able to travel so far (and return safely) because the Mongols had united most of Asia in largest empire the world had ever seen. But this remarkable political convergence was not replicated linguistically in the way the conquests of Alexander the Great had promoted the spread of Greek and Hellenism in the Middle East in the fourth century BCE. Instead, the "Mongol court conducted business in a Babel of tongues; there were scribes for Mongolian, Arabic, Persian, Uighur, Tangut, Chinese, and Tibetan, among other languages." Nor had the Ming Dynasty's epic voyages in the early 1400s across southern Asia done much to spread Chinese. Zheng He, a Chinese Muslim, headed the Ming expeditions, which included interpreters fluent in Arabic and other languages.[11]

The scope and pace of commercial and cultural expansion picked up in the late 1400s when the Portuguese and the Spanish began to spread their languages, trade, and religion along the African coast, across the Atlantic, and around Indian Ocean. The Dutch joined the Iberians in the 1600s, and mostly after 1700 the French and English added their resources. In the process, the languages of these European trading states gained importance in different parts of the world. As had been the case during Islamic expansion, changes came slowly and gradually. The spread of European languages was quite limited in Asia and Africa, in part because the number of Europeans was miniscule, a factor that inclined them to learn important local languages. When the Portuguese explorer Tomé Pires reached the important trading city of Malacca that dominated the strait that connected the Indian Ocean to Southeast and East Asia, he recorded the use of 84 languages in the markets. Four officials administered the large foreign merchant communities: one official for the very numerous Gujarati, one for other Indians and Burmese, one for other Southeast Asians, and one for the Chinese and Japanese.[12] The Dutch often used Portuguese to communicate and were more adept than other Europeans in learning local languages. In the Americas, European populations remained small before the 1800s. The growth and spread of English speakers in the Americas will be taken up in chapter 2, but it is worth noting here that even in "Spanish" America the Spanish language was less important than indigenous languages throughout the colonial period. As late as 1810, only a quarter of the population spoke Spanish at home, the rest speaking indigenous American languages. At the time of the American conquest of the Philippines, only a ninth of the population spoke Spanish, despite centuries of Spanish control.[13]

Elsewhere in the Americas the number of European immigrants remained small before 1800. Well into the nineteenth century most new immigrants and new languages came from Africa, as the result of the Atlantic slave trade.[14] As already noted, sub-Saharan Africa had great linguistic diversity. Even though some regions of the Americas imported slaves from particular regions of Africa, over time those regions often shifted and new languages were introduced. An indication of the linguistic diversity that could exist among enslaved Africans comes from the small British colony of Sierra Leone, where 160 distinct African languages were counted among those liberated from slave ships and resettled there, mostly between 1815 and 1835, by the British Anti-slave Trade Patrol.[15] Such multiplicity of mutually incomprehensible languages (not dialects) also characterized most slave communities in the Americas. Although modern research has demonstrated the importance of African cultures and languages in colonial America, the long-term linguistic outcomes followed several different patterns, as African cultures and languages competed and blended with each other as well as with European and indigenous ones. These patterns included the use of an African language, of a hybrid creole language, or the use of the European colonial language.

African languages survived in the memories of African-born slaves who left their homes as adults, whether or not they were landed with any others who spoke those languages. Many Africans knew more than one African language and many acquired a new language while awaiting shipment in Africa. Where there was a high concentration of people who knew dialects of a single African language, that language might be widely used among them in the Americas and be passed on to the next generation. This was true of some Angolan languages in early Brazil and the Yoruba language in nineteenth-century Cuba and Brazil. Africans from other regions might learn such dominant languages. In some instances, important African languages survived over many generations as secret languages used in religious contexts.[16]

Even where African languages survived and evolved in slave communities, they could not be used to communicate with overseers or with Africans who did not share that language. So a second language was needed. In some places, the working language of the plantation community was a creole or pidgin language, that is, a simplified version of the colonial language, with words derived from African languages mixed in.[17] The earliest known pidgin was "language of São Tomé," named for the Portuguese-controlled island of São Tomé in the Gulf of Guinea that served as a collection center for slaves purchased from ports along the neighboring African mainland. While awaiting shipment on the island, the enslaved Africans learned a simplified version of Portuguese combined with African usages. This pidgin also came to be used as a lingua franca for trading between coastal Africans and the Portuguese. By the 1700s it would morph into West African Pidgin English, retaining some Portuguese terms.[18] In South America, Spanish Jesuits used the "language of São Tomé" to communicate with slaves arriving in Cartagena. Another such language developed in the Anglo West Indies, today known as Caribbean English Creole. The vocabulary of the language derived principally from the "regional dialects of the English-speaking colonists" along with "[l]arge numbers of lexical items and phrases of West African provenance," while the grammar of the Creole also showed "patterns...characteristic of West African languages."[19] Connections between Caribbean English Creole and West African Pidgin English are not clearly documented, but the two languages have many similarities, raising interesting (if irresolvable) questions about to what extents enslaved Africans had learned the pidgin before sailing away, during the Middle Passage, or in the Americas. If West Africans had some familiarity with the pidgin before arriving it the Americas, it would help to explain how a version of the pidgin was transmitted so quickly from English-owned slaves in Surinam (introduced in 1651 from Barbados and withdrawn two decades later) to the newly imported Dutch-owned slaves, has ended up as the "national" language of Surinam (Dutch is the official language). Another creole known as Gullah developed in the low country of the Carolinas, which has many features in common with other Atlantic pidgins/creoles and which also seems to have been introduced from Barbados in the later 1700s.[20] It should be clear that these hybrid languages derived from interactions between different language groups with inputs from both sides. Newcomers picked up the language from the established population.

Creole languages were not characteristic of all slave communities. In many places a version of the colonial language became the lingua franca, although this could take some time to become the norm. Versions of Portuguese, Spanish, and French were widely used in the Americas and a fairly standard English became the plantation language the Chesapeake region of British North America. Two different circumstances promoted the dominance of a European language: slaves' receptivity to acculturation efforts and the proportion of African-born slaves. In Portuguese, Spanish, and French colonies, most slaves complied with authorities' encouragements to become Christians and to acculturate in other ways. In these Catholic colonies, the colonial language was used in prayers, preaching, and going to confession. However, no such acculturation was promoted in the Protestant English colonies. Slave owners in the British West Indies generally prohibited any instruction in Christianity until missionaries forced the issue during the last decades of slavery there. Patterns in British North America were more varied.

The proportion of slaves born in the Americas was probably a more important factor promoting their use of the colonial language. The resources available to acculturate African-born slaves were meager, but those born in the Americas learned the colonial culture and language naturally as children. As long as the slave trade continued, the majority of slaves in Brazil and the West Indies were African-born, because their exploitation by the booming plantation economies and high mortality prevented slaves from increasing their numbers naturally. In contrast, Spanish America received few slaves from Africa after 1650, so most people of African ancestry there were locally born and acculturated. As chapter 2 explores in more detail, the majority of slaves in mainland North America became American-born in the eighteenth century, first in the Chesapeake and later in the Carolinas. This Americanization was accelerated in part by a higher reproductive rate among slaves there than was common elsewhere in the Americas, a factor related to more balanced sex ratios, comparatively better nutrition, and healthier environments. The interruption of transatlantic trade during the period of the American Revolution also kept the numbers of slaves from Africa much lower in North America than in the West Indies and Brazil. Overall, the number of African slaves who entered what became the United States was about the same as went to the island of Barbados. After the termination of slave imports in 1808, slave populations in the United States grew rapidly through natural increase and became English-speaking.[21]

While these three different linguistic outcomes are reasonably clear, the underlying documentation of slaves' speech is spotty, depending primarily on small samples and observations by outsiders that are often contradictory or ambiguous. For these reasons different interpretations are possible and controversies abound. Nevertheless, the observations of two distinguished anthropologists in the field seem judicious and reasonable in emphasizing the agency of slaves in their cultural development. Sidney Mintz and Richard Price argue:

> All slaves must have found themselves accepting, albeit out of necessity, countless "foreign" cultural practices, and this implied a gradual remodeling of their own traditional ways of doing many things.

> For most...a new social and cultural world must have taken prece-
> dence rather quickly over...a nostalgia for their homelands.[22]

A key issue is whether such cultural changes were largely coerced by
slave masters or were the outcome of a more multifaceted process.
A related question is whether the "foreign" practices mentioned
by Mintz and Price were uniquely or even primarily European.
Support for a multifaceted interpretation comes most clearly from
cases where the issue of slavery can be removed. In some places
in the Americas there were stable communities of runaway slaves,
also known as maroon communities. One of the most famous
maroon communities was Palmares in seventeenth-century Brazil.
Although the inhabitants are described as using many terms of
Angolan origin, this was not a recreation of an African homeland.
Rather, in accommodating a population of different African origins
and including many born in Brazil, there was a more generalized
Africanization of social and political life blended with elements of
Christianity.[23] A much better documented example of the societies uprooted Africans created is the large community of Africans
liberated from slave ships in the 1800s and resettled in the British
colony of Sierra Leone in West Africa. There too, Africans from
scores of different places in Africa and speaking scores of different languages underwent a dual process of re-Africanization that
involved many alterations in identity and practices, while simultaneously the majority embraced Christianity, schooling, and English
as a lingua franca.[24] These examples reinforce the idea that cultural and linguistic change in slave communities in the Americas
was complex and multifaceted. Even though circumstances would
have made the outcomes on slave plantations somewhat different,
the best evidence suggests that the dynamics of the underlying
processes were similar.

This brief survey of language spread has touched on many patterns that later chapters will elaborate on in tracing the spread of
English. In the first place language expansion has been a common feature of the past millennium, initially of Asian languages
then European and African ones. Several became international
languages, though only English has become the global language.
Second, language expansion had many different effects on other

languages. In most cases, people added the spreading language to the linguistic mix already in existence, but in some cases of great intensity the spreading language displaced or marginalized the others, a process that took many generations in the case of Arabic in the Middle East just as it did with Iberian languages in the Americas. The chapters in this book will show that the spread of English out of its homeland roughly mirrored the earlier spread of Arabic and other trans-regional languages. In some places English displaced other languages, but overall it has spread as a lingua franca, a language people learn in addition to other ones rather than instead of them. Third, languages rarely spread by being imposed on a conquered population, for such a process would be both difficult to achieve and unpopular among the subject people. (Soviet leaders imposed the learning of Russian in Eastern European schools, but the use of Russian lasted little longer than the Soviet empire.) The more usual process is that individuals choose to learn a language because it becomes necessary or useful for them to do so.

Debates about Modern History

The phenomenon of a global language sometimes gets caught up in political and intellectual debates about the larger transformations of contemporary times. The extraordinary economic, political, social, and cultural changes of the past 60 or 70 years often get amalgamated under simple rubrics such as "modernization," "development," and most recently "globalization." Such bundles are convenient but are not always useful in analyzing the complex factors they combine. As a result, the resulting debates can produce more heat than light, and the vitriolic language used by different schools suggests that the controversies may be less about the facts than about the ideological positions being taken (or denounced). The literature on particular issues can be more enlightening than the broad generalizations, but too often layers of polemics obscure the salient facts.

A central point of contention in interpreting the modern world is the role of Western imperialism, because colonial rule was so intimately associated with the spread of global economies, communications, education systems, and values that are commonly termed "modern." It is also true that Western empires were over-turned because they exemplified forms of exploitation, discrimination, and authoritarian political control that became incompatible with "modern" values. The challenge is to interpret colonialism and its legacies in ways that take these contradictions into account. One way, characteristic of the rhetoric of the high colonial era, was a narrative that justified imperialism and its excesses as part of a "civilizing mission." In this telling, Western empire building was driven by high-minded motives, such as ending slavery and other cruel practices, and bringing the redeeming qualities of "Christianity, commerce, and civilization" to the benighted, whether they wanted them or not. The missionary travels of David Livingstone could be cited in favor of this explanatory approach. Where profit and other financial advantages were too obvious to ignore, as in the life of Cecil Rhodes, this narrative stressed that the empire builders were making good use of the colonies' natural resources and labor for the general progress of humanity, because those living in these areas had proven too ignorant or lazy to do themselves. Both are very one-sided stories: Europeans took actions; other folks were acted upon.

That familiar "white-man's-burden" approach has no real defenders today. The world has moved on. In its naive formulation it is not just bad ethics; it is bad history because it is so incomplete. The rise of opposition to European colonial empires, especially by the colonial "subjects," did much to bring the missing pieces of the story to light: exploitation, discrimination, and the values and wishes of the colonized people. The complexities of modern empires preclude simplistic interpretations. As with their ancient imperial predecessors (whose legacies ironically are generally seen as beneficial), modern empires need to be evaluated using a balanced approach that not only distinguishes good from bad but also distinguishes short-term and long-term results. Most of all, a balanced interpretation needs to take into account the actions of the colonized as well as of the colonizers.

Some recent histories of the modern world have made useful contributions to explaining the complexities of inequality in the modern world, such as the interesting and ambitious works by David Landes on the roots of inequality and Niall Ferguson on the realities of empires.[25] A more complex and revisionist insights have come from scholars trained in "area-studies" programs that were created in the wake of decolonization. Historians trained in the languages and cultures of Asia or Africa do not assume that Westerners were all-powerful or in full control even in their colonies. Rather, they insist that local circumstances and actions of local people need to be given greater explanatory importance, which has the effect of reducing the centrality of Western power and control in the colonial narrative.[26] As someone trained in African area studies and history, I am particularly appreciative of such balanced narratives, and that approach is evident in chapter 3 and elsewhere in this study.

A third approach to explaining imperialism and global transformations has been particularly influential among English and linguistics academics. It goes under different names and has different emphases, but antipathy to colonialism is a common feature. In a curious way, anticolonialist scholars tend to have a great deal in common with the white-man's-burden school: they exaggerate Western power and agency, while understating (or ignoring) the input and agency of non-Western people. They also tend to make rather rigid moralistic judgments that invariably condemn (rather than praise) Western imperialism. Just as Marx said he turned Hegel's dialectical idealism on its head, the anticolonialists turn the white-man's-burden narrative on its head. The result is that Westerners remain the dominant actors in the narrative, only instead of being the good guys, they are the villains. The victims in this telling may suffer, but they seem powerless to act and thus cannot play roles in the narrative.[27]

An influential example of this mind-set is the critique of "Orientalism" by Edward Said, who charges that Westerners in the age of imperialism held a simplistic and one-dimensional stereotype of Asians. Although partly true, Said's analysis is also full of distortions, misrepresentations, and omissions. Rather than trying to analyze the difficulties of achieving cross-cultural understanding, he seems content with demonizing Westerners for what is a common human failing. Area-studies specialists can also point out that the colonized were just as likely to hold distorted images of the Western colonizers as vice versa. In the end, as his critics point out, Said's perspective appears as simplistic and one-dimensional as the one he is attacking.[28] Many in this school carry forward this one-sided perspective in analyzing (and condemning) postcolonial globalization, producing simplistic and unbalanced conclusions. In the process of denouncing the West, they seem to end up opposing most forms of global cultural interaction.

This ideological debate about the trends of the modern world helps to explain some of the sharp polarization that exists about the spread of English. On the one hand, many scholars welcome the rise of English as the global language as "the cultural vehicle *par excellence* of modernity."[29] On the other hand, there are those who denounce the rise of English as the global language as an act of malevolent cultural imperialism. An early and influential attack on the spread of English was *Linguistic Imperialism,* by Robert Phillipson, then a lecturer in English and language pedagogy in Denmark. Phillipson makes a number of valid points: the English language has been spread by British and American imperialism, by large Anglo-American investments in teaching English, and by private language schools, especially ones that are profit-making, that is, capitalist. He acknowledges that the efforts to teach English came in response to a growing demand for instruction, but, in a classic disempowerment of people, he insists that "the demand was largely created and orchestrated by the Centre, and reflected Centre perceptions of what was needed at the Periphery." (His "Centre" is post-1945 British governments, aided and abetted by the United States and others.) He further asserts that, in the absence of such government policies promoting English, "other languages would have had much more scope for development," as was the case in "many European countries over the past century."[30] Phillipson seems doubly blinded: first by an obsessive focus on Anglophone countries' "hegemony" that makes their actions paramount by definition and second by an assumption that those in the non-Western "periphery" are blind to their own self-interest and easily manipulated. To an extent, writing when he was in the early 1990s, his blindness is understandable. He could not foresee the incredible "flattening" of world relations that would take place as the West's relative economic, political, and cultural dominance declined and as power centers in other parts of the world surged forward.

A similar group of critics charge that English is a "killer language," that is, a language that is killing off other languages.

Those believing in this "linguicide" theory combine the fact that the number of spoken languages in the world is shrinking with the assumption that this is primarily due to the spread of English.[31] The link is likewise based on an exaggerated assumption of Western power and Western malevolence, as well as a cavalier disregard of the facts. Some charges are more specific. In a more recent work, Phillipson adopts such extreme language and argues that, by becoming the dominant second language in Europe, English has endangered the survival of other European languages.[32] Despite its shaky factual basis, this theory has become influential not just among academics but also by activists concerned with language loss by slaves, Native Americans, and other indigenous peoples.

Fortunately, some prominent language specialists have challenged the factual basis of these assumptions. Robert B. Kaplan, a professor of applied linguistics at the University of Southern California for 35 years, denies that English's global reach has been the product of conspiratorial or imperialistic movements. Rather, he argues that its spread has been "the outcome of the coincidence of accidental forces." In the face of strident criticism, Kaplan, retreated to a more nuanced position:

> It would be unreasonable to assert that the introduction of English is exclusively responsible for wide-spread language death…At the same time, it would be unreasonable to claim that the huge English-language teaching activities of the English-speaking nations have played no role in language death. The role they have played is, however, not well understood.

More outspoken has been Salikoko S. Mufwene, a distinguished professor of linguistics at the University of Chicago, born in the Democratic Republic of Congo. In the first place, Mufwene argues, "Languages do not kill languages; speakers do," and, he insists, the motivations and circumstances behind individuals' decisions need to be taken seriously. Second, while he accepts that language endangerment is a serious problem, he rejects the common belief that it is largely caused by political or cultural forces alone. Rather, it is primarily the result of economic ones: people choosing to survive by learning a new language rather than saving an ancestral one. Third, Mufwene explicitly rejects the notion that the spread of English has endangered or is endangering all "indigenous" languages around the world. Both charges, he argues, are based on a misreading of the facts and a failure to appreciate "the naturalness of egalitarian multilingualism as a way of life in many parts of the world," including most of his home continent.[33]

This is not the place to pursue this heated controversy, since this book is not about whether the spread of English is good or bad, but about how it became the global language. It is worth concluding this discussion by reiterating four factual points. First, as Mufwene argues, multilingualism has long been commonplace. Since the rise of cities, empires and world religions, it has been exceptional for people to use the same language at home, in the marketplace, and in places of worship. As literacy spread, few wrote in the language they chatted in, and those that did used a more formal register. Even now, in much of the world many people do not employ the same language they speak at home when they to go to school, browse the Internet, or enjoy television and radio broadcasts. Rather, it is all-purpose languages that are the novelty. Europe was the first part of the world to promote all-purpose national languages. English, as we will see in chapter 2, gained this function earlier than most, at least among the urban elites. Standard French and Spanish languages developed a bit later, the language of the royal court trickling downward slowly through the social strata. At the time of the French Revolution only 20 percent of French citizens spoke French. Modern Italian (Tuscan) and (High) German became national languages in countries that were united only in the last third of the 1800s. In all of them, as in most of the rest of the world, standardization of languages has been product of mass education and mass media.

Second, from early times historical change has produced the death of old languages and the birth of new ones. The acceleration of change and population increase during the past millennium reversed the patterns of languages proliferating at a faster rate than they became extinct. Westerners did not originate this trend, but European expansion did create settler colonies where the imperial languages gradually gained ascendancy. However, in nonsettler colonies, the inhabitants most commonly added a European language to their repertoire without abandoning their traditional language.

Third, the endangerment and extinction of languages comes primarily from competition with national and regional languages, not with international ones. Most countries that have come into existence in recent decades incorporate populations that speak dozens or even hundreds of different languages. Their efforts to promote one national language, or more than one, have put pressure on the smallest language groups. As a result, many endangered languages will disappear as improved communication convinces people to learn the more widely used languages but many other languages will endure.

Fourth, the number of languages facing extinction is large but the number of people who are abandoning an ancestral language is small. Nigeria, for example, has over 500 spoken languages, of which some 19 are listed as endangered, that is, at risk of disappearing. In the year 2000, the largest of the endangered Nigerian languages had about 100 speakers; most had fewer than 50; the smallest had fewer than 10. Half of Nigeria's 140 million people speak versions of just six indigenous languages, all of which are gaining speakers.[34] Worldwide there are about 500 languages experiencing significant growth. Thousands of others are holding their own.

Overview

The story of English recounted in this book reflects the chronological divisions of the language's spread. By about 1900, native speakers of English were concentrated in the British Isles and North America with modest numbers of other speakers in the rest of the world. The Second World War marked an important tipping point, as the massive political, military, economic, and intellectual weight of the United States made knowing English a high priority. The third and most important tipping point occurred about 1990, when a series of events in different places started a massive stampede in favor of knowing English.

Chapter 2 sketches the long, slow history of English in the British Isles. The account of the language's evolution there is necessarily brief, because the complexity and obscurity of what occurred have little relevance to English's *global* spread. Three themes, however, do have greater relevance to the story that follows. The first is that conquest and hegemony were important in establishing English in Britain, just as these factors would be elsewhere. Old English developed from the Scandinavian invaders' languages, just as Middle English emerged in the wake of the Norman Conquest, but the key factor is the population gradually chose to adopt the language. Second, the spread of literacy and schooling among a portion of the population and education's gradual downward penetration did much to standardize both oral and written English, which is likewise a theme to be seen elsewhere. Third, English displaced the indigenous Celtic languages in Wales and Ireland for the most part quite late and with surprising speed. Here literacy and schools were major agents, as was the cultural hegemony of English. Hegemony was not new and it did not dictate a single outcome. Belatedly linguistic nationalists moved to reverse the trend by requiring Irish and Welch to be taught in schools, but so far such efforts have been little more successful in getting people to use these languages than the compulsory study of Latin in earlier generations was in getting people to speak or write that language. The chapter argues that English expanded when it did and as swiftly as it did, less because of external political or cultural pressures than because ordinary people in nineteenth-century Wales and Ireland chose to learn English to advance themselves. The agency of individuals is a recurring theme in later chapters.

Chapter 3 follows the movement of English-speaking and non-English-speaking settlers in North America. The language gradually gained a toehold in English settlements along the Atlantic seaboard, winning over some settlers with other mother tongues and expanding in annexed Dutch, French, and Spanish territories. Except among the well educated, most settlers became monolingual, but two immigrant groups, French-speakers in Quebec and many Germans in the mid-Atlantic states hung on to their mother tongues, as did many indigenous people. Some in the new American republic predicted (correctly) that the English language would soon spread across the continent; some of them believing (incorrectly) that, in the process, American English would break as decisively with its British ancestor as the 13 colonies had broken politically with their mother country. The nineteenth century brought two overlapping changes on a massive scale and of momentous importance. The first was the political and cultural westward expansion that absorbed the modest sized populations already present there. The second was the incorporation of unprecedented numbers of new immigrants, some English-speaking but many others bringing new languages that flourished and then faded. For reasons explored in the chapter, the latter immigrant populations on the whole became bilingual in the second generation and effectively monolingual in the third generation. North America thus provides a major example of many people shifting to English as their primary language, a circumstance that would be repeated on other settler colonies but not in nonsettler colonies.

Chapter 4 looks at the new overseas empires the British and Americans created by the early 1900s. The biggest empire was Britain's and its largest colony by far was British India. The British also added a significant presence in sub-Saharan Africa, including some densely populated territories, such as Nigeria, today the most populous African country. For the most part British rulers had very modest ambitions and resources for spreading English, especially in contrast to American efforts in the Philippines. The chapter argues two other groups were ultimately more important than colonial governments in increasing the use of English in these overseas empires. The first were missionaries, including many from Ireland. The second were the indigenous inhabitants who came to see the many advantages of sending their children to schools that taught English. Learning English began modestly among influential elites and overtime spread downward in society, in some places with amazing speed. A few Asians and Africans founded their own schools, some got into the few government schools, but most flocked to mission schools and partly funded their rapid expansion. When independence came to the colonies after the Second World War, nationalist leaders made different language choices in different places. Most British colonies in Africa established English as their countries' official language and the language of higher education. Responding to different circumstances, leaders in South Asia set up a transition period during which English would give way to an indigenous language—a policy that stumbled in the face of massive internal opposition.

Chapter 5 describes the expansion of English usage in different cultural spheres, largely in the twentieth century. For a time other languages were also gaining ground in international spheres. The process blended pragmatism and hegemony. As in South Asian countries, where English was used, it was often seen initially as a temporary stopgap not a permanent solution. The growing field of international relations and organizations provides one arena in which to trace the measured use of English, showing how the flood of new nations joining the United Nations after the Second World War encouraged the use of English in that body and elsewhere. Another internationalizing area was science. There the expansion of scientific writing by English speakers gradually displaced German and other languages, especially after the Second World War. The spread of English as an international language of commerce, finance, and other business arenas has been of special importance because of the massive growth of international trade around the world in the postwar decades. A more rarefied specialty where English grew was as a global literary language, used by authors seeking to reach a national audience in countries where English was not the first language of many but was the common language of the educated. Finally, the chapter takes a tour of the growing pervasiveness of English in transnational popular culture, reflecting both the hegemony of Anglo-American pop culture in the second half of the twentieth century and the utility of English as a transnational language.

The final chapter explores a series of tipping points, occurring more or less simultaneously about 1990, that moved English from just one of the major international languages to the singular global language. One of these was the creation of the World Wide Web that, with the availability of affordable computers and high-speed Internet connections, joined humanity in the largest information and communication network ever to exist. Although the dominance of English as the primary language of the Internet has not persisted, it still gave the language a boost. The second event was the collapse of the Soviet Union and its domination of Eastern Europe. Free to pursue national interests and new international connections, Eastern Europeans abandoned Russian for English and made English the primary common language of the European Union and of Europeans generally. Meanwhile a similar spread of English as the global lingua franca was occurring throughout Asia and notably in China where the reforms initiated by Chairman Deng Xiaoping promoted learning English. Other parts of East,

Southeast, and South Asia joined the trend. Finally, the need to learn English as a foreign language was accelerated by a massive increase in higher education enrollment, while the popularity of study-abroad programs also promoted English as the language of international education.

Chapter 2

The Language of the British Isles

In a sense, the English language is not indigenous to the British Isles. Over the better part of a millennium, waves of outside invaders displaced Britain's indigenous Celtic speakers and introduced a new West Germanic language. The languages of the Anglo-Saxon and Danish conquerors gradually morphed into Old English, a language best known from early epic *Beowulf,* which is quite unintelligible to modern English speakers.[1] French-speaking invaders from Normandy in 1066 prodded the transformation of Old English into Middle English, the language of *The Canterbury Tales* by Geoffrey Chaucer (c. 1343–1400), which modern readers find very tough slogging. Finally, various forces promoted the development of Modern English, in its early modern form the language of Shakespeare and the King James Bible, which most modern English speakers find familiar, if a bit quaint. This in brief is the first part of the story of English, the story of how the languages of the conquerors changed and spread in England and lowland Scotland, which is examined in somewhat greater detail in the first part of this chapter.

There is a second and much more contested part of the story in the British Isles: how Modern English belatedly became dominant into those areas where Celtic languages long had survived and remained strong, an event that occurred in Wales and Ireland only in the nineteenth century. For some that transformation can only be explained as the result of conquests or at least an insidious cultural imperialism. As will be seen later in this chapter, the actual process was more complex and less one-sided.

Evidence for the early history of the English language is fragmentary and interpreting it requires very specialized knowledge. Even then, many knotty issues cannot be resolved. Those who relish the details may ponder the impressive scholarship on morphology, syntax, vocabulary, dialects, and literary usage summarized in the thick volumes of the *Cambridge History of the English Language*. For the purposes of this book, a quicker overview of the early spread of English will be sufficient to expose the themes that have relevance to the global spread of the language. Rather than linguistics, the focus of this account is cultural power, often political, sometimes literary, and at times educational. Rather than the enormous diversity of languages and dialects that existed (and still exist to an extent), this account emphasizes how English acquired cultural prestige that gave it staying power.

Invaders

When Julius Caesar invaded Britain for the second time, in July of 54 BCE, the inhabitants of southern England were Celtic-speaking pastoralists. Over the next four centuries Roman rule expanded and introduced many notable material and cultural changes that survived Roman rule. After the collapse of the Western Roman Empire, the "Romance" languages that derived from Latin gradually became the common speech of Gaul, Iberia, and other former parts of the Empire. In Britain the story was different: the withdrawal of the Roman legions in the early 400s CE left a power vacuum that soon attracted a series of ferocious invasions by different Germanic peoples. The first waves are conventionally identified, following the eighth-century history of Venerable Bede, as the Angles, Saxons, and Jutes, though these invaders were more diverse than those three names suggest.[2] Indeed, spoken languages elsewhere in Europe (and other parts of the world) in this period would have exhibited considerable variation over even small distances. As for the indigenous British Celts, little is known for sure, except that the invasions pushed many of them westward and northward into what became known as the Celtic Fringe (or Edge): Wales, Cornwall, parts of Scotland, and the Isle of Man. The conquering Germanic peoples occupied the vacated lands, which their leaders worked to develop into kingdoms. Over time, the Germanic dialects the invaders brought coalesced into the first version of English, know as Anglo-Saxon or Old English. The completeness of the cultural displacement of the prior Celtic population may be seen in the fact that only a dozen Celtic words were absorbed into Anglo-Saxon English during that period and, aside from some place-names and other geographical terms, almost nothing of Celtic derivation now remains in general English usage.[3]

Although Roman roads, towns, and buildings crumbled in the wake of the invasions, some elements of Roman cultural and intellectual heritage managed to endure. Among the few who were literate, Latin remained the language of writing. The scribes of the courts and the clerics of the church admired its prestige and literary standards even after their own command of Latin fell short of classical norms. The fact that the Christian Church continued to use Latin in its liturgies and administration was important in preserving the literacy and learning the Romans had introduced.

Christianity had come to Britain during the Roman period, and the number of adherents to the faith grew in the sixth and seventh centuries. The dispatch of St. Augustine and a band of 50 other monks from Rome in 597 began the slow ascendancy of Christian beliefs and practices. Augustine soon persuaded King Æthelbert of Kent to become a Christian, and Augustine was rewarded by being made the first archbishop of Canterbury. The separate appearance of the Irish preacher Aiden in 635 helped speed the process of Christianization. The church introduced new words into English to describe its beliefs and practices (angel, mass, priest) and other words came through Latin from Greek (martyr, presbyter, monk, psalm) and Hebrew (Sabbath). Ironically, English adopted words the old religion for the two major Christian feasts (Easter, Yule).

Venerable Bede's *Ecclesiastical History of the English People*, completed about 731, observes that five nations were present in Britain at that time: "the English, Britons [Welsh], Scots, Picts [northern Scots], and Latins, each in its own peculiar dialect." Of these languages only Latin was used for writing and clerics like Bede were the major practitioners of that craft. Though written in Latin, Bede's *History* provides the earliest clues about the speech of the Germanic invaders, based on some 6,000 personal and place-names he recorded, along with 14 lines of poetry. This evidence appears to derive from usage in the northern areas of settlement (Northumbria).[4]

A second wave of Germanic invaders swept into Britain during the centuries after 750. These were the Vikings, including the Danes or Norsemen (who also gave their name to Normandy). By 850, the Danes' occupation of the middle part of England had been greatly destructive of the political centralization and learning underway in Northumbria. However, Alfred, king (871–99) of the West Saxon kingdom of Wessex, rallied enough allies to halt the Danes' expansion in 878 and secure a delimitation of the Danes' land from the Anglo-Saxons'. Although the settlement was essentially a political one, Alfred used language as a defining cultural characteristic of his expanded realm. Even though the Danes spoke a closely related language, Alfred used the English language to strengthen popular support and facilitate the incorporation of the new people into his kingdom. Despite the political and linguistic demarcation between the two kingdoms, over time English borrowed many Danish loan words.[5]

Even before halting the Danes' advance, Alfred had been strengthening the cultural unity of his kingdom by rebuilding the monasteries and schools. He promoted the use of English as the language of instruction and oversaw the translation of important Latin texts into English, including Bede's *Ecclesiastical History of the English People*. Alfred's justification for these translations is clearly stated in his own writing: Latin was known to too few. Alfred undertook some translation himself:

> When I remembered how knowledge of Latin had formerly decayed throughout England, and yet many knew how to read English writing, then I began among the other various and manifold cares of this kingdom to translate into English the book that is called in Latin Pastoralis.[6]

Alfred is referring to the manual written by Pope Gregory the Great (590–604) on the duties of bishops, better known in English as *Pastoral Care,* and he says he sent a copy of his translation to every bishopric in England. The translations were part of Alfred's vision that freeborn young men, who could afford it, should be trained to read in English first and afterwards, circumstances permitting, to read Latin. In his translation projects, Alfred was inspired by the promotion of learning underway in the Frankish court since the beginning of the century and he was aided and advised by clerics brought from continental Europe. The sweeping educational program he envisioned had limited success in the short run, but his promotion of English-language writing and learning foreshadowed future trends.[7]

The political vicissitudes of Anglo-Saxon England and the efforts at political unification through conquest and defensive alliance may help us to imagine what was taking place linguistically, which is otherwise very inadequately documented. Some indigenous Britons were incorporated as slaves, but over time the Anglo-Saxon speech became dominant, much as the masters' languages would on slave plantation in the Americas (see chapter 1). As in the early Anglo-Saxon kingdoms, the spoken dialects of the various waves of newer invaders were far from uniform and were highly mutable. Early regional kingdoms seem to have approximated dialect blocs, but, of course, war and trade also promoted linguistic borrowings. The centralized political and ecclesiastical institutions encouraged language standardization. Alfred's translations suggest that a common (or preferred) form of English was intelligible across dialectical boundaries.

Contacts across the borders with the Danish kingdoms and with new invaders and conquerors also introduced important changes in the spoken languages. Hundreds of new words from the Danish language (Old Norse or Old Icelandic) entered Old English, usually without displacing their Anglo-Saxon equivalents. The Danish settlers also were affected by the speech of their Anglo-Saxon subjects and over time many of them became English speakers. However, few of the early Scandinavian loan words survived the transition into Middle English.[8]

Viking raids continued during the reigns of Alfred's successors, both from the continent and from their bases in York and Ireland, but these were generally withstood. However, beginning just before 1000 a great new wave of Danish (Viking) invaders was more successful. With broad support, the Viking leader Canute made himself king of England in 1016 (as well as of Norway and Denmark), ruling the greatest territorial expanse in Britain since Roman times. Canute's English kingdom built upon the political and linguistic foundations laid over the previous century and a half by the Anglo-Saxon kings.

Just after this new Danish power peaked, another foreign invasion altered the political and linguistic landscape. In 1066, people descended from Vikings who had earlier conquered Normandy and become French-speaking conquered both the Anglo-Saxons and the Danes. Their leader, since known as William the Conqueror, took his oath as ruler of England in the three languages then of note: Norman French, the new language of the court and administration; Latin, still used by the courts, the church, and scholars; and Old English, the spoken language of the common people and the least prestigious of the three. At first, anyone aspiring to success needed to master Norman French along with Latin, the language in which the Normans issued official documents. The older tradition of issuing documents in the vernacular fell into abeyance for two centuries. Under Norman rule, many French words entered the English language, far more than had earlier been borrowed from Latin and Danish. Despite its lack of prestige, English remained numerically dominant as the language of ordinary people and showed great staying power. French would not be a "killer language."[9]

In the long run, however, it was the language of the conquered not the conquerors that prevailed. Except at the highest circles, Norman officials found it necessary to use English to communicate with their subjects. English also gained ground in the royal court after the Normans lost their territory in France in 1204. That trend reached a decisive point four decades later when the king of France insisted that no one could be loyal to him and to the Norman rulers of England. In 1258, English barons forced King Henry III to renounce his claims to territories in France and to expel the French-speaking officers he had appointed. These Provisions of Oxford were promulgated in English, the first official document issued in English in a century and a half. From then, the trend to English grew. As *The Story of English* puts it, "At the end of the thirteenth century, Edward I, who was very conscious of his Englishness, whipped up patriotic feeling against the king of France, declaring that it was 'his detestable purpose, which God forbid, to wipe out the English tongue.'" During the course of the fourteenth century English was commonly spoken and/or written in the government of London, Parliament, and the royal court. In 1362, English replaced French and Latin in Parliament and the courts of law. The linguistic threat to English was decisively removed by the long Anglo-French conflict known as the Hundred Years War (1337–1454), which shattered the ambitions of both French and English kings to have possessions on both sides of the English Channel.[10]

During the period of Norman rule, Old English evolved into Middle English, a form of which is preserved in the writings of Geoffrey Chaucer. Chaucer's language would have great influence on literary style, but oral English in this period lacked the uniformity and regularities of grammar and pronunciation of modern languages, since speech varied considerably across England to the point that people in one locality might find the language of someone from another odd or even unintelligible. Such oral diversity was less of a problem than it seems since most people never went far from home, and those who did, such as merchants and other itinerants, learned to understand the dialectical differences. Linguists have distinguished five speech areas: Northern, East and West Midlands, Southern, and Kentish, though there was much variation within each group as well. Clearly, many things had to change before one can safely speak of a single English language, recognizable across regions and classes.[11]

Modern English

During the 1500s two gradual transformations were underway in English. The first was a growing standardization of the language, especially in its written form; the second was the vernacular's growing use in literary, legal, and ecclesiastical circles. Both were promoted by the spread of printing and of schools. Standardization and prestige made it easier for the English language to spread both within the British Isles and overseas.

In earlier times, the persistence of oral English among the illiterate masses had maintained the language, but local dialects might vary considerably. From the late 1400s, greater standardization of written and spoken English worked its way downward from the upper levels of society. The most important contribution to standardizing English came from the printing press, which produced multiple identical copies of printed literary and religious works. William Caxton, retired diplomat and merchant, had introduced the first printing press to England in 1476, setting up shop within the precincts of Westminster Abbey in London and selling copies of literary works as well as compositions of his own. His decision to employ the form of English used in London in his printed works had momentous effects. On the one hand, it promoted the London dialect as the proper form of English, while, on the other, it promoted some of the oddities of spelling that abound in English. Nevertheless, speech and spelling continued to vary quite a bit, even among the literary elite. Across England differences in vocabulary could be marked. In a well-known anecdote, Claxton told of a London traveler in search of eggs in a provincial locale who needed to ask for "eyren" to be understood.[12]

Caxton also published works in Middle English and Latin. He printed the first edition of Chaucer's *Canterbury Tales* in 1478. Before then, *The Canterbury Tales* had circulated in handwritten manuscripts (of which 83 survive) among the literate of the upper strata of the royal court as well as among some merchant and middle-class families. Variations in the text abounded due to copying errors and emendations. Indeed, Caxton published a second version of the *Tales* in 1483, based on a variant manuscript. As printed works multiplied rapidly in England after 1500, many more people had access to this work, especially among the sizeable literate population of London. Even some rural people of modest standing acquired a copy. In 1484, a tenant farmer named John Boren is known to have possessed a copy of Chaucer's *Tales*.[13]

The spread of printed English helped to erode Latin's dominance. For more than a millennium, the English had regarded Latin as the superior tongue for literary expression, legal precision, and divine worship. Indeed, Renaissance humanism had rejuvenated and enhanced the use of Latin. Nevertheless, an explosion of new writing in English during the Elizabethan and Tudor-Stuart period fed the presses and expanded the vocabulary. Shakespeare alone coined hundreds of words, many of which remain in use today. Philosophers and scientists coined other new words to translate Latin and Greek terms. In all, the English language added between 10,000 and 25,000 new words during the half century between the 1580s and 1630s. Expanding English vocabulary encouraged the publication of new dictionaries that explained "hard words," beginning with Robert Cawdrey's *Table Alphabeticall* of 1604. It also encouraged some folks to imagine that the English language might gain a broader audience in the future. In *Logonomia Anglica,* an English grammar written in Latin, the scholar Alexander Gill in 1619 boasted, "Since in the beginning all men's lips were identical, and there existed but one language, it would indeed be desirable to unify the speech of all peoples in one universal vocabulary; and were human ingenuity to attempt this, certainly no more suitable language than English could be found."[14]

During the Reformation, efforts at "Englishing" were extended to the Bible and to liturgical services, though at first the vernacular movement had progressed more slowly in Britain than on the continent. After King Henry VIII's break with Rome, however, English displaced Latin in ecclesiastical usage. Printing put the new translation of the Bible produced under King James I (1603–25) into churches and private hands. The translators of the King James Bible (or Authorized Version) adopted a middle path between transliterating biblical terms from Latin and Greek and seeking out approximations in the common speech, which sought to make its translation both intelligible to the common people and an accurate rendering of the original languages. Over time this translation would have powerful impacts on both literary and spoken English.[15]

As will be seen in later sections of this study, schools have played major roles both in teaching English and in standardizing English usage. Schools were certainly a third factor (after vernacularism and printing) in the standardization of English in early modern England, but less so there than in other parts of the British Isles before 1900. In the sixteenth century, the majority of English people were illiterate, although half of adult Londoners may have been able to read. Printed religious books and other works responded to this growing literacy and encouraged its further spread. Despite their promotion of Scripture in the vernacular, Anglicans were far from being in the forefront of European Protestantism's promotion of literacy. It was the English Puritans' push for vernacular reading that had much more to do with the growth of literacy. By 1750, it might cautiously be estimated that

about half of English women were literate (compared to 10 percent a century earlier), and literacy among men had gone from less
than a third to two-thirds. Literacy rates advanced little over the
next century.[16]

Literacy in England spread by fits and starts. Historian David
Cressy usefully argues that, in contrast to its modern growth, the
reasons for rising literacy rates in early modern England had much
more do to with "pull" factors (people taking initiatives to advance
themselves) than with "push" factors (mandates and encourage-
ment from above).[17] The distinction between "push" and "pull"
factors, long common in migration studies, will be used in other
places in this book, not just in describing the factors involved in
literacy acquisition but also in language acquisition. In general,
compulsory education became an important "push" factor only
quite recently. The "pull" felt and acted upon by individuals can
be harder to document, but it seems to have been a more critical
factor in explaining the spread of the English language.

Secular as well as religious forces lay behind the standardization efforts in England taking place in the later 1700s and 1800s.
In general, forms of speech prized by the educated classes were
becoming normative. Differences in regional and class usage did
not disappear, but after 1650 nonstandard speech was increasingly stigmatized. Whether or not Samuel Johnson intended his
Dictionary of the English Language (1755) to be descriptive of
good usage or prescriptive of it can be debated, but many believed
that the *Dictionary* defined the best usage and sought to imi-
tate it, just as the *Oxford English Dictionary* (1928) would do for
later generations. There is no doubt that Johnson's patron, Lord
Chesterfield, was intent on reforming the language, lamenting
"the state of anarchy" into which English had fallen and calling
for the *Dictionary* to establish "[g]ood order and authority."[18] By
the early 1800s, printed guides to proper speech and writing had
become commonplace, as were newspapers, magazines, and novels
that appealed to a popular audience. While the speech of the better
sort of Londoner remained normative, some reformers sought to
elevate the social norm by references to the "King's English" (first
used by Thomas Wilson in 1553) or (in an early twentieth-century
formulation) the "English spoken by a simple, unaffected young
Englishman like the Prince of Wales."[19]

By the nineteenth century, the English language was in position to spread both in the British Isles and overseas. It had been a long process. Introduced by conquest and settlement, English had taken root in England, survived further invasions, enlarged its vocabulary, and became more standardized as well as more capable of literary and learned expression. The growing use of print, an accepted standard of usage, and formal education had provided a model for consolidation at home as well as for expansion elsewhere. Some of that expansion was already underway by 1800 within Britain and in overseas colonies, but the scale of enlargement lay in the future. As in England, themes of conquest, cultural hegemony, and individual self-interest would prove important in the language's spread, but the pace would be much faster. Both the "push" from above and the "pull" from below would shape the outcomes. The next section of this chapter examines the process in the British Isles, while the following two chapters look at the spread of English in North America, Asia, and Africa.

English in Scotland, Wales, and Ireland

In 1500 four Celtic languages were spoken in the British Isles: Cornish, Welsh, Irish Gaelic, and Scottish Gaelic. Cornish remained widely spoken and written in southwestern England (Cornwall) during first half of the sixteenth century; thereafter it lost ground steadily to English. By 1602, a *Survey of Cornwall* reported that "most of the inhabitants can speak no word of Cornish, but very few are ignorant of the English [language]." The last known fluent speaker died in 1777.[20] The other Celtic languages endured longer but also lost considerable ground to English, especially from the mid-1800s in the case of Welsh and Irish.

The spread of English in Scotland is in some ways a story similar to its spread in England. The early Celtic speech had been dispersed by Germanic invaders, and Scottish English was then influenced by the prestige of the education and literature of England (London). In the Middle Ages, the linguistic situation in Scotland was complex:

Six languages were in regular use. *British* or *Brythonic*...a Celtic language akin to Welsh...*Gaelic,* the majority language, a Celtic language originating in Ireland; *Inglis,* a variety of Northern English spoken in the Lowlands, and later known as *Scots; Norn,* a form of Norse spoken in the Northern Isles, Western Isles, and the adjacent mainland; *Norman French* among the Normanized nobility; and *Latin* as an ecclesiastical, academic, and legal language.[21]

By the 1400s, Norman French disappeared, Gaelic was in decline (except in the Western Isles and parts of the Highlands), and Scots had largely displaced Gaelic in the Lowlands. From 1424 the Acts of Scottish Parliaments were recorded in Scots. Many educated Scotsmen of the late 1400s considered Scots simply a dialect of English, as the older name *Inglis* suggested. Many today also consider the language a variation of English, but political and cultural nationalists ardently support efforts to reestablish Scots as a separate (i.e., non-English) language, an issue that lies beyond the scope of this study.[22]

As in Cornwall, the situation was changing rapidly by the early modern period. Scots, which had seen great literary success in the 1400s and 1500s was losing ground among the elite and expanding middle class, who favored the new English of the south as more prestigious way of speaking and writing. They admired the excellence of the southern English schools and literature. The union of the thrones of England and Scotland in 1603 under the Scottish king known as James I in England essentially sealed the triumph of English in the Lowlands. Maintaining that the two languages were one, King James himself used English as the language of his court so that all official documents were issued in that language. The Church of Scotland (the Kirk) made a similar move by adopting an English translation of the Geneva Bible. King James sponsored a new translation of the Bible into English and directed that this Authorized (or "King James") translation be used in Scotland as well. The Kirk's emphasis on literacy for Bible reading thus promoted the use of the standard English of the day. Educated Lowland Scots, such as David Hume, prided themselves on their command of good English usage, which set them apart from the provincialisms of Scots English. Interestingly, Robert Burns, whose poetry and songs celebrated the customs and speech of the common people of Scotland, himself spoke standard English with little accent. By the time of Burns's death in 1796, his efforts at recording the old tongue had preserved a substantial body of folk literature, but English, not *Inglis,* was the language most Lowland Scots preferred to speak.[23]

In the Scottish Highlands, the defeat of the rebellion of 1745 led by Bonnie Prince Charlie against the Hanoverian dynasty opened the door to the rapid spread of English, first among the clan chiefs (whom King James had ordered in 1609 to send their sons to English-medium schools) and more slowly down the social ladder. The religion of the Highlanders became the Kirk of Scotland, whose liturgical services were conducted in English. The influence of travel and employment also had their effects. When Samuel Johnson and his Scottish companion James Boswell toured the region in 1773, Johnson noted:

> Those Highlanders that can speak English, commonly speak it well, with few of the words, and little of the tone by which a Scotchman is distinguished. Their language seems to have been learned in the army or the navy, or by some communication with those who could give them good examples of accent and pronunciation.[24]

Massive emigration drained the Highlands of much of its population. Even though the Scots contributed much to the language and culture of their new lands, their descendants in North America spoke the standard English of the their new home. Only those Scots who emigrated to Ulster perpetuated something of the old way of speaking.

Wales had come under English rule much earlier than Scotland. The first English Prince of Wales dates from 1301. The Act of Union of 1536 effectively incorporated Wales into England and made English the language of administration, law, commerce, and education. The Welsh language could no longer be used in bringing suit in court and office holders had to be fluent in English. Despite these coercive circumstances, Wales went much more slowly down the path to English-language dominance than had Scotland. It seems reasonable, as some think, to see the 1588 translation of the Bible into Welsh as strengthening the language by standardizing it. At the same time, the much greater disparity between the two languages made learning English more difficult. English and Scots were both Germanic languages and closely related, so that

Table 2.1 Borrowings from Hindi, Turkish, and Welsh

From Hindi	From Turkish	From Welsh
bungalow	bosh	bug
dinghy	caftan	caracle
dungaree	caique	corgi
ghee	coffee	cromlech
loot	cossack	cwm
pajama	divan	eisteddfod
Raj	horde	flannel
samosa	turquoise	flummery
shampoo	yoghurt	
tom-tom		

Source: Garland Cannon, Tom McArthur, and Jean-Marc Gachelin, "Borrowing," in *OCEL*, 141–45; *The American Heritage Dictionary of the English Language,* 3rd ed. (Boston, MA: Houghton Mifflin, 1992).

a speaker of one with a little practice could understand the other and with a bit more experience could duplicate the sounds and rhythms of the other language. English and Welsh shared nothing linguistically. Few English speakers picked up any Welsh and English has acquired fewer loanwords from neighboring Welsh than from distant Hindi or Turkish (see table 2.1). While a few words borrowed from Welsh are familiar, such as *bug* and *flannel*, others, like *cromlech, cwm,* and *eisteddfod,* are little known outside Wales.

To function in the political and economic worlds of Britain, Welsh speakers were obliged to learn English. The Welsh gentry were the first to embrace Anglicization, sending their children to English "public" schools or having them privately tutored, so that by the eighteenth century the elite families had become quite distant from the common people. For a time the masses were much less affected. By the late 1700s, it is estimated, nearly three-quarters of the inhabitants of Wales were Welch-speaking and few of them had any knowledge of English.[25]

Nevertheless, bilingualism was beginning to increase as a result of educational efforts by religious agencies and the growing influence of the industrial revolution on the Welsh economy. From the late 1700, efforts by the Welsh Trust and the Church of England's Society for the Promotion of Christian Knowledge (SPCK) to increase literacy among the masses met with an enthusiastic popular response. A crash program by the SPCK in the mid-eighteenth century that set up three-month-long circulating schools taught a quarter million Welsh to read the Bible in English over three decades. That most of this education was in English seems to have provoked no more resistance than the use of Latin as the language of literacy had in England a few centuries earlier. Welsh parents seemed to have been enthusiastic supporters of these programs. Despite such mass literacy efforts, the level of popular education remained very low. The poorly paid teachers, an 1847 Commission to Inquire into the State of Popular Education reported, were also poorly qualified, and the very modest fees charged still kept many from staying long in school. In the 1860s, fewer than one in a thousand entered secondary school in Wales, a twentieth of the rate in Prussia at that time.[26]

British officials championed the practical advantages of English-medium instruction, even though their views were expressed with considerable cultural bias. For example, the 1847 Commission of Inquiry concluded, "The Welsh language is a vast drawback to Wales, and a manifold barrier to the moral progress and commercial prosperity of the people," a conclusion that understandably provoked a strong negative reaction locally. Nevertheless, popular demand for English-medium education increased in Wales during the latter 1800s since those who had a good command of English were able to move up to better jobs in Wales' expanding coal mining and manufacturing sectors. By 1870, a network of English-medium schools, both private and public, covered Wales. Primary education in English became universal and compulsory a decade later. By the end of the 1800s two-thirds of the Welsh were bilingual.

Although the Welsh language held on for a time, Welsh speakers declined during the twentieth century both absolutely and as a proportion of the population. The number of Welsh speakers fell from nearly a million in 1911 (out of 2.42 million) to just over half a million in 1991 (out of nearly 3 million), while the proportion of the population able to speak Welsh fell even faster—from more than half of the population to less than a fifth. This precipitous decline took place despite the efforts of an influential pro-Welsh movement that supported the establishment of Welsh-medium education (1939), Welsh-language radio (1974) and television stations (1982ff.).[27] What had happened? Any explanation that emphasizes British discrimination has no lack of evidence, but linking external bias to the timing and speed of the changes is more difficult. In the first place, it seems clear that bilingualism was due to the "pull" of English on the masses, who saw was great advantages in learning it. The movement from bilingualism to monolingualism in English is more complicated, but some insight comes from examining the success and failures of coordinated efforts to revive the language.

Beginning in the 1990s under the leadership of Welsh nationalists, the language has made something of a comeback, especially after Welsh gained legal parity with English in 1993. Beginning in 2000, the study of Welsh became compulsory for students up to the age of 16, creating a new generation who are familiar with the language. In the 2001 census, the proportion of people saying they could speak Welsh rose to 20.8 percent. This was the first increase reported in 90 years and was due to the great increase in number of speakers in the 10–16 year age group. A survey in 2004 found those able to speak Welsh had increased to 21.7 percent. However, it is far from clear that compulsory study is reestablishing the language in general use. There is insufficient demand to support a Welsh daily newspaper, though a weekly manages to survive. After the age of 16 most students, including those whose first language was Welsh, prefer to continue their studies in English, especially those in science and mathematics. Despite the recent rise in the number of Welsh speakers, the proportion of families speaking Welch at home continues to decline, to a great extent because households with two Welsh-speaking parents are rare. Other factors are that a quarter of the residents of Wales were born elsewhere, that the Welsh population is aging and dying rapidly, and that native Welsh people also emigrate in significant numbers. One recent estimate is that Wales loses three thousand Welsh speakers a year.[28]

The story in Ireland is similar. English had begun to penetrate Ireland in the Middle Ages as contacts with England increased. Self-interest led Irish involved in commercial and other contacts with the English to learn some of their language. Such incentives increased from the mid-1500s as rural Irish had to communicate with locally resident English-speaking employers. King James I of England, who had inherited the throne of Ireland as well as Scotland in 1603, implemented policies of Anglicization in Ireland (similar to those in Scotland) in language, law, and religion. The gentry were encouraged to educate their sons in English. An Englishman who accompanied this occupation and who later became speaker of the Irish House of Commons expressed the views of many when he wrote that "we may conceive and hope that the next generation [in Ireland] will in tongue and heart, and every way else, become English; so as there will be no difference or distinction but the Irish sea betwixt us." He included in the changes to be made the displacement of the Catholic Church.[29]

The conquest of Ireland and its incorporation as British territory in the late 1600s introduced many of the features of English incorporation of Wales two and a half centuries earlier—but at a much swifter pace. Policies of assimilation were reinforced by long-standing English disrespect for Irish culture, religious beliefs, and political organization. A key aspect of Anglicization was to erase as much of Irish life and language as possible. The Irish generally succeeded in resisting efforts to change their religion and other cultural ways, and eventually succeeded in regaining their political independence, but using the English language was another matter. As elsewhere in the British Isles, the process moved downward from the top, with members of the elite eager to advance themselves with their overlords through proficiency in English. English also made rapid gains in the cities and towns during the eighteenth century. After the Act of Union (1800), the ruling classes regularly sent their sons to be educated in England, much as the Scottish landowners had done two centuries earlier. Local schools were also an important medium of spreading English speech, and, as in Wales, the quality of instruction in English often left a great deal to be desired, from the perspective of a speaker of standard English.

English spread even more rapidly in the nineteenth century. By 1800, just over a third of Irish people were exclusively Gaelic-speaking, with the rest of the population about equally divided between those who were bilingual and those who spoke only English. A national education system that was introduced in 1831 mandated English-medium classes. Students who dared to speak

Gaelic at school received corporal punishment. At mid-century the Great Famine increased the trend to English by removing many Irish speakers from the poor west counties and by enhancing the need to know English among those who emigrated to cities in England and North America. By 1851, the percentage of Irish able to speak Gaelic was down to 30 percent, while the number able to speak English had risen to over 90 percent. As historian Joseph Lee interprets this dramatic change, the national schools did not kill off the Irish language, as some nationalist histories would have it; rather Gaelic had "committed suicide before 1845," as Irish people embraced English for the opportunities it could bring them. By 1900, 85 percent of the adult population of Ireland spoke only English, while exclusive Gaelic speakers had fallen to less than one percent, largely confined to the poorest areas of the West coast.[30]

Irish nationalists have taken quite different positions on the decline of the ancestral language. The "great advocate" Daniel O'Connell (1755–1847) saw the Irish language less as a national treasure to be preserved than as obstacle to national unification. Though fluent in Gaelic he conducted his rallies in English. Once independence was achieved, nationalist views changed. The 1938 Irish Constitution proclaimed Irish as the "first official language," and the schools have been used to acquaint Irish youth with the ancestral language through compulsory instruction. In practice, as in Wales, the ancestral language is more revered in the abstract than actually spoken.[31]

This remarkable transformation was due to British educational policies similar to those applied in Wales, but the outcome would not have been possible without a similarly high level of eagerness to master English on the part of most Irish. As was quite evident in the independence movement of the early twentieth century, English had become a language of liberation and a key to successful independence. As later chapters will relate, the gradual emergence of English as the dominant language in the British Isles had important repercussions in the global diffusion of the language. England and America would play obvious leading parts in the spread of English, but the Celtic peoples had remarkably influential supporting roles. Scottish, Irish, and Welsh emigrants carried the English language to North America and other British colonies. Irish and Scottish soldiers and missionary educators were of great importance in spreading English in British colonies in Asia and Africa. Celtic writers used English to claim an honored place in the canon of global literature. As the second English-speaking country in the European Union, independent Ireland helped check the dominance of French in that body until the balance finally tipped and English became the language of European unity.

Conclusion

This overview of the spread of English in the British Isles raises a number of themes that resonate with discussions in other chapters of this work. One theme is that, although English was introduced in Britain through conquest and colonization, the people of what became England made it their mother tongue. They resisted the new languages of subsequent Scandinavian and Norman conquerors, while enriching English with borrowings from these and other languages. As the next two chapters recount, overseas colonization by English-speaking people would also introduce English to lands overseas, whose local people might also make it their own while enriching English with expressions from their own languages.

The diversity of English, or the "Englishes," is a popular topic in recent studies of the global reach of the English language. Some of this emphasis reflects the legitimate concern of linguistics with divergent trends, while some writers also seem to harbor a thinly disguised disparagement of foreigners who don't measure up to the standards of native speakers (or those of the better classes). People are entitled to their prejudices, but diversity of accent, syntax, and vocabulary has been equally characteristic of the long history of English in Britain. Even in recent times there has been more diversity of speech (more "Englishes") in Britain than in North America, as is discussed in chapter 3. Nevertheless, a growing standardization of English in modern times has been essential for the language to find global acceptance. Some standardization came about through powerful political, ecclesiastical, and literary leadership and some through the rise of printing, guides to proper usage, and the growth of education. These forces, too, would have their counterparts overseas.

This chapter has also shown that the spread of English among the ordinary people of Wales and Ireland came later that it had among the people of England and lowland Scotland. Despite a long association with England, it was only in the nineteenth and twentieth centuries that English became the language of the masses in these Celtic lands. Many interesting issues and controversies have arisen concerning the speed with which English became the second language of most Welsh and Irish and then equally fast became the primary or only language. On the one hand, the first part of the process, the acquisition of English as a second language, invites comparisons with the spread of English as a second language in much of the rest of the world. On the other hand, the displacement of the Celtic languages by English has suggested a false parallel with the spread of English more globally, since there is little evidence that learning English is leading nonnative speakers in Asia and Africa to abandon their first languages (see chapter 4). However false the analogy may be, it appears to be at the root of some scholars' portrait of English as a "killer language."

The three themes just mentioned—conquest and acceptance, diversity and standardization of speech, and the use of English as a first and as a second language—raise another issue: what caused English to spread in the British Isles? The answer is not simple, but it seems reasonably clear. Part of the answer concerns "push" factors from above: the Anglo-Saxon conquests, the promotion of English by rulers and ecclesiastical authorities, campaigns to purify and standardize the language, and the teaching of a standard English to the masses. This is the most obvious and best documented part of the explanation, but it is not a sufficient answer. The "pull" English exercised over ordinary people is much harder to document but very obvious in the outcomes. Learning a second language (or a more prestigious register of speech) requires a lot of effort. While people made such an effort because of English's prestige or "cultural hegemony," it was not abstract expressions that motivated people. What appears salient is that individuals saw improving their command of English (or a register of English) as in their self-interest and acted to bring it about. Ironically, the best example documented in this brief survey comes from the campaigns to promote Gaelic and Welsh by requiring their study in schools and use in public places. Such "pushes" from above have been successful in ensuring the survival of these historic languages, but they have not succeeded in displacing the enormous "pull" of the English language in people's lives. Here too is a lesson to be applied in examining the global spread of English.

Chapter 3

The Language of North America

In the early 1600s, when William Shakespeare was penning elegant plays in the language of London and scholars were preparing the King James translation of the Bible, few could have foreseen that English would one day become the dominant language of the vast continent across the North Atlantic. Spanish would have seemed more likely to establish its mastery in North America, since Spain had dominated the population centers of Mexico and the Andes for a century and was expanding its influence northward.[1] By the late 1700s, however, some visionaries were predicting that English would become the dominant language in the Americas. By 1900, the dominance of English north of the Rio Grande was a reality, as the territories from the Atlantic to the Pacific had absorbed a rapidly multiplying population of English speakers from the British Isles and had assimilated an even larger influx of other Europeans, Africans, and Asians.

Some English settlers saw the mastery of a continent as providential, the fulfillment of their God-given destiny to triumph over geography, adversity, and other peoples. Historians find destiny an unsatisfactory explanation and American triumphalism an unpleasant pose. The hand of God is invisible, but the hands of humans—rapacious, hard working, or just lucky—can be seen vividly in the expansion of English across the North American continent. The amazing speed with which English spread from the Atlantic coast to the Pacific was not providential, but it was a major step in the language's global rise.

Colonial Beginnings

It took a long time before the small colonies founded by English-speaking people along the Atlantic coast of North America in the 1600s had much impact. Entering a land where other peoples and languages were well established, early English settlers had little choice but to learn the languages of the Native American groups among whom they settled, much as French traders and Jesuit missionaries were doing in the lands further north. Some Indians learned the Europeans' languages. In New England in the mid 1600s, Protestant missionaries proselytized using religious texts and schoolbooks they had translated into native languages. Many words entered American English from the Eastern Algonquian languages of New England (see table 3.1).

By the last quarter of the century, however, such policies began to be reversed. Finding enough teachers familiar with indigenous languages was difficult, and attitudes toward native North Americans had hardened after major military conflicts, such as King Philip's War (1675–76). The new plan was to make the indigenous people learn English. Citing the failure of England to subdue the Irish in the previous century, Daniel Gookin, the Indian superintendent for Massachusetts, advocated "changing the language of a barbarous [and conquered] people" to reduce them "unto the civility and religion of the prevailing nation." Especially at the urging of

Table 3.1 New vocabulary in colonial American English (excluding place-names)

From Algonquian			From Dutch	New words
animals	*plants*	*other*	boss	bullfrog
chipmunk	hickory	papoose	cookie	cold snap
moose	squash	toboggan	dope	popcorn
opossum	pecan	tomahawk	Santa Claus	snowplow
raccoon		wigwam	snoop	
skunk			scow	
woodchuck			waffle	

Sources: Garland Cannon, Tom McArthur, and Jean-Marc Gachelin, "Borrowing," in *OCEL*, 143; John Truslow Adams, "Provincial Society, 1690–1793," in Mark C. Carnes, and Arthur Schlesinger, Jr., eds., *A History of American Life*. Revised and Abridged (New York: Scribner, 1996), 287; John Algeo, "American English," in *OCEL*, 39–40.

the Rev. Cotton Mather, boarding schools for Amerindians were established in the 1700s. The schools in New England and Virginia mostly failed to alter the Amerindians' cultural preferences and beliefs, but they did spread their familiarity with spoken and written English. The cultural assimilation of the Amerindians and their Anglicization became government policy particularly through the use of missionaries and the Bureau of Indian Affairs (established 1824). It is notable that the Bureau for its first quarter-century was a part of the Department of War.[2]

Besides dealing with native inhabitants, settlers in the southern colonies faced the challenge of assimilating substantial numbers of enslaved Africans, who spoke many different languages. The mainland English colonies had imported over 15,000 Africans by 1700, and nearly 300,000 more arrived before the importation of slaves became illegal in the United States in 1808.[3] As was discussed in chapter 1, African-born slaves in the Americas could remember their native languages, but no single African language was spoken by a critical mass of people. In most cases, the language of plantation communities was either the colony's European language or a hybrid creole, which blended African usages with the dominant European language. In the Carolinas, a creole know as Gullah developed, which is still spoken on some coastal islands in South Carolina. In contrast, the slave communities around the Chesapeake Bay used English to communicate with each other and with their masters.

On the North American mainland, historian Philip Morgan argues persuasively, the adoption of English or Gullah was not unilaterally imposed by the slave masters but due to four other factors. First, the number of slaves imported was small, averaging only a couple of thousand a year in the eighteenth century in the case of Virginia and South Carolina. Second, African arrivals spoke a large number of distinct languages. Only occasionally in eighteenth-century Virginia were half of the African-born slaves from a single African coast, and each coast of Africa drew on societies speaking a multitude of languages. In South Carolina the mix was even greater. Third, most slaves were American-born after 1700. The percentage born in Africa shrank to single digits after 1770 in Virginia, although percentages were larger in South Carolina, which imported many more slaves after 1750. Fourth, slaves were a minority of the population in the Chesapeake area. He notes, "Although black speech in the Chesapeake...had certain distinctive characteristics, some of which derived from Africa, most [eighteenth-century] observers were more impressed by the ability of Chesapeake slaves to speak Standard English, or its near equivalent."[4]

Historian Ira Berlin uses Morgan's research to examine the transition in the mid-1700s from societies in which most slaves were African-born to ones where the majority were creoles (American-born). Compared to slaves brought from Africa, the American creoles were healthier, lived longer, and had a more balanced sex ratio, all of which favored a much higher rate of natural increase then was possible among African-born slaves. As a result, the Chesapeake region (and later the Carolinas) needed to import far fewer slaves to keep up with demand than did the plantation colonies of the Caribbean where most slaves remained African-born. "Perhaps most importantly," Berlin argues, "the new creoles had control of the word, as English was their native tongue." American-born creoles were eager to perfect their English, Berlin explains, because it brought them knowledge that would eventually enable them to challenge their owners. The cultural transformation that was forming black Americans' speech was also making them scornful of African ways. As creole slaves embraced the Christian religion that itinerant preachers introduced them to, they shunned African names in favor of Christian ones.[5]

A third linguistic challenge in the English mainland colonies was the large number of European settlers who were not native speakers of English. Tom Paine suggested that not more than a third of the population in the 13 colonies was of English origin in 1776.[6] Paine would not have included as "English" the many Irish, Scots, and Welsh, most of whom would have known English. Their inclusion would bring the proportion of English speakers up to half the population. Even so, in Pennsylvania where Paine was writing, a quarter of the settler population was German-speaking, and there were the large of Native Americans as well as some Africans.

The Germans were the most numerous of the early European immigrants who were not English-speaking. By 1790, about 100,000 German speakers had settled in North America, with many more to follow. In some parts of Pennsylvania and other states, German appeared to be the principal language in use. In a private letter in 1753, which disparaged the Pennsylvania Germans' intelligence and character, Benjamin Franklin stated that few of their rural children learned English and that adults read and wrote in German, including legal documents. A more positive account published in 1789 by the American physician Benjamin Rush noted that, although the Pennsylvania Germans settled in clusters, always accompanied by a clergyman, and continued to speak German among themselves, most of the men who traveled to towns learned English. Literacy was nearly universal among them, supporting a large number of German-language newspapers and printers.[7] Rush's description captures the two exceptional features of German immigrants in North America (which will be explorer further later in this chapter): their preservation of their ancestral language and their bilingualism. In suggesting that all of the diverse free residents of the colonies would support a break with Britain, Paine implies a third characteristic of the Germans and other later immigrants: their political loyalty to their new homeland.

The American victory in the War of Independence was a tremendous turning point in the linguistic history of North America. The new nation threw open to settlement the lands across the Appalachian Mountains, ending the prohibitions that had helped provoke the break with Britain. By 1800, the European settler population had grown to about 5.4 million and their slaves numbered about a million. Though modest, the combined settler and slave population was six times the surviving Native Americans in the territories of the future 48 states, who numbered about 600,000. The stage was set for a massive territorial expansion and population increase during next century.

The War of Independence also promoted many visions of a special future for the new nation, only a few of which came true. One farsighted individual was John Adams, who was led to "prophesy" (the word is his) both the continental and the global expansion of the English. When he was writing in September 1780, while ambassador to France, the embattled American rebels were still clustered along the Atlantic coast, and the decisive victory at Yorktown lay more than a year in the future. In less-populous Canada, English speakers were just pulling even with French speakers. Yet Adams confidently predicted that, fed by continuing rapid population growth and expansion, English speakers in North America would outnumber those in Britain within a century. That alone would have been a remarkably prescient vision, but the Ambassador Adams went on to predict that British and American connections and commerce with other parts of the world would have the effect of making English the most widely read and widely spoken language in the world. He had a clear sense of the historical context of his prediction. Latin, he knew, had been the universal language of Europe until the 1700s; French was then gaining a similar ascendancy. Soon, Adams argued, it would be English's turn: "English is destined to be, in the next and succeeding centuries, more generally the language of the world than Latin was in the last or French is in the present age."[8]

Writing a century later, in the wake of the Spanish American War and on the eve of the annexation of Hawaii, Theodore Roosevelt confirmed Adams's vision of the spread of English in North America and other parts of the world: "During the past three centuries the spread of the English-speaking peoples over the world's waste spaces has been not only the most striking feature in the world's history, but also the event of all others most far-reaching in its effects and its importance."[9] Not only did Roosevelt consider the global spread of English momentously important, but he also believed it was a positive force for good. Such ideas may not have been shared by all those compelled by circumstances to add English to their linguistic repertoires, but modern cultural relativists might be surprised how little opposition there was in North America to learning English at the time. Those who had added English as a second language might not have used Roosevelt's self-confident, bombastic rhetoric, but they might well have shared his belief that their new language was of positive personal value.

Other linguistic visions competed with Adams's in the aftermath of Revolution. Not least among them was suggestion that the new Republic should signal its uniqueness by replacing English with a different national language. French and German were proposed, as were resurrected classical ones such as Hebrew and Greek.

Arguing that there were more pressing reforms to be implemented in the new Republic, the pragmatists prevailed.[10] In fact, as the great lexicographer Noah Webster argued, the new nation already had its own distinctive language, American English. In words that echoed Adams's, he prophesied with remarkable accuracy in 1789 that within 150 years "North America will be peopled with a hundred millions of men, *all speaking the same language*" (his emphasis). He was wide of the mark, however, in predicting that isolation from Britain and the force of local circumstances would make American English "as different from the future language of England, as the modern Dutch, Danish and Swedish are from the German, or from one another."[11]

As a linguist, Webster was correct in expecting that American English would change and evolve over the next century, but he could not have foreseen how changes in communication and education would impede the tendency of languages to drift when transmitted orally and in isolation from linguistically related communities. Perhaps no one could have foreseen the fact that American and British English would in fact diverge very little over the next century and that their distinctive accents would remain mutually intelligible.[12]

Other contemporaries had different insights into the linguistic situation in North America. The Rev. Timothy Dwight, the president of Yale from 1795 to his death in 1817, for example, agreed with Webster that American speech was different, but he argued it was distinctive not so much for its divergence from British English but for its greater uniformity and purity. Based on his indefatigable travels in the early nineteenth century, Dwight reported that "the English language is in this country pronounced more correctly than in England," explaining that by "correctly" he meant the standard pronunciation "of well-bred people in London" and that deviations from this standard by class and region were far less common in the United States than within England. He continued, "It is no exaggeration to say that from Machias [Maine] to St. Marys [Georgia], and from the Atlantic to the Mississippi, every American descended from English ancestors understands every other as readily as if he had been bred in the same neighborhood." Dwight believed that the uniformity of American speech could be attributed to the example of the well-educated teachers in the schools, of the clergy in the churches, and of freer communication among social classes, which retarded the development of class accents.[13]

Writing a few years later (in 1828), novelist James Fennimore Cooper voiced the same view of language quality and uniformity. His fictional New Yorker, John Cadwallader, offered the judgment that "the people of the United States with the exception of a few of German and French descent speak, as a body, an incomparably better English than the people of the mother country," a language that is perfectly intelligible to any Londoner but varies much less than the speech of Londoners. Cadwallader added that American speech had grown even more uniform in the previous 20 years rather than splitting into regional dialects.[14] European visitors made quite similar observations about the quality and uniformity of American speech. For example, based on his travels in the coastal states in 1822–23, the Englishman Isaac Candler concluded, "As far as pronunciation is concerned, the mass of people speak better English than the mass of people in England."[15]

In spite of the near unanimity of such contemporary testimony about the uniformity of American English, some modern scholars, such as historian David Hackett Fischer, have put forward the thesis that regional and class accents from identifiable waves of British immigrants persisted in North America. Perhaps, as historian Joey Lee Dilliard suggests, Fischer's views have been influenced by the work of philologists, who have traditionally given greater attention to language diversities than uniformities. Dillard notes that the trend among recent scholars is to pay more attention to the standardization of American English, which he says was "as relatively complete as such things ever are" in the thirteen English colonies by the early 1770s. The standard history of English by Albert Baugh and Thomas Cable also concurs on the greater uniformity of the American language compared to national languages in Europe, wisely noting how easily minor differences can be blown out of proportion. However challenging it is to make a clear pronouncement about historical continuity and change in something as complex as culture, the essential point seems clear: the language spoken in public by most people in the early Republic was a very standardized English.[16]

Expansion and Assimilation

What followed, as the nation expanded across the continent and absorbed tens of millions of immigrants, was infinitely more complex than what had occurred during the two centuries following the colonies' establishment, even if the ultimate result was similar. A less obvious factor shaped the linguistic impact of this massive territorial expansion and immigration: the homogenization of the American population. The blockades and perils of the French Revolution, the Napoleonic Wars, and the War of 1812 had greatly slowed immigration to North America. In 1830, an estimated 98.5 percent of Americans were American-born and similarly large proportions were English-speaking and Protestant. Coming just at the beginning of the nation's westward expansion and its absorption of massive numbers of foreign immigrants, this moment of homogenization stabilized the nation still further and dampened the tendencies that might have pulled it apart culturally. This cultural consolidation also fed the expansionist mentality known as manifest destiny. The goal and justification of territorial growth was to fill as much of the continent as possible with English-speaking, Protestant Americans. Expansion also added new words to the language (see table 3.2).

The first steps in expansion beyond the Appalachians were in the Ohio Valley. The Louisiana Purchase of 1803 added vast new lands for settlement. Florida and the Gulf of Mexico coast were added in 1819, and much more was in the offing. In 1821, Stephen

Table 3.2 Loanwords in nineteenth-century American English

Mexican Spanish	German	Italian
ranch (1808)	frankfurter	tutti-frutti
lasso (1819)	wiener	spaghetti
corral (1829)	hamburger	
lariat (1831)	delicatessen	
stampede (1843)	kindergarten	
bronco (1850)	gesundheit	
chaps (1870)		

Source: Stuart Berg Flexner, I *Hear America Talking: An Illustrated Treasury of American Words and Phrases* (New York: Van Nostrand Reinhold, 1976), 218, 163–68.

Austin had established an American colony in the Mexican province of Texas, and when initially friendly relations with Mexican authorities soured, the Republic of Texas declared its independence in 1835. The admission of Texas to the Union in 1845 set off a bitter war with Mexico that, at its conclusion in 1848 added vast new territories to the United States. While the war was underway, the California gold rush brought numbers of English-speaking Americans to the Pacific.

Between 1836 and 1914 the United States also absorbed more than 30 million immigrants, mostly from Europe. At first immigrants came from the same lands as had their predecessors: the British Isles and Germanic Europe. The Great Famine of 1845–51 drove nearly two million Irish to the United States and Canada from the British Isles and the failure of the revolutions of 1848 convinced a million Germans to cross the Atlantic as well. Smaller numbers of Scandinavians were attracted by the availability of rich farmland in the sparsely populated continent. By 1880, arriving immigrants included large numbers of so-called new immigrants from southern and eastern Europe, as well as Chinese, most of whom arrived with little or no knowledge of English.

The 20 million European immigrants who settled in the United States during the 40 years after 1880 came during the final decades of the country's westward lunge to the Pacific. Even so, in 1900 over 40 percent of Americans still lived in just 7 (of the 46) states: New York, Pennsylvania, Illinois, Ohio, Missouri, Massachusetts, and Indiana (in descending order). Many of the German and Scandinavian immigrants went into farming, but most other new immigrants, too poor to buy land or travel far, stayed in East Coast cities where jobs were available.

The proportion of foreign-born residents had risen to nearly 10 percent by 1860, when the census began to collect such information for the first time. At its peak the foreign-born made up 15 percent of the population of the United States. That modest proportion may have been the national averages, but the actual distribution of immigrants was anything but even. For one thing, the South received many fewer immigrants than the rest of the country. In 1890, less than 7 percent of the population in the South were foreign born or the children of foreign-born parents, whereas about 45 percent of those in the Northeast,

Midwest, and West fell into that category.[17] One should also note that many nonimmigrants annexed along with the Mexican lands from Texas to California spoke Spanish or Native American languages.

Incorporating these new territories, immigrants, and other non-English speakers was a mighty test of the primacy of English. Language was not the only cultural issue. The large Catholic component of the Irish, Italians, south Germans, and Poles further diluted the proportion of Protestants, if not their power. In highly literate America, many immigrants stood out and were looked down on because they were illiterate. The Irish at least spoke English, if few could read or write it.

Other demographic factors shaped the evolving process. The tripling of the American population between 1850 and 1900 (from 23.3 million to 76 million) was only partly due to new immigration. Natural increase among native-born Americans was also high, ensuring that English speakers were a substantial majority almost everywhere in the country. Moreover, population distribution in the United States changed from over four-fifths rural as late as 1860 and more than half urban after 1920. Thus, assimilation was an urban process for a substantial part of the new immigrants.

In the cities language was a key issue because immigrants were surrounded by American-born native speakers of English and English-speaking immigrants from the British Isles. Learning to function in a new language was a slow and painful process for adults, but a necessary one to communicate with the English-speaking majority, as well as with the babble of other immigrants in the cities. Younger immigrants and the children of immigrants picked up English more readily. Urban public schools made a massive effort to teach people of all ages to speak, read, and write the language.

Even before the American Civil War, public schools in the northern states had been the chief mechanism for sustaining Standard English and for teaching the children of non-English-speaking parents the American language. Boston, for example had opened a grammar school for boys in 1682. Girls were admitted a century later in 1789, and from 1818 were there primary schools for both boys and girls. The early schools in Boston and Salem charged fees, although the poor might be exempt, but it was in the rural communities of New England where a remarkable American innovation appeared: free schools open to all without distinction.[18]

Tax-supported elementary schools had become the norm in the North by 1850. Led by the reformer Horace Mann, the Commonwealth of Massachusetts, New York State, and other states had introduced compulsory attendance and teacher certification programs, like those begun in Prussia. After the Civil War public schools expanded rapidly in the South, aided by funds from the federal government during Reconstruction and substantial bequests from wealthy New Englanders, especially for the education of poor blacks. Then the national passion for education exploded. Between 1870 and 1900, attendance became compulsory in the North and West, typically up to age 14, and the number of public high schools went from 160 to 6,000, although in the impoverished Southern states the quality and the number of schools continued to lag behind. Overall 15 million American children were in school at the end of the century, including half a million in the expanding secondary school system.[19]

Because New York City was such a center of immigration, its schools were immensely important in Americanizing immigrants culturally and linguistically. As early as 1860, the majority of the city's residents were foreign born and by 1890, immigrants and the children of immigrants constituted 80 percent of the population. At first, the city's 1874 compulsory-education law was unenforceable among immigrant slum dwellers because the capacity of the existing schools was inadequate to absorb all those of school age. Ten years after the law went into effect the president of the New York City's Board of Education conservatively estimated that 20,000 school-age children were not in school. New evening schools for working children provided some relief, but thousands each year were still being turned away from schools in the late 1880s for lack of space. The situation worsened in the 1890s as thousands of new Italian and Jewish Eastern European immigrants flooded into Lower East Side tenements and school expenditures failed to keep pace.[20]

Nevertheless, New York City's failures pale in comparison to the extraordinary numbers of students its schools managed to provide with a good education. Even if the city's schools never managed to catch up with the numbers of new immigrants that flooded into it before First World War and even if its extensive building program never provided enough buildings, classrooms, and desks, New York did manage to become a great engine of assimilation and Anglicization.

Among non-English-speaking immigrants in North America the general pattern was to be exclusively English-speaking by the third generation. The first generation learned enough English to get by, but spoke their mother tongue at home. Their children learned the ancestral language at home, but the English they learned at school was the language they were most skilled at reading, writing, and speaking. When that generation raised families, they used English as the home language, and their children rarely learned more than a few words of the ancestral language. North American immigrants were not unique in this regard, but it is a notable characteristic of the North American experience that immigrants preserved an ancestral ethnic identity far longer than any facility in an ancestral language. Why was this so?

As already seen, the public schools played a large role in transmitting the English language, as did the parochial school established by Catholic immigrants. There were also significant social and political pressures at work. Theodore Roosevelt voiced a popular sentiment in the United States at the time of the anti-immigrant "Red Scare" of 1919: "We have room for but one language here, and that is the English language; for we intend that the crucible turns our people out as Americans."[21] Using German in public had been banned during the First World War. During the Second World War similarly strong pressures were employed to curtail the use of the Japanese language and over a hundred thousand Japanese Americans and legal immigrants were interned in camps.

External pressures to use English were accompanied by a genuine desire to assimilate among most immigrants. America was not just a new home; it was a passionately desired new homeland. Putting aside the dress and speech of other places and embracing America's language and customs was a major assertion of that new identity, although ethnic foods, festivals, and other folkways were treasured, too. Finally, one should not underestimate the pragmatic importance English played as the lingua franca of immigrants new lives, as the linguistic gateway to success.

Language learning took place locally, so in a big country assimilation did not mean homogenization in language any more than it did in food and customs. As the country had grown, regional speech patterns naturally developed. Within the large dialect groups stretching westward from the Atlantic coast, there developed many local variations, in cases even within cities such as New York. Public schools often made efforts to promote more standard pronunciation and usage, but teachers themselves usually had local accents. Nevertheless, the tendency for the American language to diverge was held in check by three factors: the high literacy rate universal education produced, the development of national broadcast media, and the great mobility of the American population.

Even if people spoke differently, they often read the same things. The period from about 1840 to 1920 saw a tremendous growth not just in public literacy in the United States but also in the availability of things to read. The rapid growth of daily newspapers was a notable phenomenon, culminating in the influential publications of the newspaper barons at the turn of the century. The literary quality of the popular press was not high, but American book publishing was also coming into its own during this period. The oldest presses in Atlantic port cities like Boston and New York were joined my many others. Book prices fell as the market grew and paperback editions ("dime novels") made books affordable for the masses. The most popular writer of the nineteenth century was Horatio Alger, whose heroes' rise from rags to riches captured the imagination of the American public, including many immigrants. Even more important in reaching a mass reading audience were free public libraries, another American phenomenon. In the early twentieth century, Andrew Carnegie, an immigrant from Scotland who had risen from the shop floor to the owner of the giant steel-making conglomerate U.S. Steel, gave away most of his mammoth fortune to build nearly three thousand free ("Carnegie") lending libraries, making reading materials available to a large share of the population. Helping feed the demand for books was the ongoing development of a distinctive American literature that also helped to calibrate the language. Colonial writers had made a notable beginning in creating an American literature, but nineteenth-century writers solidified the field even as the country expanded its boundaries. Special attention goes to the distinctively American voice of Mark Twain. William Faulkner considered Twain the grandfather of American writing, "the first truly American writer...all of us are his heirs."[22]

Beginning with the development of national radio networks from the 1920s, the national language could be heard coast to coast, even if it was not on the lips of the listeners. Radio networks devoted only a part of their airtime to national news programs; local programming and entertainment serials took up the rest, and these often embodied quite distinctive local accents. So radio's overall impact was not to erode local accents so much as to make regional speech familiar nationally. Southerners heard and learned to understand the speech of people from northeast and Midwest. Rural folk heard the speech patterns of the big cities. In a still highly segregated society, the immensely the popular *Amos 'n' Andy* radio program, first broadcast in 1929, spread familiarity with black speech, even if the program parodied that way of talking for comic effect. Similarly, the patrician accent of President Franklin Roosevelt was familiar from his "fireside chats," as were the rich tones of Hans von Kaltenborn (1878–1965) and Edward R. Murrow (1908–65). The popularity of moving pictures had a similar effect in promoting recognition. The surge in television broadcasting after 1945 became the most powerful of all the media, with four-fifths of American households having a TV set by 1960.[23]

An even more powerful force for homogenizing American speech came from the widespread mobility of Americans. Pushed by poverty and hardship or lured by opportunity, vast numbers moved from one part of the country to another and from rural communities to large cities. Accents did not change suddenly, but interaction gradually modified the speech of the immigrants (and sometimes of their hosts). As with immigrants from abroad, the next generation readily assimilated the speech of the host community.

Persistence of Other Languages and Bilingualism

Except where immigrants from one language were few or scattered, it might seem perfectly reasonable to expect that ancestral languages would have persisted in North America. After all, the world is full of examples of immigrant groups living side by side with other people for centuries yet preserving their separate languages. Because bilingualism has not commonly persisted in North America north of the Rio Grande, it is instructive to look at some examples of enduring bilingualism and the reasons for them. Four examples are considered: Germans in the United States, the French in Canada, Spanish speakers in the American Southwest, and indigenous North American peoples.

As discussed earlier, German immigrants in colonial America had been the most likely to preserve their language. The great wave of new German-speaking immigrants in the 1800s continued that tradition of bilingualism. Their continued success in preserving the German language was due to a number of factors. One is that state and federal governments were remarkably tolerant of the German language—at least up to the First World War. Beginning in the 1790s and continued in the 1830s and 1840s repeated efforts were made to mandate printing federal documents in German as well as in English. Even though none was successful, in 1870 a US Commissioner of Education argued that German was in fact the country's second language, which every well-educated American should know.[24] The high degree of literacy among German immigrants is even more fundamental in explaining why they preserved their language while most other immigrants did not. German communities established secular, Catholic, and Protestant schools that taught primarily or exclusively in German. German signage and speech were common on the streets in some cities and neighborhoods.

A German observer in 1829 surveyed the evolving preservation of German in the eastern United States as well as the inroads English was making. From northeastern Pennsylvania, he observed, an "uninterrupted chain" of German settlements stretched south into Maryland, Virginia, North Carolina, and Tennessee, where the German language was widely spoken and sometimes dominant. German-language churches abounded. Professorships in German language and literature had been established at Harvard and the University of Virginia. However, the author noted, some prosperous German-Americans had begun pushing for English in the churches, arguing that their wives and children could no longer understand

German well enough to follow the service. Some parishes, in fact, had completely dropped German. Sermons in Lutheran churches in Philadelphia had been in English since 1806 and in Harrisburg since 1812. By mid-century a more critical German observer deplored the gradual loss of German language in Pennsylvania where German had become a "broken language," a "senseless *mischmasch*," reduced to a few thousand words.[25]

However, when those sentiments were written, a great new influx of German-speaking immigrants was already underway that would keep the language thriving in the United States. The failed revolutions of 1848 pushed many educated Germans to emigrate to North America and other new immigration spread German communities across the Midwest. German immigration to the United States reached a peak in the decade 1881–90 when nearly a million and a half German speakers arrived, and another million entered the United States by 1920. In the national censuses of 1890, 1900, and 1910 foreign-born residents in the United States from Germany and Austria numbered over 3 million. Like the earlier German immigrants, these newcomers made a substantial commitment to perpetuating their language and learning in churches and in schools, both parochial and secular.[26]

The persistence of this bilingual community suffered a substantial blow after United States entered the First World War in 1917. Concerns about the loyalty of German-Americans and their devotion to German language and customs led to mob attacks and ridicule, and a 1918 law mandated the use of English as the primary language of instruction in all schools. In response to these pressures, German-Americans abandoned many of the outward expression of their German heritage. The postwar generation was much less likely to be bilingual.[27]

The French speakers who came to North America about the same time as English settlers were founding colonies in Virginia and Massachusetts spread themselves more rapidly across a much larger geographical expanse than their English-speaking counterparts to the south. French trappers, lumberjacks, and traders penetrated down the St. Lawrence River, through the Great Lakes, and down the Mississippi Valley. Initially, the number of native speakers on the ground was much thinner than in the English settlements, but during the century after 1650 the tiny band of just over 10,000 French-speaking immigrants multiplied to some 70,000.

The acquisition of New France by the British in 1760 opened up the territory to competing English-speaking settlers. A small flood of 35,000 Loyalists after the end of the War of the American Revolution doubled the number of English speakers there. By about 1800, the size of the populations speaking French and English were about the same, with still more English-speaking Scots and Irish to follow. Meanwhile, French expansion in North America had been curtailed by the American acquisition of Louisiana and the Mississippi Valley. Some French speakers there became English-speaking, but the French language and identity remained dominant in the heartland of Quebec and in neighboring parts of Maine and New York. In an effort to win the loyalty of their new subjects, the British had promulgated laws in 1774 protecting their language and their Catholic religion. Language and the Catholic faith were powerful unifying forces against the rising sea of English-speaking Protestants. The British expected that the unification of Upper and Lower Canada into a single colony by the Act of Union (1840) would draw the French speakers into greater association with English speakers and weaken their separate identity. That proved not to be the case.

The Union and the continuing influx of British immigrants, however, further tipped the language balance in favor of the English speakers. The peopling of the Canadian West was by many nationalities, most of whom ended up speaking English. As Theodore Roosevelt suggested in 1889, "The extension of the English westward through Canada since the war of the Revolution has been in its essential features merely a less important repetition of what has gone on in the northern United States."[28]

Nevertheless, the amalgamation of all of the British possessions in 1867 gave birth to a country deeply divided by language and culture. For a time the Quebecois preserved their separate identity by turning inward, though the price was a smaller share of Canada's rising prosperity. In the more aggressive political contests of the twentieth century, however, their successful resistance and population growth served French Canadians well. Canada's modern language politics recognize the permanence of Canada's two separate languages. As Prime Minister Stephen Harper put it in 1997: "Canada is not a bilingual country. It is a country with two [official] languages."[29]

However, there is another way to frame that reality. Like the German immigrants to the south, the Quebecois ultimately preserved their language by becoming bilingual. Bilingualism among English speakers in Canada is not much greater than among their counterparts south of the border, but bilingualism is much more common among French-speaking Canadians. Even though more than a fifth of Canadians speak French at home, 85 percent of Canadians speak English as their first or second language. As in the United States, English is Canada's primary language.

A third and more ambiguous example of bilingualism has occurred among the people of the American Southwest, annexed at the end of the Mexican War in 1848 and augmented by the Gadsden Purchase in 1853. The greatest numbers were the block of over 60,000 people (in what is now New Mexico), most of whom spoke Spanish, Navajo, or other Amerindian languages. Many English speakers subsequently settled in the territory. When New Mexico became a state in 1912, voters, using a ballot in both English and Spanish, approved a constitution that provided for both Spanish and English to be used in official documents for 20 years. In fact, the practice has continued, although English is the de facto official language. At the end of the twentieth century, 514,000 (nearly 30%) of the state's population of 1.8 million spoke Spanish at home, and most of them could also speak English very well.[30] Like the French in Canada, the Spanish in New Mexico were incorporated into an English-speaking country but have managed to retain their language.

Another set of non-English speakers incorporated by the rapid westward expansion of the United States and Canada were the indigenous peoples of these regions. At the time these peoples were generally called Indians. Today they are most commonly referred to Native Americans in the United States and First Peoples in Canada, but they commonly call themselves Indians or use their tribal or clan names.[31] Efforts to assimilate the native peoples after the Civil War followed many of the programs in use for the assimilation of immigrants though with some different outcomes. In his monumental study, historian Francis Paul Prucha described the movement for Americanize them this way:

> A concerted drive on the part of earnest men and women who unabashedly called themselves "the Friends of the Indians" made Congress listen at last....Convinced of the superiority of the Christian civilization they enjoyed, they were determined to do away with Indianness and tribal relations and to turn the individual Indian into a patriotic citizen, indistinguishable from his white brothers.

Although free of the hatred and greed characteristic of some frontiersmen, these well-meaning reformers had a notable fault, ignorant paternalism. As Prucha puts it: "Lacking all appreciation of the Indian cultures, they were intent on forcing on the natives the qualities that they themselves embodied. It was an ethnocentrism of frightening intensity."[32]

A key strategy was education, similar to the public schools that were Americanizing the droves of immigrant children. There was a key difference: most European immigrants were urban; most Native Americans were rural. To become properly "civilized," the large nations of the Plains not only had to be taught to dress, speak, and worship like white Americans, but they also had to be taught farming to replace the hunting and gathering practices that the reservation system and the destruction of the bison were making impossible. The supporters of this cultural and agricultural makeover focused on a key institution, a boarding school using manual labor. The boarding school separated young Native Americans from what the reformers considered the corrupting influences of their homes, enabling them to be trained in the manners, language, and religions of white Americans. All instruction was in English. Equipped with livestock, equipment, and land, the schools taught students mixed farming, with student labor partly offsetting the costs of such operations. As in white America, farming was to be a male task primarily; female students were trained in domestic skills and were put to work keeping classrooms and dormitories clean.

Practice fell short of theory in many respects. It was some time before there was enough money to make this form of education universal. By 1884, the federal government had opened 143 schools, about half of which were boarding schools. By 1887, there were 231 government schools of all kinds for Native Americans. As impressive as this expansion was, the ten thousand students attending government schools in 1887 constituted a small fraction of the school-age population. By 1914, the number of Native Americans attending federal government schools had climbed to 27,755, while 25,180 others were enrolled in public schools, and 4,943 in mission and private schools. The peak of enrollment in government boarding schools came in the 1970s when there were about 60,000 attending.[33] Canada had a similar system of residential schools for its native peoples.

From the beginning the government schools had many critics, and criticism mounted during the latter part of the twentieth century, a time of mounting political activism by Native Americans and First Peoples. Criticism focused on the deculturation of the students as well as on instances of physical and sexual abuse. Particular criticism was aimed at the prohibition against using native languages in school. Ultimately both America and Canada abandoned these policies. In the United States, the Indian Self-Determination and Education Assistance Act of 1975 provided for direct federal grants to federally recognized Indian tribes, which they could administer in ways that gave them greater control over education policies. In Canada, Prime Minister Harper apologized for the harm done to native peoples by the residential schools, and the Anglican Church of Canada (which administered many of them) issued its own apology and had to make court-ordered settlement payments to settle abuse claims.

The concession of greater say over education to native authorities did not resolve the tension between wanting to preserve ancestral languages and needing to know English in North America. Among the Navajo the percentage of children entering school who were fluent in Navajo actually dropped from 95 percent in the mid-1970s to 50 percent in the mid-1990s, which must reflect the language parents were using with their young children. A survey of Navajo parents found broad support of teaching Navajo in school, but respondents were divided about equally over whether the goal should be to acquire basic knowledge, competence, or fluency in the language. In any event, knowledge of

English was also a high priority, and most instruction in the upper grades continued to be in English.[34]

The charge that the compulsory use of English in schools is the root cause of the decline in native languages needs to be tempered by considering other factors that are commonly associated with language switching. As with other populations, there is linguistic safety in numbers. Fifty to sixty percent of the members of the three largest indigenous groups in North America can speak their ancestral languages. These are the Navajo of the American Southwest (numbering 300,000), the Cree of Canada (200,000), and the Inuit of Canada, Alaska, and Greenland (150,000). A greater percentage of members of the much smaller Zuni nation of New Mexico (about 10,000) can speak their ancestral language. For these peoples the greatest linguistic change of the past century has been the addition of English as a second language. According to US Census Bureau data for 2007, only 3 percent of Navajo speak Navajo exclusively, but the number of people acquiring the language is increasing. The number of native Zuni speakers is also increasing.

The indigenous peoples with the smallest number of members generally have the most endangered languages, a circumstance also common elsewhere in the world. However, many other factors besides size and concentration have affected language retention among the native peoples of North America. Large nations in the eastern part of the continent who have had longer association with the European frontier have lower rates of retention than western nations like the Navajo, Hopi, and Zuni. Thus, only a quarter of the estimated 220,000 Ojibwe (Chippewa) in the United States and Canada can speak their ancestral language. Lower retention rates also are characteristic of those nations that were conquered and forced to relocate, such as the Choctaw (numbering 120,000 and found in every state in the United States) and the Cherokee (13,000 in North Carolina and 300,000 in Oklahoma). Less than 10 percent of these two groups speak the ancestral languages. Western nations that experienced violent frontier wars and have undergone substantial language shifts include the 100,000 Sioux, about a third of whom speak the ancestral language and 56,000 Western Apache, 22 percent of whom speak the ancestral language.[35]

The conclusion to be drawn from all this is a familiar one for historians: too much emphasis on a single factor, such as government language policies, leads to misleading conclusions. The harm done to native peoples by government policies, even when well intentioned, was real and serious. But even persecuted peoples have been able preserve their languages and cultures. As linguist Salikoko Mufwene has argued, English-medium boarding schools have not led to the extinction of healthy indigenous languages in postcolonial Africa, and there is no reason to see education in a different language as the key factor in the decline of native languages in North America. Most indigenous people in North America speak English and, as discussed above, the percentage of those who are bilingual varies considerably. The number of indigenous people has also risen significantly in recent decades in North America and in some cases, as noted earlier, so has fluency in native languages. Whether bilingualism will be sustained in the future is an open question. There is evidence of both declines in the use of indigenous languages at home and increases in instruction in them in schools.[36]

These examples of the persistence of languages and the growth of bilingualism require some explanation because they go against the general tendency in North America toward monolingualism in English. The German case seems pretty straightforward. No other language besides English had as many immigrant speakers as German before 1950. Few other immigrant groups had such high literacy rates as the German speakers. Literacy and the devotion to education and publication in German helped extend the perpetuation of the language in subsequent generations. Most other immigrants were doubly dislocated: first by a voyage to North America and then, especially after the colonial period, a second dispersal from the port of entry that scattered them among other people. To be sure, all sorts of immigrant communities abounded in North America: German towns, Polish towns, Irish towns, and so on, but they were havens, not ghettos. Immigrants had to interact and communicate with other people, which was usually through English.

Because the Navajo are numerous and concentrated on large reservations in New Mexico and Arizona, they have been less affected by the scattering that affected many European and other immigrants and many other Amerindian nations. French Canadians and Spanish-speaking New Mexicans also benefited from being concentrated in particular locations. Those who stayed put were most likely to retain an ancestral language, even if circumstances warranted learning English as a second language.

In other cases, English displaced immigrant languages, in part because of official policies but even more because of other circumstances. As one scholar puts it, "America's linguistic history has been a mix of tolerance and intolerance that has had the overall effect of mitigating against the use of non-English languages."[37] The expectation by the majority that immigrants would learn English made them do so, while this push was matched by a strong pull to acquire the language that was so important for success. The pull to be assimilated is most evident in the loss of the ancestral language among most immigrants, although that was not the only possible outcome.

Bilingualism in North America may be on the increase, as it is in most of the rest of the world. The three decades following 1980 saw a massive resurgence of immigration into the United States and Canada. During both the last decade of the 1900s and the first decade of the 2000s, immigration to both countries surpassed the previous peaks set in 1901–10. In this period the number of legal immigrants to the United States from sub-Saharan Africa surpassed the numbers who had arrived during all the decades of the Atlantic slave trade. By 2010, fully 25 percent of Americans were immigrants or the children of immigrants. What is distinctive (besides their numbers) about these new immigrants and their descendants is that air travel and telecommunications make it possible for them to retain contact with relatives in their ancestral homelands and thus with their ancestral languages.

As a result the newest waves of immigrants to North America may not become monolingual. This possible trend toward bilingualism has become the subject of an intense national debate in the United States about bilingual education for the new waves of immigrants. The greatest attention has focused on the rising Hispanic population of California, Texas, Arizona, and other places, often on the part of that population who lack legal residence documents. Proponents of bilingual education insist on the educational value of continuing instruction in English and the mother tongue, often framing the debate in terms that go against the assimilationist ideology that dominated the previous two centuries of the country's history. Pragmatists worry about the high costs of providing mother-tongue (and dialect) instruction to a large number of different immigrant groups and about the deterioration of educational quality resulting from the hiring of under-qualified teachers who may be imperfectly bilingual themselves. Opponents of bilingual education in some states have moved to make official the long-standing primacy of English. Voters in California, a state with large number of immigrants, voted to curtail bilingual education in 1998.[38] Not far below the surface in many places was a dislike of people speaking a foreign language in public, whether or not the individuals were also proficient in English.

This chapter has examined how North America became the part of the world with largest concentration of native speakers of English. It would be possible to complete this story of settler colonies examining other English-speaking populations in Australia, New Zealand, and South Africa. Such completeness would also lengthen this study, but these details would be unlikely to reveal new patterns.[39] Including their particular stories also risks distorting the narrative of the rise to global English since these smaller settler populations were not as influential in making English the global language as were the British and North Americans. For these reasons this study turns instead to areas of the world where English has gained importance as a second language, for that form of English's growth has been the major factor in the rise of global English.

Chapter 4

English in Imperial Asia and Africa

English meant different things to different people in British India. For Ram Mohan Roy, a prominent Indian intellectual in the early 1800s, the English language was "the key to all knowledge—all of the really useful knowledge which the world contains." A century later, the Indian nationalist leader Mohandas K. Gandhi felt it "a matter of deep humiliation" to have to address an Indian audience in English rather than a vernacular language and charged that the time spent learning English was a waste of six years for Indian youths. In Africa, such principled resistance to using English was much rarer, though the reason was not due to African nationalists' lack of passion. Rather a dozen former British colonies there (plus Ethiopia and Liberia) chose English as a necessary and powerful tool for uniting their disparate populations and modernizing their societies. As Edward Wilmot Blyden, an Afro-Caribbean educator in Liberia, had predicted in the mid-1800s, when colonies were still few, "English is, undoubtedly, the most suitable of the European languages for bridging over the numerous gulfs . . . caused by the great diversity of language" among the peoples of Africa. In a postindependence essay in 1965 the Nigerian novelist Chinua Achebe voiced a similar theme:

> Let us give the devil his due: colonialism in Africa disrupted many things, but it did create big political units where there were small, scattered ones before . . . And it gave [Africans] a language with which to talk to one another.

Similarly, Tanzanian professor Ali A. Mazrui celebrated the role English has played in building pan-African unity, playfully referring to the great number of black English speakers as "Afro-Saxons."[1]

This chapter explores the factors common to the spread of English in Anglo-American colonies, as well as the differences in outcomes that resulted. Added to the establishment of English as the dominant language in North America, the spread of English across Asia, Africa, and the Pacific was a giant step in making English global. Who was responsible for this global spread? While it might seem obvious that the imperial powers were, the facts on the ground suggest a more complex answer, in which the actions and views of the colonized count equally—or more.

The spread of English in Asia and Africa cannot be attributed primarily to British and American colonizers for two key reasons. In the first place, the power of imperial forces to effect cultural change was more limited in most colonies than many people assume. Colonial administrations were very small and social engineering was allotted a tiny amount of their limited budgets. Second, policy makers in the huge British Empire were reluctant to promote English, even if they had had the funds to do so. Their imperial administration needed comparatively few English-speaking Asian and African employees, and administrators correctly feared the disruptive effects large cultural changes would have on the peoples they ruled and thus on their imperial power. In places like Hawaii and the Philippines, American imperialists promoted English more aggressively (as they had with regard to Native Americans), but the global effects of such actions were limited because America's overseas empire was so much smaller than Britain's.

Two other groups were more effective agents in spreading English in these colonies. As in Wales and Ireland, fervent Christians were of major importance as agents of cultural change. Although some colonial officials who were sincere Christians also affected policy decisions, independent missionaries acted far earlier and did much more to promote the study of English, both on their own and in tandem with colonial officials. Some may view missionaries and educators (often one and the same) as cultural imperialists. Neither missionaries nor educators were likely to be cultural relativists, since they believed they possessed universal truths and knowledge necessary to leading a proper life. Because they set out to transform people from within, altering basic belief systems and transforming ways of life, missionaries and educators helped bring about far more substantial changes in people than the purveyors of Western clothing, food, gadgets, or music.

Even so, calling missionaries and educators cultural imperialists seems intellectually lazy. Part of the problem is in the metaphor. Political empires have a center of command. Missionary movements were far more diffuse, and, while they might receive assistance from colonial authorities, missionaries and imperial officials pursued quite separate (and sometimes antithetical) agendas. To be sure, some in the British Empire were affiliated with the established Church of England, but many other missionaries came from other traditions that are hard to see as part of a grand plan. In British Africa, for example, Irish Catholics were notably active and often had considerable antipathy both to British power and its established church.

An even greater flaw in the notion of cultural imperialism is the assumption that missionaries and educators possessed some sort of coercive power. In reality, while they might expose people to new cultural possibilities, they lacked the power to compel people to accept what they preached and taught. For cultural change to occur, then, it had to come from within and required considerable fervor and effort. The power of missionaries and educators came from their ability to convince others to change themselves. For that to occur the people who embraced Christianity, Western education, and English had to see advantages for themselves in doing so. To disregard the importance of African and Asian agendas in bringing about cultural transformation is to miss the heart of what was occurring.

It is much harder to denigrate the intentions of the second group instrumental in spreading English in colonies since they were the colonized themselves, and they were arguably the greatest force for its spread. A report by the private American foundation, the Phelps-Stokes Fund, about British colonies in East Africa in the early 1920s concluded that Africans "are as a rule eager to learn an European language," because they believed that English would open doors for advancement and enhance their abilities to communicate with colonial officials.[2] In contrast to the settler colonies in the Americas and Australasia, most Asian and African colonies in had relatively few white settlers or none at all. In every African and Asian colony, the indigenous populations were the majority and their interests and welfare were of paramount concern to authorities, though imperial interests and resource constraints meant that welfare measures were implemented slowly. Colonial governments were much less powerful than is often imagined and the subject masses, though not greatly empowered, were far from powerless.

As has already been discussed with regard to the British Isles and North America, the pull to master English accompanied and often exceeded the governmental push from above. Elite individuals among colonial subjects were the first to recognize the benefits English might bring them in dealing with imperial authority and economy. Later, more subordinate members also sought to improve their standings by learning the language of the more powerful. Ultimately the nationalist movements that helped end these empires made extensive use of English (and the ideas learned by reading works in English), whether they endorsed or opposed continued usage of English. Ironically, the English language helped overthrow those who introduced it.

British Colonies in Asia

The spread of the English language in southern Asia had its beginnings in the trading ventures of the East India Company (EIC) in the 1700s. Although the Company was a business first and foremost, it became a political and military force as well. As the EIC's power grew, some Indian rulers looked to it as a useful ally. Some local individuals learned enough English to gain employment with the EIC as local agents, interpreters, and servants. Yet, on the whole, the EIC opposed English-language education, fearing its promotion might generate disturbances. Instead, the small educational efforts it made were confined to institutions that promoted the study of Arabic, Sanskrit, and Persian, the best established South Asian languages of learning. After taking control of Bengal in 1765, the Company promoted the teaching and mastery of local languages, founding institutions such as the Calcutta Madrasa in 1781 and the Sanskrit College in Banaras in 1791. Fort William College in Calcutta was added in 1800 to train EIC officials in

Indian languages. The Company's press at Fort William printed rules and regulations in Bengali. Christian missions and some Indians in Calcutta soon added their own publishing programs in vernacular languages. In all, some 15,000 works in Bengali were printed and distributed between 1810 and 1820.[3]

In addition to the small number of Indians who worked for the EIC as servants, clerks, and translators, some high-caste Hindus who prospered from the Company's presence in Calcutta appreciated the advantages they could gain from fluency in English. Most eminent among this "new breed of baboos" was Ram Mohan Roy (1772–1833), the freethinking son of an aristocratic Hindu family, who had educated himself to a remarkable degree in the languages and scriptures of Asia and then took up the study of English. Often seen as the father of modern India, Roy believed Hindu society needed to be reformed using liberal and scientific ideas from the West. Besides founding newspapers in English, Bengali, and Persian to spread his ideas, Roy played a leading role in planning a new educational institution that would introduce Indians to Western ideas. He was a powerful force behind the foundation of Hindu College in Calcutta in 1817 (renamed Presidency College in 1855), although Roy withdrew from the enterprise lest his unorthodox religious views offend Hindu moderates. Although not the first English-medium school in Bengal (one for indigent Christians having been founded nearly a century earlier), Hindu College set the standard for all that followed, both in its devotion to the study of English and in the high standards of its diverse curriculum. Anticipating the later Anglicist/Orientalist debates among Company administrators, Bengali intellectuals of this era also debated how much of the reform Indian education should come from Western models. In 1824, Sanskrit College opened its doors across the street from Hindu College with more traditional "Orientalist" curriculum.[4]

Christian missionary societies were a third force in Bengal educational development, as were evangelical Christians in the EIC. Missionaries' early efforts in India had echoed those of the EIC in focusing largely on education in the vernaculars. Even so, the Company was concerned about their promotion of Western Christianity and resisted legalizing missionary activities until 1813. Thereafter, missionary activities in Bengal expanded, particularly among the lower classes. In addition to these vernacular efforts, some missionaries began to encourage the use of English. Already in 1792, Charles Grant, a Company official with evangelical views, advocated English-medium schools to replace the "darkness" of Hinduism with the light of Christianity and modern Western education. In a break from missionary focus on converting the lower classes, the first Church of Scotland missionary in India, Alexander Duff, pioneered the proselytization of the upper classes. His new school that opened in Calcutta in 1830 (later known as Scottish Church College) followed an English-medium curriculum that combined Western secular subjects with the compulsory study of the Bible and the study of Bengali literature. With the help of Ram Mohan Roy, the new school won support from prominent Bengalis, who were reassured that students could read the Bible without having to become Christians.[5]

The policy of the Europeans immersing themselves in Indian culture, promoted by Governor General Warren Hastings (1773–85), began to lose ground in the early nineteenth century to evangelicals' idea of assimilating Indians to English culture. This policy of "Anglicism" is often traced to the famous Minute on Education (1835) of Thomas Babington Macaulay, the son of the evangelical leader Zachery Macaulay, but this important policy shift was the product of larger forces that emerged under the liberal Governor General William Bentinck (1828–35). Bentinck was an admirer of the utilitarianism of the Scottish economist and philosopher James Mill (1773–1836), and the Anglicist policies he pushed had pragmatic ends. In 1833, Bentinck secured the opening of administrative appointments to Indians, partly in response to pressure from educated Indians for inclusion in government but even more as a way to reduce the expense of European civil servants.

The Orientalist/Anglicist tug-of-war for the meager government funds allocated to education was unresolved until 1833 when Governor Bentinck appointed Charles Trevelyan to the committee in charge of education, where Trevelyan pushed tirelessly for a broadening of English-medium instruction. The controversy this stirred among the education committee members led Bentinck to refer the matter to Macaulay, the newly arrived legal committee member. Macaulay's famous Minute on Education championed the policy Bentinck and other Anglicists had begun. Given the modest sums available for education, Macaulay concluded that the best policy was "to form a class who may be interpreters between us and the millions whom we govern—a class of persons Indian in blood and colour, but English in tastes, in opinions, in morals and in intellect." That class, in turn, would import Western scientific nomenclature into the vernacular languages of the mass of Indian subjects. Among the justifications Macaulay offered for this policy was that Indians favored English education, as was evidenced by the fact that they were already paying for such schooling out of their own pockets, while the government had to subsidize the study of Sanskrit and Arabic. In response, the governor general and his education council established English schools in the major towns of Bengal, but the new policy remained controversial in official circles for another dozen years. Many Hindus and Muslims in India, including those who supported English education, voiced opposition to the new plan since it would shift educational funding exclusively to English-medium schools at the expense of the existing Sanskrit and Arabic schools. As a result, the Company directors revised the policy and assured critics that sufficient funding would be made available for the new English schools without reducing the funding of the Oriental schools. Special funding was also made available for continuing the publication of vernacular translations of major European books.[6]

In a dispatch to the governor general of India in 1854, Sir Charles Wood, the British chancellor of the Exchequer, tipped Indian educational policy in a decisively Anglicist direction. Once celebrated as "the Magna Charta of Indian education" in the nineteenth century, the Wood's Dispatch of 1854 was more evolutionary than revolutionary, envisioning a broader system of education using vernacular languages in the elementary schools, but with English being the medium of instruction at the secondary level and above. Over the next half century a great expansion of publicly funded and assisted education took place in the five provinces the EIC administered (Bengal, Madras, Bombay, the North West Province, and the Punjab), but such assistance was disproportionately directed to the English-medium secondary schools opened by Indian private organizations and Christian missionary societies. Government policies clearly shaped this line of expansion, but its pace was also driven from below by the strong demand from urban Indians wanting to advance themselves by becoming fluent in English. Poorer classes seeking advancement also joined in. By 1882, there were about 180 secondary schools, of which only 4 used vernacular languages. By that year the number of colleges affiliated with the universities of Calcutta, Bombay, and Madras had risen to 72 from the 27 existing at the time of the universities' establishments in 1857. Punjab University opened in 1882 and Allahabad University in 1886. Meanwhile, a tremendous expansion was taking place in elementary education, which enrolled over 20 million pupils by the early 1880s. This was a significant achievement, but in the vastness of British India, it was just a drop in the bucket, and few went on to the secondary level.[7]

Nevertheless, the patterns put in place in the nineteenth century guided educational development in India during the rest of the colonial period. The entire system grew steadily at all levels, fastest at the primary level where funding was primarily local. However, it was the growth of secondary and tertiary (postsecondary) education that had greatest effect on the knowledge of English. At the tertiary level, Indians were active in founding new private colleges. At the instigation of Governor General Lord Curzon, a number of educational reforms were introduced in the early 1900s aimed at improving the quality and broadening base of Indian education. The census of 1901 had documented that only a tenth of Indian males were literate and only 0.7 percent of females. On the issue of using English, there were only minor changes to the established system of beginning instruction in the vernaculars, teaching the English language in the upper grades, and then moving to instruction very largely in English in secondary school.[8]

Since the English language conveniently symbolized British imperial domination, the spread of English was an easy target for Indian nationalists. Mohandas K. Gandhi in particular railed against the tyranny of the English language in India, though he was a late convert that position, having once prided himself on his good English speech, dress, manners, and London law degree (1891). By 1916, however, Gandhi could give a speech at the opening of Benares Hindu University bemoaned the time so many Indians lost in studying a foreign language, arguing that India would have been much better off if education in the previous half century has been in the vernaculars. His question, "Is there a man who dreams that English can ever become the national language of India?," drew cries of "Never!" from his audience. Gandhi apologized for posing the question in English, but he did not suggest which Indian language might be the alternative to English. There was great irony in Gandhi's position, but his position was not disingenuous. He freely admitted that individuals benefited from learning English but argued that the nation suffered as a result. Indians, he charged, were complicit in Britain's rule and needed to make personal sacrifices if a new, independent India was to emerge. In the 1920s, the Indian National Congress (INC) took up the issue of national education, urging a gradual withdrawal from government schools and colleges in favor of institutions run by Indians and making far greater use of Indian languages. However, the practical difficulties of such a program led Gandhi and Congress to reverse that gradualist position in 1922.[9]

Gandhi's critique of English education was inaccurate in many respects, notably his charges that it had come at the expense of vernacular education and that it had been imposed from above. Such inaccuracies and distortions as his attacks contain, however, seem pale in comparison with the venomous assaults on traditional Indian culture in Macaulay's Minute (see above). Gandhi was not alone in advocating greater use of vernaculars. After the First World War, nationalists (and some officials) had criticized the educational system as too elite and had called for a broader national education system. The creation of provincial assemblies in 1921 opened the door to promoting more broadly based systems using mother tongues and the establishment of high schools offering instruction in Hindi and Bengali. For example, in 1934 Bengali was made the medium of instruction in Bengal, and Urdu came into wider use in Hyderabad schools. Still, many elite schools and all Indian universities continued to teach in English. In 1938–39, British India had a combined student population of about 13.5 million at the primary through secondary levels (out of a population of some 400 million), plus 120,000 university students.[10]

As independence approached after the Second World War, the language question became an important issue in British India. English was well established across the colony and had become the de facto language of the Indian National Congress and the link between the leaders of the INC and the Muslim League. Even so, those who supported greater use of the vernaculars correctly criticized English as the language of the elite. In 1944, a prominent Indian educator declared, "India is the only country in the world which presents the curious spectacle of young pupils learning in school through a foreign tongue which they can only imperfectly understand."[11] Educators elsewhere in the world would have been surprised at that claim, since most students in some lands and some students in most lands were schooled in a language other than their mother tongue. At the time examples of non-mother-tongue education ranged from non-Arab Muslims in Koranic schools to immigrants in schools in North America and elsewhere. Nevertheless, support for vernacular language education was a popular issue at the time.

Choosing a national language was a separate issue. More than 30 Indian languages had a million speakers or more on the eve of independence and no vernacular language was understood by a majority of Indians. Finding a language to unite them was a daunting task. For a time there was much support for Hindustani, which had been the language of the Mogul Empire and in its spoken form was the lingua franca of much of northern and western India. However, when it became evident that the INC and the Muslim League could not overcome their differences and partition was inevitable, Hindustani lost support. By a narrow margin Indian nationalists opted for Hindi, which was understood by a considerable number of the INC leadership. For its part, Pakistan chose Urdu, a language commonly used as a lingua franca in West Pakistan, but spoken by few as a first language. Linguists consider the spoken forms of Hindi and Urdu as dialects of Hindustani, but the literary forms of the languages differ widely with Urdu having many Persian and Arabic influences.

Jawaharlal Nehru, India's first prime minister, supported the continued use of English in India but agreed that a national language had to be known by more than the elite. He argued that Hindi would be a better choice because so many more Indians already knew it, but allowed that English "must continue to be the most important language in India."[12]

Each of the new South Asian countries recognized that it would take time to move to new national languages. Each proposed a 15-year transition period, during which English would remain in official use and would serve as the basis for interprovincial communication. Then the designated indigenous language would become the sole national language.[13] None of these transitions worked out as planned. Pakistan's choice of Urdu was unpopular among the Bengali-speaking population of East Pakistan, where few understood that language. The language issue helped fuel the separatist movement that led to the breakup of the federation in 1971. East Pakistan became Bangladesh and chose Bangla (Bengali) and English as its national languages.

In the island republic of Sri Lanka to the south, nationalists had chosen to install Sinhala as the official language, a move that helped further alienate the large Tamil-speaking population and led to decades of conflict. Despite this decision to push Sinhala, English remained important in many internal contexts from business and tourism to scientific higher education and was essential for international communication. Ever since the British takeover from the Dutch in 1796, English-medium private and missionary schools had been producing a middle class whose understanding transcended narrow nationalist visions. As internal and global pressures multiplied in the 1980s, the Sri Lankan government relented recognizing the importance of English as a "link language," validating the existence of "international schools," and, in 1995, proclaiming English a national language.[14]

In India, as the transition period drew to an end in 1965, many who were not native speakers of Hindi feared they would be unable to compete for government jobs with those who were. In the southern province of Tamil Nadu there were riots against being forced to use Hindi. Under growing pressure, the government announced a new compromise permitting the continued use of English in the national parliament and in non-Hindi-speaking states. Language choices were placed in the hands of the individual states, whose boundaries were adjusted to correspond more closely to linguistic frontiers. In most states a local vernacular functioned as the principle medium of communication, with English being taught as a second language, and Hindi as a third. In the end the states established 33 vernaculars as official languages, along with three foreign languages (English, French, and Portuguese). Unofficially, as historian Paul Brass commented in the late 1980s, not much changed:

> In practice English has continued the dominant language of elite communication in the country as a whole...It is still accepted as the medium of examination for admission to state services, along-side the official state languages, in every state and union territory in the country. Hindi has not succeeded in displacing English as a lingua franca for the country.[15]

By the 1990s, nearly all Indians were able to receive several years of English instruction during their first ten years of school. However, mastering English was still confined to the elite, as a distinct minority of the population remained in school for ten years, and only about a tenth of those who did so attended English-medium schools. More recently English has been gaining popularity because of its international importance, as will be discussed in more detail later in this chapter. New English-medium schools are springing up, and there is considerable pressure on state schools to expand the teaching of English, in some places by making it the medium of instruction.[16]

In their smaller colonies in East and Southeast Asia, the British had followed policies similar to those in India, using English in the upper levels of governance but also encouraging local languages. Local people who could afford to attend a Western school made their own choices. For example, during the first 60 years of British rule (1842–1902) in Hong Kong, students had the choice of English-medium, Chinese-medium, or mixed-medium government schools. Initially, Chinese language schools were the most popular, but by the 1880s, the mixed-medium schools were attracting students in equal numbers. Thereafter, the mixed-medium schools pulled ahead. For a long time the English-only schools catered largely to the children of the colony's European residents and a very small number of Chinese from elite families. So it is not surprising that in 1910 a recognizable approximation of standard English was spoken by only 1,000 to 1,200 Chinese in Hong Kong, all of whom were graduates of Queen's College, an elite secondary school known as the "Eton of the East."[17]

Under pressure from local nationalists, especially after the emergence of the People's Republic of China in 1949, the British government in Hong Kong moved to fund Chinese-medium primary schools in the early 1950s and made nine years of education free and compulsory in 1978. A Chinese-medium university opened in 1964, complementing an English-medium one that had operated since 1911. Chinese was made the second official language of the colony in 1974. Given Hong Kong's extensive foreign trade and banking, knowing English gave residents considerable employment advantages. By 1991, nearly all of the residents spoke Cantonese (the language of the earlier Chinese settlers), a third could also speak English, and only 18 percent knew Mandarin, the language of many recent immigrants from mainland China and a compulsory subject in schools. After Britain ceded the territory to China in 1997, the government of Hong Kong moved to improve the quality of English and Mandarin instruction. Because spoken Cantonese shows no sign of declining, Hong Kong seems destined to be trilingual for the foreseeable future.[18]

In the cluster of British colonies and protectorates in Southeast Asia known as the Straits Settlements, language policies followed lines similar to those in India: vernacular primary education, with English-medium schools, mostly missionary run, for the elite. Chinese and Indian immigrants added to the diversity of the population and complicated language policies. After independence in 1957 the Federation of Malaysia (briefly including Singapore) opted for making Bahasa Malaysia, a standardized form of Malay, the national language. Over the next quarter century to government gradually implemented a transition from using English in government, and English-medium schools were fazed out. Resistance from the Chinese and Tamil communities led to their being allowed to operate their own vernacular schools. The Chinese have moved to make Mandarin the language of instruction, even though most of them have spoken other dialects from southeastern China. All schools teach English as a second or third language. It might appear that the Malay population were advantaged because they only had to master two languages, but in fact many rural Malay had difficulties because they spoke a different dialect of Malay at home and were unlikely to have had any exposure to English before entering school. The challenge of mastering three languages by the end of secondary school was unevenly met. By the 1990s, Malaysia had made good progress in establishing Bahasa as the national language, but the country was slipping behind other Asian countries in training people in English to a level of proficiency that was competitive with other Asian countries.[19]

Like Hong Kong, Singapore is a city-state with a Chinese majority and has great importance in international trade. Under British rule Singapore's economic rise went hand in hand with the use of English. By 1954, English-medium schools had surpassed Chinese-medium ones in popularity among the colony's residents. Higher education was exclusively in English. Since separating from the Federation of Malaysia in 1965, the government of Singapore has made English the first language of the republic, while Mandarin, Malay, and Tamil also have official status. It has pursued policies that promote bilingualism in English and the vernacular, as well as the use of Mandarin as the standard form of Chinese. Outside of a handful of special schools, all education is English-medium, except when studying the mother tongue. Echoing earlier policy statements by President Lee Kuan Yew, the Minister of Education in 1986 explained the policy this way:

> Children must learn English so that they will have a window to the knowledge, technology and expertise of the modern world. They must know their mother tongues to enable them to know what makes us what we are.[20]

Proficiency in English remains crucial for gaining admission to higher levels of education. Because of parents' recognition of the language's importance for their children's future, the number of Singapore households using English as the primary home language has risen very rapidly from 9 percent in 1980 to over 32 percent in 2010. The 2010 census reported that 80 percent of the population is literate in English and 70.5 percent are literate in two or more languages.[21]

This overview of British imperial influences in Asia highlights two important facts. First, British policies promoting the use of English were limited, although actions by missionary societies and individual Asians enhanced the language's usage. Second, postindependence policies have been a greater force in shaping language changes, although with multiple outcomes. Singapore is unusual in committing itself to using English as its first language and in achieving such extensive growth in the use of English as a primary language and as a secondary language. It is interesting that Hong Kong, though similar in ethnic composition and economic circumstances, has seen much less language displacement by English, even though it remained a British colony much longer. Elsewhere in the former parts of Britain's empire, the decision to promote a local language as the national language and reduce the importance of English has also produced mixed results. Malaysia appears to have had the greatest success in creating a new national language, but in the process it has struggled to keep its citizens sufficiently fluent in English to compete for international business with other countries in the region. Bangladesh already possessed a national language and Pakistan was moderately successful with promoting Urdu, although both countries have found it necessary to use English in higher education, military cadres, and international relations. In India and Sri Lanka efforts to build new nations around a vernacular language ran into difficulties, not only because of opposition from the speakers of other languages but also because of English's continuing growth as the premier international language. The next section examines the quite different outcomes in former British Africa, where the most important former colonies have promoted English as their national language.

British Colonies in Africa

The spread of English in Africa followed patterns similar to those in Asia, though the affected populations were smaller. By 1700, the presence of English traders in West Africa had led to the transformation of the lingua franca of the coast from a Portuguese-based pidgin to one using mostly English words. A number of West Africans became fluent enough in Standard English to act as translators and agents and some West African traders sent their children to England to master the language. Some of these, in turn opened English-medium schools in coastal West Africa. An African trader in the coastal port of Old Calabar even kept a diary in English in the 1780s. In 1846, the Church of Scotland opened a mission in the same port, which soon led to the establishment of English-medium schools in the area.[22]

Expanding English trade in the Indian Ocean helped spread English in southern Africa. An African from the Cape Town area named Autshumao (also known as Harry) learned English working on an English ship to Java in the 1630s. Because he also had a command of Dutch and local African languages, Harry was able to become the chief interpreter for the Dutch East India Company outpost at Cape Town. The fact that ships of many nations called at the port on their way to Asia favored the use of English over Dutch. Britain took over the Cape Colony from the Dutch East India Company in 1805, intending to use it as a way station on the route to India, but circumstances would draw them deeper into the interior.

After a series of calamitous frontier wars, many of the Xhosa peoples abandoned traditional practices and embraced Christianity. Mission schools introduced English. The Free Church of Scotland's Lovedale Missionary Institute, founded in 1841 in territory not then a part of the Cape Colony, pioneered in the education of the "Church Xhosa," teaching generations of Africans an English-based curriculum to a high standard. In 1916, the South African Native College at nearby Fort Hare raised the standard even higher.[23]

Meanwhile, another small British colony was emerging in Sierra Leone on the Atlantic coast of West Africa. In 1808, Britain acquired the remains of a bankrupt settlement of free blacks from London, North America, and Jamaica, and soon began to use the harbor at Freetown as the headquarters of its naval squadron patrolling the Atlantic coast to intercept ships illegally engaging in the slave trade. Over the course of the next several decades some 94,000 Africans rescued from the slaving ships were liberated in Freetown, and most were resettled in its hinterland under the care of missionary societies that opened English-medium schools. Lacking any common language, liberated Africans often used English to communicate with each other and with their benefactors. For example, an African named George Crowley Nicol testified to a parliamentary committee in 1849 that his own parents, born in different parts of Africa, spoke to each other in English.

The spread of English in Sierra Leone was sped by the numerous schools, mostly run by missionary societies. The schools were staffed primarily by English-speaking blacks from the Atlantic diaspora who had settled there earlier, by growing numbers of newly trained liberated Africans and their descendants, as well as by a few Europeans. The liberated Africans' pursuit of education remained passionate even after school fees were imposed. By 1840, Sierra Leone had over 8,000 children in its schools (a fifth of the total population), giving the small colony a literacy rate (in English) higher than that in many European countries. A secondary school opened in 1845 and shortly thereafter an old seminary at Fourah Bay was revitalized and again became an important center for African education. Fourah Bay College (affiliated in 1876 with the University of Durham and later the basis for the University of Sierra Leone) turned out many notable graduates who earned advanced degrees elsewhere, much like their Asian counterparts. As will be recounted later, a number of other Africans from Sierra Leone became active in Christian missionary efforts in southern Nigeria.[24]

The small colonies of Cape Colony and Sierra Leone were followed in the last decades of the 1800s by much larger British annexations associated with the general European "Scramble for Africa." When the dust settled, Britain had acquired three more territories in West Africa: tiny Gambia, the rich Gold Coast, and densely populated northern and southern Nigeria (merged in 1914), five in eastern Africa: the Sudan (administered jointly with Egypt), the Protectorate of Uganda, British East Africa (later Kenya), British Somaliland, and Zanzibar, and three colonies in southern Africa: Nyasaland, Southern Rhodesia, and Northern Rhodesia (the latter two administered by the British South African Company until 1923), as well as three protectorates known as Basutoland (now Lesotho), Bechuanaland (now Botswana), and Swaziland. After the defeat of Germany in the First World War, Britain's African responsibilities were expanded to include administering former German possessions under League of Nations mandates: Tanganyika (former German East Africa), Southwest Africa (administered by the government of South Africa), and parts of Togoland and Cameroon in West Africa. Of these, the most populous by far was Nigeria, now the most populous country in Africa.

In the new colonies, British policy followed policies much like those devised in South Asia: a few government schools and subsidies to approved schools (missionary run for the most part). Although some officials realized the utility of an educated, English-speaking elite, many distrusted the loyalties of educated Africans to the colonial government and to their fellow Africans. As Nigeria's first governor general, Frederick Lugard (1858–1945) argued, it should be "a cardinal principle of British colonial policy that the interests of the large native population not be subject to the will...of a small minority of educated and Europeanized natives who have nothing in common with them, and whose interests are often opposed to theirs." Although educated Africans had held important posts in the small British colonies of Sierra Leone and Lagos in the nineteenth century (and on the Gold Coast in the 1700s), during the first half of the twentieth century views similar to Lugard's were used to block the appointment of educated Africans to administrative positions. Another important British official in West Africa, Sir Alan Burns, spoke for most of his peers in deploring educated Africans as "bad imitations of Europeans instead of good Africans."[25] Such views persisted among British officials well after the 1930s, even as the number of educated Africans was growing, the cultural division between them and the masses was narrowing, and the educated elite were emerging as the spokesmen of incipient nationalist movements.

British language policy was quite similar in its nonsettler colonies in Asia and Africa. As a general rule indigenous languages were not to be interfered with beyond efforts to standardize their usage and orthographies for the purpose of their use in schools, broadcasts, and printed works. This was consistent with the pragmatic policy of interfering as little as possible with the cultures of the subject peoples by governing through traditional chiefs. As governor of Northern Nigeria, Lugard had raised this use of traditional rulers to an influential theory of colonial rule, which he called "indirect rule."[26] The promotion of English, therefore, was to be limited to producing a small number of locals who were needed to assist with the tasks of administration that required them to deal directly with British officials. Near the top of the administration, highly placed traditional rulers (or their translators) needed

English to comprehend and carry out policy. Lower down in the ranks clerks, messengers, and some in the police and military forces needed to have a command of English. Other English-speaking Africans acted as assistants to British merchants, transporters, and missionaries.

The official policy of limited educational opportunities for Africans ran counter to the wishes of Christian missionaries and humanitarians, who pressured British colonial governments to subsidize mission schools. It also ran contrary to the wishes of a growing number of Africans. The Scotsman J. H. Oldham, a dominant figure in the Protestant efforts as head of the International Missionary Council from its founding in 1921, called for more schools as an essential part of preparing Africans for eventual self rule. An American foundation, the Phelps-Stokes Fund, sponsored two influential investigations on the state of African schooling in the 1920s that pointed out the need for educational reforms and better coordination between government and private voluntary efforts. British policy soon shifted to providing grants and subsidies to all schools that met standards of quality, which permitted the missionary societies to expand their schools more rapidly. Some missionaries were suspicious of the government regulations that came with the subsidies, but the larger missionary bodies recognized the greater good that subsidies brought. For example, the Roman Catholic apostolic delegate to British Africa in the 1920s strongly urged Catholic missionaries to cooperate fully with colonial educational policies and, if necessary, even "neglect your churches in order to perfect your schools." As a result, Catholic education expanded rapidly in Africa, with Irish missionaries taking the lead in many places, and in places surpassed the older efforts by Protestant missions.[27]

The populous British colony of Nigeria is a good illustration of how official policies, missionary activities, and African aspirations interacted to produce dramatically different regional outcomes. English was taught in the early grades of Nigerian schools and became the medium of instruction in the upper grades. By the year 1938–39, Northern Nigeria had 25,000 students, nearly all in government-sponsored schools, a modest number in a territory of 11.5 million people. That same year in the somewhat less populous southern half of Nigeria there were 268,000 students in

Table 4.1 Education in Nigeria and India, 1938–39

	Northern Nigeria	Southern Nigeria	British India
Population	11,500,000	8,500,000	400,000,000
Students, primary & secondary	25,067	267,788	13,500,000
Students, university	0	0	120,000
Students, primary & secondary per 10,000 population	22	315	335

Source: Michael Crowder, "White Chiefs of Tropical Africa," in L. H. Gann and Peter Duignan, eds., *Colonialism in Africa, 1870–1960* (Cambridge: Cambridge University Press, 1970), 2:322; Syama Prasad Mookerjee, "Schools in British India." *Annals of the American Academy of Political and Social Science* 233 (May 1944): 30–38.

schools: 14 times as many students per capita as in the north. Only a small number of these were in the three government schools in the southern region (see table 4.1).

What had produced such diverse results in two regions of the same colony? Both precolonial histories and responses to new conditions were critical, along with, more indirectly, some British policy decisions. A Muslim reform movement had gained control of northern Nigeria at the beginning of the nineteenth century, and the new Sokoto Caliphate had greatly expanded the existing Koranic school system. After the Caliphate was forcibly incorporated into Northern Nigeria in 1900, its emirs (governors) continued as key parts of the colonial administration. British policy promoted not only the continued rule of Muslim elite, but in many ways also encouraged the spread of Islam. Christian missions were excluded from Muslim-majority areas, so as not to antagonize the Islamic elite on whose cooperation British power rested. An unintended effect was that schools and other social changes spread much more slowly than in southern Nigeria.

Southern Nigeria had a different precolonial history and a different experience of the colonial era. The coastal part had been in continuous contact with European traders for four centuries. As already mentioned, by the eighteenth century many coastal people could speak English, some rather well. During the nineteenth century a number of African Christians freed from slavery in Brazil, Cuba, and Sierra Leone had moved back to their southern Nigerian homelands and some Christian missions were also established. The head of the first Anglican diocese, Bishop Samuel Ajayi Crowther, was an African born in southwestern Nigeria who had been rescued from a slave ship and educated in Sierra Leone and England. This precolonial introduction of Christianity was limited, although it would affect the pace of later developments. Africans who were English speakers and Christians in southern Nigeria constituted a small percentage of the region's total population.

As in northern Nigeria, the events of the colonial period were more critical. Despite a Muslim presence among the Yoruba of the southwest, colonial authorities gave missionaries pretty much a free hand throughout southern Nigeria. For complex reasons of their own, large numbers of Africans in southern Nigeria responded positively to the Christian evangelists. Irish Catholic missionaries were particularly active in promoting Christianity and English-medium schools in southeastern Nigeria, but one must be careful not to assign too much credit to foreign missionaries and too little to their African auxiliaries. Among the Igbo people of southeastern Nigeria, historian Adrian Hastings had pointed out, the rapid growth in the number of Catholics from under 5,000 in 1906 to 74,000 in 1918 cannot be explained by the actions of the foreign missionaries working there, who numbered only about 30 and lacked facility in the Igbo language. Rather, he argues, "the Igbos converted themselves," both because the actual evangelization was in the hands of Igbo catechist-teachers, whose numbers swelled from 33 to 552 in those dozen years and because the decision to embrace Catholicism was a very personal individual response. It is worth noting that the rapid expansion of Catholic schools (from 24 to 355) among the Igbo in those years took place before government subsidies were authorized, which means that Igbo villagers largely financed and constructed that educational base.[28]

The subsequent spread of Christianity and schools in southern Nigeria and other British colonies in Africa depended on economic considerations. One factor was government expenditure on education, which, as table 4.2 indicates, varied widely from colony to colony. Some variation was due to differences in policy, but the key factor was how much revenue each colony took in. A poor colony, such as Nyasaland, could spend only meager amounts

Table 4.2 Annual expenditures for education in British African colonies, 1926 (£ per 1000 population)

Gold Coast	78.20	Northern Rhodesia	8.00
Nigeria	11.75	Nyasaland	3.30
Sierra Leone	24.24	Bechuanaland	24.50
East Africa (average)	22.60	Basutoland	73.50

Source: Raymond Leslie Buell, *The Native Problem in Africa* (New York: Macmillan, 1928), II: 980.

on education compared to a richer colony like the Gold Coast. Another factor was how much money parents had to spend on their children's education, which varied similarly among colonies. Although government expenditures for education in Nigeria were modest on a per capita basis, the colony spent much more on education in southern Nigeria where schools were many than in the north where they were few. The number of schools in the south was due to both parents' decisions to send their children to mission schools and their ability to divert income they received from selling cocoa of in the southwest and palm oil in the southeast. Many in the north has income from selling peanuts but were less inclined to spend it on schools. The highest expenditures on education per student were in the Gold Coast, where cocoa revenues enabled African parents to pay school fees and where Governor Sir Frederick Gordon Guggisberg (1919–27) had championed educating Africans as a viable and cheaper alternative to employing high-cost labor from Europe. Guggisberg began by building up sufficient well-trained African teachers. He also founded Achimota School to train Africans for government service. Nigerian support for education trailed that in the Gold Coast until Governor Donald Cameron (1931–35) adopted similar policies for producing a cadre of educated Africans and spearheaded the founding of Yaba Higher College to that end.[29]

In places like southern Nigeria, illiterate, rural African peasants were well ahead of government policy makers in seeing education as the road to success for the next generation. In contrast to British India, African colonies, except in Muslim areas, saw little debate about the Western content of such schooling or the use of English in the upper grades. In non-Muslim areas of Africa,

Christian missionaries were active partners in the explosive growth of schools. Between the world wars education in some British African colonies increased dramatically. In Northern Rhodesia (now Zambia), school enrollment rose from some 40,000 in 1924 to 120,000 in 1939. In Nigeria, the number of students in primary and secondary schools increased 740 percent between 1919 (90,000) and 1947 (667,250).[30] The postwar decades saw further rapid growth of school enrollments.

Vernacular education dominated the first years of primary school in southern Nigeria, which necessitated indigenous teachers, with English being introduced during the early grades and then becoming the medium of instruction in the upper grades. Teacher-catechists thus needed a basic grasp of English in order to teach as well as to communicate with the foreign missionaries who employed them. Once educational subsidies were introduced vast numbers of teachers had to be trained to keep up with the demand from below. Especially in southeastern Nigeria, African communities competed with each other to fund primary schools and later secondary schools. Not just Catholics but Anglicans, Methodists, Presbyterians and others saw their school systems grow rapidly. At independence in 1960, 90–100 percent of school-age children in Nigeria's southern provinces were attending school, versus 5 percent in the north. Such an enormous disparity owed much more to the enthusiastic groundswell from below than to colonial policy.

During Nigeria's transition to independence there was some public discussion of adopting an African language as the country's official language. Some intellectuals admired the symbolic importance of choosing an indigenous language, but which language? The only serious contender was Hausa, a language spoken by about 38 percent of the population in the north and known more widely there as second language, but there was very little support for it among the much better educated southerners who were at the forefront of Nigeria's nationalist movement. In contrast to the contentions debates in Asia, Nigeria's nationalist leaders gave serious consideration to only one language—English. Though apprehensive about southern domination, the northern political leaders were also fluent in English and accepted it as the only language that could unite the diverse peoples of Nigeria.

After independence Nigerian governments pushed to expand English-medium education to promote national unity and development. Elementary education became free and universal; secondary education was expanded at a rapid rate; and great efforts were made to build high-quality universities. Between 1960 and 1984, the number of elementary students increased fivefold and secondary enrollments rose more than 20 fold. Reflecting on the early years of independence in former British colonies in Africa and Asia, political scientist David Abernathy put his finger on a key factor in explaining their different choices in language policy: "The language controversy that had bedeviled the politics of India, Ceylon, Malaysia, and other Asian countries has been averted in Africa precisely because African vernaculars were not vehicles for the written transmission of culture before the coming of the European." In South Asia, he notes, the benefits of vernacular education had come at the expense of national unity, whereas in Nigeria, while ethnic and religious conflicts were all too vividly present in the early years of independence, the spread of English as a common tongue helped break down communication barriers among different groups.[31]

Writing shortly after independence, the celebrated Nigerian writer Chinua Achebe defended the literary use of English on pragmatic and nationalist grounds: only English could reach the myriad peoples of the new Nigeria and, along with French and Arabic, serve to communicate among the new nations of Africa. It is worth repeating the brief excerpt quoted at the beginning of this chapter in Achebe's larger context:

> Let us give the devil his due: colonialism in Africa disrupted many things, but it did create big political units where there were small, scattered ones before...And it gave them a language with which to talk to one another. If it failed to give them a song, it at least gave them a tongue for sighing. There are not many countries in Africa today where you could abolish the language of the erstwhile colonial powers and still retain the facility for mutual communication. Therefore those African writers who have chosen to write in English or French are not unpatriotic smart alecks with an eye on the main chance—outside their own countries. They are by-products of the same process that made the new nation-states of Africa.[32]

Most of the rest of British West Africa followed this same road, as did British Central, Southern, and East Africa. In the latter region, Swahili, an indigenous language widely used as a lingua franca, was also accorded official status, but English dominated higher education. Even though Ethiopia had been under British administration for only a few years after the British liberated it from Italian rule during the Second World War, it also made English its official language and the language of instruction in secondary and postsecondary education.

South Africa is another interesting example of the language decisions in former British African colonies—one that shows both contrasting and similar choices. South Africa had the largest white settler population of any African territory, as much as a quarter of the population in 1910. White settlers were about equally divided between those who spoke English and those who spoke Afrikaans, a language derived from Dutch. Following the election victory of the National (i.e., Afrikaner) Party in 1947, white minority government there attempted to entrench its supremacy after 1947, using a system of racial and cultural segregation, best known as *apartheid* and then as "separate development." Under these programs Africans were to be encouraged to develop "along their own lines," that is, according to their ancestral traditions, despite many decades of coerced incorporation into a Western economic and political regimes and of their widespread acceptance of Christianity and other Western cultural values. A key component of apartheid/separate development was that Africans would use their ancestral languages. From 1956 to 1979 all instruction in African primary schools was to be in the mother tongue. In rural areas, most Africans never completed the primary grades. In urban areas, a modest number were able to go to secondary schools, where they had to switch to English-medium instruction. A few managed to go on to higher education.

Two events dramatically illustrate the degree to which Africans rejected this effort at cultural isolation as an effort to keep them subordinated. In the cities in 1976, there were prolonged and often violent demonstrations by young students in response to curriculum changes that mandated increase instruction in Afrikaans at the expense of English. Afrikaans was regarded as a provincial language used very largely only in South Africa and associated with political oppressors, whereas English was perceived as a language associated with internationalism, economic progress, and black liberation. This great upheaval ultimately led to the abandonment of the Afrikaans language requirements and the introduction of English-medium instruction after three years of primary education, a transition followed in many other African countries. The second event occurred in the rural "homelands" after they were made self-governing. Free to decide their own internal agendas, the homelands turned overwhelmingly to English-medium education. In other words, when not constrained by settler agendas, South Africans followed the same course as most of the rest of former British African colonies.

The continued use of English in former British colonies in Africa after independence was a pragmatic decision. In most cases, employing an African language nationally would have been even more difficult than in newly independent Asian lands, both because of greater linguistic fragmentation and because few African languages had much history of literate usage. Arabic was a notable exception, as it was adopted as the official language of the former British-occupied territories Egypt and Sudan. The Swahili language, the coastal language of East Africa, had spread inland, making it a viable alternative to English in Tanzania and Kenya, but it has been used only in the lower grades of school (see table 4.3), thereafter replaced with instruction in English. In southern Africa, even though the former British protectorates of Botswana, Lesotho, and Swaziland were exceptional in having viable national languages, all three chose to make English their official language because of its regional value and its established use in education.

The former British colonies that adopted English at independence, along with Liberia and Ethiopia, constitute a substantial bloc of half a billion people using English as a second language. This is half of the continent's population. Nigerians make up a third of that bloc. As the members of this bloc joined the United Nations and other international organizations, they contributed to the use of English internationally. Thus, Africans have been particularly important in making English the global language.

Table 4.3 African countries using English officially in education

	Population est. 2012, in millions	English-medium instruction begins	Other official language(s)
Botswana	2.0	Upper primary	
Cameroun	20.7	Lower primary	French
Ethiopia	93.8	Secondary	Amharic, Arabic
Gambia	2.3	Lower primary	
Ghana	25.2	Upper primary	
Kenya	43.0	Lower primary	Swahili
Lesotho	2.1	Upper primary	Sotho
Liberia	3.9	Lower primary	
Malawi	16.3	Upper primary	Chewa
Namibia	2.2	Upper primary	
Nigeria	170.1	Upper primary	
Seychelles	0.1	Upper primary	
Sierra Leone	5.5	Lower primary	
South Africa	48.8	Upper primary	10 others
South Sudan	10.6	Lower Primary	
Swaziland	1.4	Upper primary	Swazi
Tanzania	43.6	Secondary	Swahili
Zambia	14.3	Upper primary	7 others
Zimbabwe	12.6	Upper primary	
Total	518.5		

Source: CIA, *World Factbook,* accessed August 30, 2012; UNESCO Institute for Statistics, Data Centre, accessed July 9, 2012.
Note: UNESCO calculates that 63 percent of sub-Saharan African adults were literate in 2012. Literacy is higher among those 15–24; lower among the oldest.

American Colonies in Africa, Asia, and the Pacific

The United States acted overseas before 1945 on a much smaller scale than Great Britain and its language policies affected fewer people. At the same time, the Americans adopted more aggressive policies in promoting English overseas than the British. The differences in British and American actions may reflect historical circumstances more than imperial philosophies. As was shown above, Britain was quite aggressive in promoting English in Wales and Ireland and overseas in settler colonies in North America and Australasia. But British policies in nonsettler colonies were quite different, since the size of these Asian and African colonies would have made Anglicization prohibitively expensive and would have sparked considerable resistance. Philosophical considerations reinforced these practical ones: the nonsettler colonies were regarded not as permanent outposts but as temporary strategic holdings. Admittedly, the line between the two types of colonies was sometimes confused, as when Britain favored white settler interests in South Africa and Southern Rhodesia over those of the African majority, but the distinction was clearly enunciated in Kenya. A 1921 White Paper declared that Kenya was an African colony not a white man's colony (nor, as one administrator had put it in 1901, was East Africa to be "the America of the Hindu,"[33] i.e., a place to absorb surplus South Asian population); ultimately African rights should be paramount. Americans, on the other hand, were much more inclined to see their overseas colonies as extensions of their transcontinental expansion across North America, as a part of nation building as much as empire building. Despite their smaller size, the scattered American colonies were additions to Anglophone world.

Two quite different American colonies in the nineteenth century, Liberia and Hawaii, shared a similar devotion to the promotion of Americanization through English as well as Christianity. Like Britain's West African colony of Sierra Leone just to the north, Liberia was founded in the nineteenth century as a place of refuge for free people of African descent, in this case by the American Colonization Society in 1821. Although Liberia was never officially a colony of the United States, the American Congress had chartered its foundation, and the American government treated it as a protectorate throughout the 1800s, both before and after its independence in 1847. African American settlers in Liberia knew no other language than English, a circumstance (along with their Christianity) that they believed distanced them from the indigenous peoples of the region, whom the settlers generally looked down upon. Like Sierra Leone, Liberia was an English-speaking outpost from the beginning, but its growth was much slower.

The case for English was made unambiguously by the Afro-Caribbean educator Edward Wilmot Blyden, who was born in the Danish Virgin Islands where English was the common language. "Next to the Christian religion," he declared, "the most important element of strength and prosperity in Liberia is her possession of the English language." He noted the external advantages of English in connecting Liberians to other nations, especially the United States, "the most vigorous and progressive of modern nations." Blyden predicted that English would gradually diffuse in the region, an outcome that he equated with advancement.[34]

Education spread slowly in Liberia. By 1924, there were 1,900 students in Liberia's 55 government schools, two-thirds of which stopped at the third grade. Mission schools enrolled another 7,000 students, though the quality of their education was often lower than in the government schools. Only ten mission schools, enrolling about a hundred students, went beyond the eighth grade. The premier institution was the Methodist's College of West Africa, in theory a secondary school preparing students for admission to the government-run Liberia College, but in fact its standards were higher than those of Liberia College. Most students in mission schools were native Africans and studied English from first grade with half the curriculum being taught in English by the fourth grade. Over the next half century education expanded slowly as did government investments in schools. By 2000, there were nearly 150,000 students in primary schools, 55,000 in secondary schools, and about 10,000 in postsecondary institutions. The spread of the English language has been considerable with adult male literacy in English over 50 percent.[35]

A second American overseas colony was Hawaii. In the early 1800s, the isolated island chain in the central Pacific had been united under King Kamehameha, who opened the islands to American traders seeking Hawaiian sandalwood for their growing China trade. The first American missionaries arrived in 1820 and British missionaries followed. As in other lands, early missionaries set out to learn the spoken Hawaiian language and used the Roman alphabet to create a written form of the language. The first schools were conducted in Hawaiian and quickly created a literate core among the population, including members of the royal family. As elsewhere, a desire for more advanced schools to expand the range of Western knowledge led to the creation of English-medium schools. Oahu Charity School (later Honolulu High School) was established in 1833 and five years later, in response to a request from Hawaiian chiefs, an English-medium boarding school was founded (later called the Royal School). Other schools soon followed, including more select schools for the children of the missionaries and other Americans. At mid-century, English-medium schools were established for Hawaiians in addition to the "common schools," but budgetary constrains limited the expansion of both systems. The Hawaiian monarchy favored the continued use of English but moved to curb other aspects of missionary teaching. Meanwhile the population of the islands was undergoing other transformations: as unfamiliar infectious diseases were decimating the indigenous people, thousands of contract laborers were recruited, mostly from East Asia, for the growing sugar plantations. English continued to function as the lingua franca, but it evolved into two distinct forms: the standard English of the schools and a popular pidgin, Hawaiian Creole English, which emerged as the common language of the plantations, markets, and, to the distress of the educational establishment, the school corridors.[36]

By the census of 1900, the first after Hawaii's annexation by the United States, the native Hawaiian or part Hawaiian share of the population had fallen to just under one quarter, while Japanese and Chinese immigrants and their offspring constituted more than half the population. Annexation as an American territory led to an acceleration of efforts to Americanize society, including the 1896 provision that all instruction in public schools be in English. As had been taking place on the mainland, a key purpose of public education was to assimilate people of diverse origins to a common Americanism. More controversial was the segregation of English-speaking white students in English Standard schools, set apart from the common schools for those who spoke other languages at home and Hawaiian Creole English on the streets. In 1949, a new law mandated that all schools be brought up to the standards of the elite English Standard schools.[37]

While the annexation of Hawaii was underway, the United States was acquiring other new colonies in the Pacific and Caribbean as the result of the Spanish-American War. Spanish was widely used in Puerto Rico, but centuries of Spanish rule had had limited linguistic impact on the inhabitants of the Philippines, the most important colony claimed from Spain. Spanish or a sort of Spanish, Philippine Creole Spanish or *chabacano,* was spoken in only three communities in the islands; elsewhere a tremendous diversity of vernacular languages dominated. To unify the islands, the Americans adopted an aggressive policy to establish English as the principal language of education. There was no provision for vernacular instruction. Faced with a large number of unwritten languages, especially on the island of Mindanao, using English alone seemed the best strategy, a policy that also promoted the agenda of Americanizing the colonized people. One difference was that education in the Philippines was much more secular than in Liberia and Hawaii.

By 1908, the Director of Education reported that public schools were using English exclusively, and it was the expectation that students would be able to read an ordinary book or newspaper and write simple prose after three years. He described a method of instruction, effective if still controversial, that today is known to Americans as "immersion" and in Europe as "content and language integrated learning" (CCIL):

> The child who enters schools entirely ignorant of English will understand ordinary directions of the schoolroom within a very few days; after that he picks up the language rapidly, and by use of the chart and primer he learns to read, to write, and to speak it at the same time. A child, under favorable conditions of instruction, may learn in the course of the school year to read and write about 250 words, with a conversational acquaintance of nearly as many more. This is considered a good foundation, but it is obviously of small value to the child if he is to stop here. It is observable, however, that second-grade pupils use their English pretty well, are able to carry on a conversation upon limited topics with a stranger, tell him about their town, and give him directions. By the time a child has completed the third grade he has secured a knowledge of the language which will remain with him, and which he will constantly amplify after he leaves school.

This description concerns the elementary schools, which was as far as most students went. At that time in the Philippines (1908), there were 467,253 students in 3,701 primary schools (grades 1–4), 17,780 students in 193 intermediate schools (grades 5–8), but only 1,643 students in the 38 secondary schools. A working knowledge of English was largely confined to the graduates of these schools in 1908, although night classes in English for adults were being offered to about 1,800 in Manila. Spanish continued to be used for some aspects of government at that time, but the administration moved to make English the language of government and of the courts from 1911.[38]

Over the years the number of schools and students increased steadily, creating an ever-growing population literate in English. By the time of independence in 1946, about two-fifths of the Philippine population could function in English, usually as a second language. The independent government took over the existing school system and in time began the promotion of Filipino/ Pilipino/Tagalog, an Australasian language spoken in the capital region, as a second language of education. In 1974, a compromise Bilingual Education Program ended competition by making Pilipino and English the languages of instruction in public schools, marginalizing the Philippines' 80 other spoken languages. Pilipino is widely used in the capital and in government, while English dominates business, higher education, and international relations.[39]

In conclusion, there can be no denying that British imperial expansion was a powerful force for introducing the English language to many parts of the world, as was American empire building on a smaller scale. The English language's continuing importance owes even more to the decisions made by individual Asians and Africans and the policies pursued by their newly independent governments. The fact that most African countries chose to adopt English as their official language at independence while most Asian states opted for an indigenous language requires some explanation. On both continents nationalists wished to champion indigenous traditions as well as to build modern societies. Even where a vernacular language was to become the nation's official language, English showed remarkable persistence. Those vernaculars that were not made official languages mostly suffered no diminished vigor. In Asia, the turn to indigenous languages occurred in part because there had been a proud tradition of writing in those languages. In Africa, the practical utility of English as a unifying and modernizing force mostly won out, in part because African vernacular languages in non-Islamic areas were usually oral. The greater diversity of languages in sub-Saharan Africa also made it harder for any other language to become a viable alternative, except for

Swahili in East Africa and Arabic in Sudan, although in states like India linguistic diversity stymied the ascendancy of both a single indigenous language and English. Whichever course was adopted, many practical difficulties stood in the way of raising literacy and educational standards. Even where a local language was successfully adopted, the rising importance of globalization meant that a national language had to be complemented by one or more international ones—a topic examined in the chapters that follow.

Was the spread of English language usage in British Asia and Africa an act of cultural imperialism? If saying no seems impossible, saying yes seems to provide little insight into the underlying process. The British were imperialists and they viewed the world through lenses that exaggerated their cultural superiority and their subjects' cultural inferiority to degrees that can still shock. In his Minute on Education, Macaulay famously asserted that "a single shelf of a good European library was worth the whole native literature of India and Arabia," despite freely admitting he knew not a word of either Sanskrit or Arabic. In his view, the vernacular languages of India merited even less respect, since they contained "neither literary nor scientific information and [were] so poor and rude" they were almost untranslatable. Writing of Nyasaland (now Malawi) in east-central Africa on the eve of its colonization in 1890, a generally moderate British official (later knighted), Harry Johnston, recommended sending in Christian missionaries, because they would "strengthen our hold over the country...spread the use of the English language...induct the natives to the best kind of civilization." In fact, he concluded, "each mission station is an essay in colonization."[40] Although some held more extreme views (and a few more moderate ones), there is no point in multiplying quotations. For the issue here is not the imperialists' biases, but the reasons their actions succeeded. In the first place, as this chapter has argued, imperial policy on language was not uniform, varying both over time and from colony to colony. Second, government was only one player, so that outcomes reflected, inter alia, the roles played by missionaries as well as by Asian and African students and their families. Third, British rule was remarkably parsimonious and thus incapable of any great successes in any cultural arena. Finally, Africans generally saw English as culturally neutral, while Asians initially chose to denounce it as a product of colonialism. In this arena, as in others, the less powerful in colonies were far from powerless in shaping outcomes.

By 1975, the era of imperial expansion was largely over, but it had added millions of new speakers of English to the expanded core in the British Isles (60 million) and North America (220 million). They included European settlers in Australia (13.5 million), New Zealand (3 million), and South Africa (3 million). To this total of 300 million native speakers, one needs to add the very considerable number of people to whom imperialism introduced English as a second language. The African total in 1975 would have been about 125 million; the South Asian perhaps 75 million. With a few million more from the Caribbean and Pacific, this amounted to over half a billion English-speaking people.

People in former British colonies have been notable for maintaining ties based on language. The (British) Commonwealth was founded in 1931 by former settler colonies but has grown to include 54 member states, which meet regularly to discuss matters of mutual concern. The English-Speaking Union, an association of individuals founded in 1918 with a view to strengthening British and American connections, has also grown to include branches in a similar number of countries, some of which (Albania, Chile, Estonia, France, and Moldova) were never British or American colonies. Branches conduct various cultural activities and delegates attend international meetings every few years.[41]

Chapter 5

Cultural Worlds

The world was shrinking in the late 1800s. Growing global contacts, conflicts, and exchanges were eroding societies' isolation and autonomy. One particularly influential response to the world's need for improved communication came from L. L. Zamenhof (1859–1917), a Jewish student with strong interests in languages and international peace. He had grown up in Bialystok (then in the Russian Empire), whose population was divided into four mutually hostile communities: Poles, Russians, Germans, and Jews, each with its own language and religious tradition. His experience convinced him of the need for a universal language that would facilitate trade, diplomacy, and cultural exchanges, while reducing misunderstandings and conflicts. Like others with similar ideas, Zamenhof believed that no existing language could become a universal language, both because it would be resisted as foreign (perhaps imperialistic) and because of the practical difficulties of mastering the sounds, grammar, and idioms of the leading international languages. Instead, he argued, the world needed a new, "artificial" language, designed to be politically neutral and, by means of a simplified vocabulary and grammar, to be much easier to learn than any existing language.

Zamenhof's contribution was Esperanto, which he devised while in high school and which went on to become the most successful artificial spoken language ever devised. For his efforts Zamenhof was nominated for the Nobel Peace Prize in 1910. The new language first found support in Russia and Eastern Europe and then spread to Western Europe, the Americas, and the Far East.

Esperanto gained the support of many organizations during the twentieth century, including official recognition by UNESCO in 1954, and it still has a solid base of supporters. However, Esperanto never gained sufficient adherents to perform its intended global functions.[1]

The spread of English, rather than Esperanto, as the global language is a vivid example of how historical forces can push aside logical solutions to human problems. Even though English has been the language of British and American imperial power and expansion, people around the world have come to accept it as sufficiently neutral to be the global language. Compared to Esperanto, English is quite difficult to learn because of its immense vocabulary and numerous idiomatic expressions along with its irregular spelling, uncommon vocalizations (notably the two "th" sounds), and other pronunciation challenges. So how did English overcome such impediments? As the previous chapter has detailed, the imperial ventures of Britain and the United States produced enough acceptance of English to partially offset the opposition they also aroused. *The Economist* recently declared: "English...has emerged as the lingua franca of business, science, and much culture."[2] This chapter examines five specialized cultural arenas where English gradually gained prominence or preeminence: international relations, science and technology, global business, global literature, and global popular culture.

International Relations

When the representatives of international bodies meet they need to be able to communicate clearly and precisely. One way such communication may be achieved is to allow participants to speak in their own languages and provide translations to the others. Although this procedure accords equal dignity to all, as the number of languages grows translation of speeches and published accords may become expensive and impractical. The European Union, for example, began with four official languages, but the addition of new members has raised the number to over 20. To avoid this situation, other organizations have recognized only a limited number of languages that may be used for official purposes. The

United Nations, for example, began with only five official languages (Chinese, English, French, Russian, and Spanish). Despite the enormous growth in its membership, only Arabic has been added for official use in the larger UN bodies. However, in many settings UN delegates use only one or two to facilitate deliberations. For example, up until 1983 the UN Security Council used only French and English as working languages.

Because the history of modern international relations grew out of the conflicts and alliances of European states and because European languages (as the United Nations illustrates) have tended to dominate in modern global organizations, Europe is a prime venue for exploring how English rose to the fore in international relations. The predominance of English in Europe is a fairly recent phenomenon, just as it is in most of the rest of the world. Despite Britain's rising importance as an industrial, military, and imperial power, few in nineteenth-century France bothered to learn English, preferring German as a foreign language. In Germany, the study of French (mandatory in Prussian *Gymnasien* from 1831) remained much more important than English throughout the 1800s, though students in some secondary schools studied English as a second foreign language. Not until the twentieth century did English's growing importance as a "world language" lead to its being promoted ahead of French in Germany.[3]

The French statesman Georges Clemenceau (1841–1929) played a pivotal role in the ascendancy of English over French and German in European diplomatic usage. Unlike most of his compatriots Clemenceau was a committed anglophile, a position shaped by his political opposition to the imperial pretenses of Napoleon III and to the power of the Catholic Church. To escape political persecution Clemenceau went into a self-imposed exile in the United States, where he perfected his English and married an American. His successful political career, following his return to France in 1871, culminated in his service as prime minister in 1906–9 and 1917–20.[4]

In recognition of its valiant role in the First World War, France was accorded the honor of hosting the Paris Peace Conference called in 1919 to write the terms of the peace settlements, but the two English-speaking countries, the United States and Britain, were the dominant players. In the plenary sessions, Prime Minister Clemenceau, as chair, sat in the center of the head table, flanked on the right by President Woodrow Wilson and the American delegation and on the left by Prime Minister David Lloyd George and the British delegation. Clemenceau readily accepted English as the Conference's second language. In the smaller Council of Ten (two each from France, Britain, the United States, Italy, and Japan) Clemenceau frequently addressed the assembled delegates in English. Following the passage of the Anglo-American sponsored League of Nations Charter, the Conference's key sessions were in the so-called Council of Four (Britain, France, the United States, and Italy). Since Italy's foreign minister rarely attended, English predominated.[5] The exclusion of Germany and Austria-Hungary as Conference participants also derailed German's prewar gains as a diplomatic language. The use of English in Paris stemmed as much from the fact that the combined importance of Britain and the United States and their empires in the war had made English the obvious lingua franca for discussion as it did from Clemenceau's gracious accommodation of English. Nevertheless, the Paris Peace Conference may be seen as marking the emergence of a new international language of diplomacy, even if other languages remained important.

The establishment of the first global organization in 1919, the League of Nations, more squarely raised the issue of what language(s) the diplomatic world would conduct its business in. Reflecting the fact that the League at its inception was predominantly a European organization, British English, French, and Spanish were made the official languages. The refusal of the United States government to join the League kept English from being considered more important than the two other official languages. In fact, the League actually promoted Esperanto as the future working language of this and other international bodies. The fact that Esperanto is heavily based on Romance and other Indo-European languages may explain its support among delegates from European countries, but a key player in the League's debates about Esperanto was Wellington Koo, the head of the Chinese delegation. Koo had earned a doctorate from Columbia University and later served briefly as acting premier of China, interim president of China, and ambassador to the United States. Chinese interest in Esperanto came from contacts with

Japanese students and Russian merchants, who had embraced it as the ideal world language.[6]

The subsequent rise of English as a global language was not simply the result of the geopolitical importance of the Anglo-American alliance, but in international relations it was closely tied to that phenomenon. The Second World War saw a significant shift of leadership and power to Anglophone countries. With Belgium and France out of the war and the Soviet Union facing a furious assault by Germany, the belated entry of the United States enabled the Allies to snatch victory from the jaws of defeat. The British and the American generals who launched the assault on the Western Front naturally created Anglophone command structures. In 1942, the Voice of America began radio broadcasting in cooperation with the BBC, using English along with several other languages. The 1944 Convention on International Civil Aviation mandated the use of English in communication between aircraft and between aircraft and ground control personnel. This convention was modeled on the use of English in maritime communication.

In the postwar years, English usage in Europe took off. American voices seemed to be everywhere: running the occupation of Germany, directing the Marshall Plan for rebuilding war-torn Europe, chatting in the streets, and teaching in the schools. Americans dominated the North Atlantic Treaty Organization in many ways, but British English and French were NATO's official languages. There were also many Anglo-American efforts to teach English in postwar Europe. Government-funded Fulbright Fellowships supported study in the United States, and American English-language classes were offered on US military bases in Europe. The Ford Foundation began training English-language teachers in the United States in 1952 and from 1961 in Britain. The British Council was also active in teaching English to nonnative speakers. Both countries funded volunteer programs overseas in the 1960s, and many of the volunteers taught English.[7]

The post-1945 period also saw a great increase in the member states at the United Nations, many of them countries that used English as their official language. Seven of the original members fell into that category: Australia, Canada, Liberia, New Zealand, South Africa, the United Kingdom, and the United States. Other Anglophone countries joined in the 1950s: Ireland, followed by newly independent African states of Sudan and Ghana. In the 1960s, 11 other new African nations using English joined, along with 4 newly independent Anglophone Caribbean nations. Sixteen Francophone African nations also joined between 1958 and 1962. More Anglophone former colonies in the West Indies, and South Pacific followed in the 1970s, plus St. Christopher and Nevis in 1983. The addition of Zimbabwe in 1980 and Namibia in 1990 tipped the linguistic balance further in favor of the Anglophone bloc. The dominance of English as a lingua franca is evident from the fact that two-thirds of the countries listed in the UN directory in 2001 indicated that they preferred to receive email messages in English.

Something similar has been happening in other multinational bodies. One observer estimated that 97 percent of the political and commercial elite around the world prefer to conduct their international communications in English. In global business the growing internationalization of management has been a significant factor in this trend. Much the same is true of the Catholic Church. Under Pope John Paul II (1978–2005), English all but displaced Italian as the language of Vatican diplomacy.[8]

Scientific English

In 2001, a collection of essays alternately cranky or celebratory about the dominance of English in science appeared—in English—from a scholarly press in Berlin. The editor, himself a German, opened the volume with the observation, "That English is today's dominant language of science is stating what would be called a *Binsenweisheit* in German, a trivially obvious insight."[9] Whether the dominance of English in science is a tragedy to be mourned or a truism not worth mentioning can be debated, but it is a remarkable fact that requires some explanation. How has it come about that 80–85 percent of all scientific papers are now published in English or with English summaries?

Science has never been linguistically democratic. In earlier times, only a few languages developed the capacity to tackle the arcane realms that are now called "science." In East Asia, Chinese was the medium for spreading science. In the West, the ancient

Greeks were important pioneers in devising subtle terminology needed for philosophical discourse, and their language remained integral to many fields long after leadership had passed elsewhere. Roman translations of Greek science passed to Western Europe, first in Latin and then in the Romance languages. Alexander the Great spread Greek learning eastward to Persia, which developed its own scientific tradition. Scientific works were translated from Greek and Persian into Arabic during the intellectual renaissance in Bagdad under the Abbasid Caliphate in the eighth to tenth centuries. Persians also spread Hindu science westward, including the misnamed "Arabic" numerals.[10]

The "Scientific Revolution" in early modern Europe gave explosive new life to European science, then still a branch of philosophy. Pioneers as far flung as Nicolaus Copernicus (1473–1543), Galileo Galilei (1564–1642), and Johannes Kepler (1571–1630) wrote not in their native Polish, Italian, or German, but in Latin, still the language of Western learning. Early English scientists like Francis Bacon (1581–1626) and William Harvey (1578–1657) likewise published their pioneering works in Latin.

Scholarly publication in French and some other European vernaculars became more common during the 1700s, the era of the Enlightenment. The great *Encyclopédie* spread science and all sorts of other knowledge in that language. Most European vernaculars were still considered inadequate to precision for specialized descriptions and reasoning. In the preface to the *Encyclopédie*, the editor Jean d'Alembert declared, "The use of the Latin language can be very useful in works of philosophy [i.e., science]." The great English scientist Isaac Newton (1642–1727) agreed, and he wrote both in Latin and English. His *Principia Mathematica*, for example, appeared first in Latin in 1687 and was not translated into English until 1729. On the other hand, he first published his *Opticks* in English in 1704 with a Latin translation coming two years later. Although the pioneering Swedish botanist, Carl Linnaeus (1707–78), wrote in Latin (still the universal language for biological classification), vernacular scientific writing was in the ascendancy in the 1700s. The great reformer of chemical theory and language, Antoine-Laurent Lavoisier (1743–94), wrote in French, as did his colleague, Louis-Bernard Guyton de Morveau (1737–1816). All of the key scientific works written in Latin (or French) were readily translated into English and the other Romance languages, all of which could easily make use of scientific terminology derived from Latin and Greek roots. German translators had to invent many new scientific terms.[11]

The movement to the vernaculars was promoted by the growing importance of national academies of science, notably the Royal Society of London (founded 1660) and the Académie Royale des Sciences in Paris (founded 1666). The Royal Society, which did much to sort out conflicting theories and to disseminate the latest findings to the English-literate public, was very much an international (European) body. Its first secretary Henry Oldenburg (c.1619–77) was German-born and educated. He originated the practice of sending out submissions for expert commentary and translated those that passed muster into English from French, German, Italian, or Latin for publication in the *Philosophical Transactions of the Royal Society,* the first peer-reviewed scientific journal. [12]

Germans led the way in scientific research, and during the 1800s their language naturally followed. From the inception of the Nobel Prizes in 1901 until 1918, Germans won or shared twice as many of the awards in science as people from any other nation. (France was second.) Though the perception of German as the language of science lingered, the Nobel lists also document how Germany fell behind the United Kingdom and the United States in scientific achievement after the end of the First World War, and German scientific leadership slipped badly under misguided Nazi policies.

Anglo-Americans dominance in science grew even more rapidly following the Second World War. The United States was the only major country to emerge from the war with its research and educational institutions intact, a fact that helped attract many foreign scientists and large numbers of foreign students. The trend to English moved quickly in the postwar decades. To stay competitive, scientific journals publishing articles in other languages began offering English summaries and publishing entire articles in English. By the early 1980s, for example, nearly two-thirds of scientific articles by French authors were published in English. By the mid-1980s, 95 percent of the articles published in the German journal *Zeitschrift für Tierpsychologie* were in English, a fact that led the journal editors in 1986 to give it an English name, *Ethology*. These were not isolated instances. In an effort to keep competitive, the Mexican journal *Archivos de Investigación Médica* had been publishing English summaries of all of its articles; but in 1991, it threw in the towel, hired an American editor, changed its name to *Archives of Medical Research,* and began publishing only in English. By the early 1990s, 31 percent of all scientific articles appeared in journals based in the United States. Nearly 50 percent were published in journals in the major English-speaking countries, not counting the many journals in other countries that published partly or entirely in English. A study of German academics in the early 1990s found that between 72 percent and 98 percent used English as their working language, with physicists reporting the highest use. In comparison only 20 percent of German historians used English that way.[13]

In smaller countries, the trend to English has often been even more pronounced. Finland, Israel, and Hungary may serve as examples. Finland made great strides in science in the twentieth century, keeping abreast of what was happening elsewhere. In the four decades before 1950, most Finnish students in the natural sciences wrote dissertations in their native language but nearly as many chose to use German, while only about 6 percent wrote in English. In the 1950s and '60s, however, 73 percent of science dissertations in Finland were written in English, and the trend advanced so steadily that by the mid-1990s 95 percent of Finnish scientific dissertations were written in English. The new state of Israel made great efforts to make modern Hebrew a language of science, and Israeli universities have had strict policies against foreign language usage in academic contexts. Nevertheless, a study found that over two-thirds of the dissertations in science at Tel Aviv University in the 1990s were written entirely or largely in English. Like Finnish and modern Hebrew, Hungarian is a language little used outside a single small country, so it is not surprising to find that by the end of the 1990s two-thirds of scientific publications by Hungarians were in English. To do otherwise most of the scholars surveyed agreed would be a waste of time.[14]

The dominance of English in the hard sciences has an interesting parallel in science fiction. Some credit Mary Shelley with creating science fiction with her *Frankenstein* in 1817 and none dispute the contributions of H. G. Wells (*War of the Worlds*, 1898), Aldous Huxley (*Brave New World*, 1932), or the *Star Trek* series (1960s onwards). Anglo-American writers very largely created the many scifi subgenres. The hard-science end has been well defined by the prolific American Isaac Azimov and the United Kingdom's Arthur C. Clark. Tom McArthur, editor of *The Oxford Companion to the English Language,* declares, "English may be the second language of Europe, but it is the first language, sometimes it seems the only language, of science fiction." An essay entitled, "Why is English the Language of Science Fiction?" lists French, Israeli, Finnish, and Dutch writers who choose to write science fiction books in English. And why not? Wherever the annual World Science Fiction Convention is held, more than half those attending are from the United States and the United Kingdom.[15]

Business English

As in science, the leadership of international business has become increasingly internationalized. For similar reasons, the English language has also become dominant at the top tier of global commerce and finance. "English is the lingua franca of business," Carlo Brumat, dean of an Anglophone business school in Monterrey, Mexico, points out. "Not recognizing that is like shooting yourself in the foot." Dr. Brumat is Italian.[16]

The paramount importance of English in international business is the culmination of a process similar to what has happened in science: the globalization of what was once regional. To facilitate commercial exchanges regional trading networks gravitated toward one or more dominant languages. The Lingua Franca used by merchants around the Mediterranean as a common tongue is a good example, and its name has become the generic term for similar languages elsewhere. In the 1200s, for instance, the Venetian merchant Marco Polo apparently acquired enough Persian while traversing its homeland that he was able to use it all the way along the Silk Road that stretched across inner Asia, as well as in the court of Kublai Khan in China where it was a lingua franca of the many foreigners.[17] Similarly, Arabic and Islam spread among the markets and merchant communities of the Indian Ocean and northern Africa during the Middle Ages, making Arabic the most useful lingua franca of that region. All of these trading languages overlay the many existing local and regional languages that continued in use. Nor has spread of English as the language of business and commerce displaced regional commercial languages, but in places it has demoted them.

As Western nations expanded their trading networks and empires after 1450, they took their languages with them. Portuguese spread along the Atlantic coast of Africa and around the Indian Ocean in the wake of Portugal's commercial ventures and is still used in places as distant as Goa, Macao, and East Timor. The Dutch were better capitalized but made a smaller linguistic impression, since their multilingual merchants often made use of Portuguese, English, or other languages. The English and French trading companies that followed the Dutch added to the linguistic diaspora, but by the 1700s, Britain's greater military and commercial power was pushing versions of English to the fore in ports of call from Hong Kong to Latin America. Britain's dominance in the eighteenth-century Atlantic slave trade helped spread the use of English along the Atlantic coast as well as in the various ports in the Americas that depended on British suppliers. A French observer in the late 1700s lamented, "English is spoken all along the coast of Guinea [West Africa]; consequently the English have the advantage that they don't need an interpreter."[18]

This push of Western trade and trading companies overseas was a major imperial venture and was accompanied by the usual push from below. The Gold Coast of West Africa provides interesting examples of local people using English for personal advancement. Settlements that grew up around the small trading British forts there were inhabited by Africans who depended on British trade for their livelihood. They included laborers, such as washerwomen, porters, and canoeists, whose knowledge of English need not have been more than minimal, as well as a variety of African intermediaries, whose positions depended on a good command of the language. Among these critical intermediaries were the "linguists," who were as much diplomats as translators, as their duties required them to bridge the cultural gaps between the British and their African trading partners. The head linguist at Cape Coast Castle in the mid-1700s, an African known as Cudjo Caboceer, sought to promote local Africans' familiarity with British culture by establishing an English school at the castle. One of the first pupils, Philip Quaque (1741–1816), proved so adept that he was sent to Britain for further education. He chose to pursue a clerical career. When he returned to the Gold Coast as the Anglican chaplain in 1766, he also became a schoolmaster for the African population. African merchants and intermediaries also sent their sons, and sometimes daughters, to be educated in England.[19]

The English spoken in coastal trading communities varied from fairly standard English to formalized pidgins and creoles. English-based pidgins were widespread from West Africa to the Far East, as well as in the Americas and the South Pacific. On the China coast in the early decades of the 1800s, Tom McArthur reports, "Pidgin or 'business' English was already the lingua franca in Canton...using a Chinese word order, but with loanwords from Arabic and Portuguese as well as English." As in West Africa, it was local Chinese, not Europeans, who were the principal culture brokers. Interestingly, while pidgins and creoles have declined in importance in commercial transactions in recent times, a standardized "business English" remains of major importance globally, as is evidenced by the large number of learners and teachers of this specialized language.[20]

The key tipping point in English's dominance in business came with the rise of multinational corporations (MNCs). Initially, many of these were British or American in whole or in part so it was natural that English was used in their corporate communications with (and usually within) their overseas operations. The British were also skilled creating sophisticated corporate networks. An example is the Hongkong and Shanghai Banking Corporation (founded in 1865 and still surviving within the giant HSBC).[21] However, as MNCs originating in non-English-speaking countries became more international in their upper administration and operations in the later twentieth century, more and more of them found it expedient to use English as their internal corporate language. Some also used English to communicate with their shareholders. Even where there is no official policy favoring English, the managers of MNCs based in countries whose national language is little known elsewhere may also use English for internal communication in a semiofficial way.

Some interesting examples come from Finland. Beginning in the 1960s Kone, a Finnish elevator manufacturer, expanded operations into Sweden, Austria, and Germany. Kone began issuing its financial reports in English, which also served as the common language of communication among its executives and managers. This informal practice eventually became official policy and all upper-level employees had to be fluent in English. A similar transition to using English as the corporate language occurred at the Finnish metals group Outokumpu in the early 1990s after it made foreign acquisitions. The much larger and more global Nokia, best known for its cell phones, also uses English for intra-corporate communication.[22]

The German engineering and telecomm firm Siemens AG made English its main "corporate language" in 1998.[23] In 2011, Deutsche Bank appointed its first chief who was not fluent in German: Indian-born and English-speaking Anshu Jain, who had served as in DB's London branch, became co-CEO.[24] Upon the retirement of its founder (Stan Shih) in 2005, Acer Inc., Taiwan's largest computer company, named an Italian (Gianfranco Lanci) as its new president (and CEO in 2008) and designated English as the company's official internal language.[25] English is also the official language of the European Central Bank, headquartered in Germany, as well as Louis Vuitton in France and Antonio Merloni in Italy.[26] What is happening in the boardroom is also going on in the business schools, where instruction in English is increasingly common to accommodate the international student body (see chapter 6). Analogously, faculties and administrators are growing more international. In July 2010, for example, the prestigious Harvard Business School appointed its first dean born outside North America, Indian-born Nitin Nohria.[27]

The use of English in business provides a common language both among executives and managers and with clients around the world. A case study of the global company, TechComp, detailed how one manager in Germany began his day making deals over the phone with Chinese clients in English, then communicated with various Europeans in English or other languages, and ended the day on the phone to North Americans. Despite the variety of accents and usages of English involved in these transactions, the level of mutual understanding was adequate to the tasks at hand.[28]

The spread of English in the top ranks of MNCs has been paralleled by its adoption as an entry-level requirement in other businesses. This includes hotel employees and tour guides in much of the world, but the most striking examples are the call centers in Bangalore. They are an interesting example of companies' efforts to cut the cost of customer service by employing educated young Indians who are eager to find good-paying jobs. As American companies tried to trim costs they automated many tasks, such as providing balances on bank account of credit cards, and set up phone centers in lower-cost regions. Some of these centers were in lower-wage states, such as Utah or Texas, but the sharp fall in telecommunication costs in recent decades still made using locations half way around the world an attractive possibility. Centers in the south-central Indian city of Bangalore, operating round the clock seven days a week, are staffed by young English-speaking Indians who have been specially trained to understand and speak American English. Sometimes using American aliases that their phone contacts will find easier to understand than their actual names, call-center employees either initiate calls to sell products such as credit cards or answer customer-service calls about lost luggage, bank statements, and other topics. Even though only 6 percent of applicants get through the tough screening process at the better centers, nearly a quarter of a million Indians held such jobs in the early 2000s. Competition is fierce because such jobs are high paying by Indian standards, have pleasant air-conditioned surroundings and high-tech equipment, and offer unusually generous benefits, including free meals, insurance, and educational subsidies. Many Indian employees can earn business or technology degrees while working full-time at such centers and see these jobs as a big step up the ladder of success. Indeed, learning English as a way out of poverty has become a major obsession of poor Indians, as the next chapter explores.[29]

Global English Literature

Besides scientific and business reports, people from almost every country in the world are writing novels and poetry in English. In part, this literary trend reflects the fact that so many talented people from around the world have studied or lived in English-speaking countries and are most comfortable writing in English. For many the use of English as a literary language may be a strategy for reaching an international audience. Writing in English is also a means of reaching a national audience, since in countries with many vernaculars English is often the common tongue of the educated. Whatever the reasons, lists of best-selling books and literary prize winners show it to be a booming phenomenon.

English literature's global drift has followed the spread of the English language. As English spread in the British Isles, major literary works appeared in English from the Celtic lands. Similarly, in North America and other former colonies, literary works have been written by both native speakers and those a generation or two removed from another primary language. Beginning with works in the colonial period, American literature has grown to include a larger corpus of works than British literature and includes authors whose ancestors came from Africa, Asia, or continental Europe and by native peoples as well. Writers in Canada, Australia, New Zealand, South Africa, and other former British settler colonies have made major contributions as well. A substantial and distinguished body of English literature has also come from authors indigenous to former British colonies in Asia and Africa, as well as from among the descendants of Africans and Asians in the West Indies.

One may conveniently begin the story in Ireland, where literature in English has a distinguished history. By the 1800s, Irish poets and playwrights, such as W. B. Yeats, George Bernard Shaw, and Oscar Wilde, "were among the most internationally renowned writers in the English language."[30] In rapid succession Yeats and Shaw received Nobel Prizes in Literature in 1923 and 1925, the first of the Anglophone Irish writers to do so. The twentieth century continued this trend with the distinguished fiction of James Joyce, the explosive and humorous plays of Brendan Behan, the brooding novels and drama of Samuel

Beckett, and the poetry of Seamus Heaney, the latter two also winning Nobel Prizes (in 1969 and 1995). Members of this distinguished group differed in their physical relationship to their Irish homeland. Joyce lived in France and Switzerland. Wilde and Shaw preferred England, Shaw claiming his Nobel Prize as a citizen of the United Kingdom. The greats deserve their due, but from a historical perspective the most significant point is that the most revered of Irish writers were but the tip of a mountain of Irish writers in English.[31]

For some outside the United Kingdom, writing in English was more an individual choice than a national trend. Joseph Conrad (1857–1924), born in the Ukraine of Polish parents named Korzeniowski, is "perhaps the most famous example of English being acquired and used as a foreign language." Having learned English working on British ships, Conrad became a British subject in 1886, before penning his major works, *Typhoon* (1901), *The Nigger of the Narcissus* (1898), *Lord Jim* (1900), *Heart of Darkness* (1902), which are still widely read.[32] One might be tempted to question Conrad's claim to special preeminence in light of the extraordinary literary achievements of Vladimir Nabokov (1899–1977), a Russian émigré, who switched to English after taking up residence in the United States, having earlier written novels and stories in Russian and German.

By the time Conrad went to the Congo Free State, some coastal West Africans had been writing in English for more than a century. A number of people sold into slavery from West Africa penned accounts of their experiences in the Atlantic world in the 1700s and early 1800s, of which Olaudah Equiano's *Interesting Narrative*, first published in 1789, was the most widely read both in his own time and in recent years. English writing became well established in trading town of Old Calabar in what is now southeastern Nigeria so that a number of letters by Africans as well as a personal diary have survived.[33] Letters from Africans on the Gold Coast have also survived, notably by the versatile Philip Quaque mentioned above.

Enthusiasm for writing in English grew still more in the British Crown Colony of Sierra Leone, annexed in 1808, which became the headquarters of the British patrols intercepting illegal slave traders and the place where thousands of African captives were liberated. Missionaries introduced schools and at one point the colony had a higher literacy rate than many parts of Europe. Notable among the educated Africans in the colony were Samuel Ajayi Crowther (1806–91) who became the first Anglican bishop in West Africa and James Beale "Africanus" Horton (1834–83), an Edinburgh-trained physician and author of several pioneering books about West Africa.[34]

The expansion of Britain's colonial empire in Africa from the turn of the century resulted to the penetration of English much deeper into the continent and the foundation of African literature in English. One of the earliest to achieve fame was Nigerian James Ene Henshaw (1924–2007) of Calabar (the "Old" having been dropped from the city's name). A physician (like Horton) by trade, Dr. Henshaw became well known in Nigeria for his English-language plays about traditional life and the early encounters with European missionaries and colonial rulers. Equally popular at home, but much better known internationally, was the Nigerian novelist and professor of literature, Chinua Achebe (born 1930), whose early books also explored the same period. In the decades following Nigerian independence in 1960, there was an explosion of excellent fiction and poetry too large to catalog here. Distinguished playwright, poet, and novelist Wole Soyinka (b. 1934) won the Nobel Prize in Literature for 1986, the first African to be so honored. The first Nigerian women to achieve international fame, the prolific Buchi Emecheta (b. 1944) has won many awards including the Order of the British Empire in 2005; her novels probed women's lives in the precolonial and colonial eras.

It is not surprising that populous Nigeria has produced the lion's share of African literary giants, but other parts of Africa where English is the primary language of literacy have also made important contributions. Achebe was the founding editor of an "African Writers Series" from Heinemann that grew to over 250 titles. Some titles were translations (mostly from French), but the overwhelming majority were novels, plays, short stories, and poems composed by Africans in English. As elsewhere in Africa, the first black writers in South Africa achieved prominence for compositions in English after the Second World War: Peter Abrahams (b. 1919) was the first to gain widespread attention in 1946 with *Mine Boy*, the story of an rural African who goes to Johannesburg seeking work in the gold mines. In East Africa, the Kenyan James Ngugi (b. 1938) was the first to gain attention with his powerful novels of colonial Kenya: *Weep Not Child* (1964) and *The River Between* (1965). Ngugi is also notable for the dramatic turn his life took in his middle years, when he renounced Christianity and began to write in his native Gikuyu under the name Ngugi wa Thiong'o. In his 1986 book, translated as *Decolonizing the Mind*, he explained, "Language is...inseparable from ourselves as a community of human beings with a specific for and character a specific history, a specific relationship to the world."[35]

Ngugi was not alone. The Ghana novelist Ayi Kwei Armah (b. 1939) voiced similar thoughts about the European languages being alien to Africa. However, the reality was that no African language was going to attain pan-African acceptance and very few even found acceptance at the national level because most African countries had dozens or hundreds of spoken languages. In the name of being authentic, Ngugi chose to write in a subnational language; ironically he regularly translated his own works into English so as to reach a larger African audience.

The intellectual roots of needing to use an authentic language are problematic, since they came from outsiders steeped in Marxist paradigms, such as the French intellectual Jean-Paul Sartre and the Afro-West Indian Franz Fanon.[36] Not surprisingly, most African writers have taken a quite different view of the burden of the African past and the dynamics of modern African cultural development. Chinua Achebe has been particularly outspoken: in the language of his own storytelling and in a 1965 essay, "English and the African Writer," and in later pieces. In that essay, he explicitly acknowledges that modern African nations and the modern idea of pan-African identity are themselves, like it or not, the products of colonial rule. "The only reason we can even talk about African unity," he notes with a clear eye on reality, "is that when we get together we can have a manageable number of languages to talk in—English, French, Arabic." Finally, he challenges the notion that authentic African realities can be described only in ancestral African languages: "I feel that the English language will be able to carry the weight of my African experience. But it will have to be a new English...altered to suit its new African surroundings."[37] Achebe's readers would likely agree that his novels successfully evoke the speech and sensibilities of his Igbo people while remaining intelligible to others who know only standard English. In a 1975 work, Tanzanian scholar Ali Mazrui also defended the use of English despite its colonial baggage. He described English as "undoubtedly, the most suitable of the European languages for bridging over the numerous gulfs," ethnic and linguistic, that divide Africans. He argued its special suitably comes from the fact that English was "a composite language...made up of contributions by Celts, Danes, Normans, Saxons, Greeks and Romans, gathering to itself elements...from the Ganges to the Atlantic."[38]

Some Indians began writing in English in the 1800s. According to Braj B. Kachru and Tom McArthur, the first surviving works were Carvelly Venkata Boriah's *Account of the Jains* (1809) and the translations of the Upanishads by Rammohan Roy published between 1816 and 1820. A Bengali published poems in 1830; another Bengali published a novel in 1874. In 1913, Rabindranath Tagore won the Nobel Prize in Literature for his poetry in English. However, the first Indians to achieve popular success while writing in English were the novelists R. K. Narayan (1906–2001) and Mulk Raj Anand (1905–2004), whose stories of ordinary Indians attracted an international readership previously restricted to the Indian novels of British writers like Runyard Kipling and E. M. Forster. With the help of Graham Greene, Narayan published his first novel in Britain in 1930. E. M. Forster wrote the preface to the first edition of Anand's *Untouchable,* published in Britain in 1935, a work that was reprinted by Penguin in 1940 and kept in print ever since. However, much more than Kipling and Forster, Narayan and Anand also found immense popularity among the growing numbers of Indians literate in English. To meet Indian demand for his works during the Second World War Narayan printed his books himself. One can see in their success the foundation of an Indian national literature using English, a foundation on which a large number of other South Asian writers have built.[39]

Since the Second World War many more Indian writers have made contributions to literature in English. Some are well known, such as Ved Mehta, the blind Indian who became a staff writer for the *New Yorker*, whose autobiographical and family histories reached a large audience. Because the names of many others will be much less familiar to the readership of this book, listing them might become tedious.[40] What is worth emphasizing is that since about 1980 Indian writing in English has become so common, so well known, and of such quality that the notion of Indians writing in literature in English requires no more explanation than Americans or Australians doing so. The tipping point in global consciousness was Salman Rushdie's winning the prestigious Booker Prize in 1981 for *Midnight's Children*. Arundhati Roy also won a Booker Prize in 1997 for her highly successful novel, *The God of Small Things*, which both in India and abroad sold more copies than any previous Indian novel in English or any other language. Kiran Desai won the Booker Prize for *The Inheritance of Loss* in 2006; her mother Anita Desai, had been short-listed three times for the prize.

In a provocative essay in the *New Yorker* in 1997 Rushdie took on the critics of using English because it was a "foreign" language. "English has become an Indian language," he declared, by virtue of having gained "the aura of lingua-franca cultural neutrality," especially in South India and other regions where Hindi is regarded as much more foreign and culturally alien. He conceded that modern Indian writers in English generally come from elite backgrounds but denied that they represented the views of just their own class, anymore than did the stories that Narayan and Anand told about the lives of ordinary or oppressed people. Rushdie celebrated the fact that Indians writing in English were both international and Indian, and described them as "holding a conversation with the world" as well as with each other. In the most provocative part of the essay, Rushdie concluded that literature created "by Indian writers working in English is proving to be a stronger and more important body of work than that produced" by vernacular writers. He reached his conclusion after reviewing the current crop of Indian novels in English and in vernacular languages (which he read in translation).[41]

In an op-ed essay in the *New York Times* a few years later, Indian novelist and diplomat Shashi Tharoor made similar points. He defended using English because it was the dominant language of communication among India's elite and of elites around the world. He suggested "few developments in world literature have been more remarkable than the emergence, over the last two decades, of a new generation of Indian writers in English." Although the percentage of the Indian population who are fluent in English is small, their numbers are large, and, Tharoor argued, they write "as naturally about themselves in English as Australians or South Africans do."[42] Another writer of Indian ancestry, Trinidadian-born V. S. Naipaul, winner of both the Booker Prize (1971) and the Nobel Prize for Literature (2001), refers to this phenomenon as the emergence of a "universal civilization."[43]

Popular Culture: Rap and Mac

Universal civilization is not just literary and elite. To any global traveler American fast food chains and pop music seem ubiquitous. Even more pervasive is the English language, which may be less noticeable because it is partly hidden in the minds of so many people. Around the world people have a passive recognition of English words and phrases, whether or not they are able to speak the language. In addition, there is a widespread admiration for the cultural cachet that English carries, if not among some intellectuals, then among the masses. Such an influence is by no means uniquely American, even if American culture influences have become the most prominent of late.

A monumental transition figure in France was Johnny Hallyday (born Jean-Philippe Smet), who not only adopted an Americanized name (borrowed from his aunt's American boy friend's stage name, Lee Hallyday) but, more importantly, introduced a version of American rock and roll music in 1960 that became wildly popular among the French. Although Hallyday usually sang in French, sometimes he sang the original English-language versions of popular songs.[44]

The French love affair with American popular culture had earlier beginnings, notably with the arrival of American Negro entertainers in France between the world wars. The most famous of these was Josephine Baker, a dancer and singer known to the French as "La Baker," who became a French citizen in 1937. Baker sang in French, but she attracted other African Americans, without her language talents, notably jazz musicians and singers, such as Sidney Bechet, Louis Armstrong, and Archie Shepp. From 1979 Carole Fredericks achieved popularity similar to Baker's, learning to sing in French and appearing in French film. She was buried in Montmartre Cemetery in Paris.

While Anglophone music (heavily American) had been invading the rest of the world for some time, during the decade they remained together (1960–70), the Beatles became the premier representatives of the wave of popular music groups Americans called the "British Invasion." The global impact of this phenomenon was greatly enhanced by the most popular communication device ever invented, the transistor radio. By the 1960s, small, cheap transistor radios were bringing shortwave news and music to places that did not have electricity or phones. Not only were transistor radios much less costly and smaller than battery-powered vacuum tube radios; they were also cheaper to operate because they needed much less power.[45] Whether at home or on a bicycle one could listen to shortwave broadcasts from the BBC or the Voice of America (the latter perhaps broadcasting in "special English," i.e., in abnormally slow and precise speech). Before long, the even more portabile "pocket radio" brought the latest pop hits to even more listeners rich and poor.[46]

ABBA occupies a special place in the spread of Anglophone pop music. The Swedish group sang an engaging and well-produced music that achieved enormous popularity in Europe, throughout the Anglophone world, and in Latin America, selling at least 375 millions records, not only during their period of performance from 1972–82, but long afterwards.

American (especially African American) culture also had enormous appeal south of the Sahara. Manthia Diawara, now a professor of African literature and film at New York University, moved as a boy with his family from his native Guinea to Bamako, the capital of Mali, another former French colony. There Diawara fell under the thrall of American popular music. In the late 1960s, he and his secondary-school friends, who called themselves "the Rockers," would gather at his home to listen to the records of artists ranging from Wilson Picket, Ike and Nina Simone, and B. B. King to the Rolling Stones, Bob Dylan, Paul Simon, and Steppenwolf. In particular their imaginations were "captured by the defiant images" of African America's Black Power movement, the Black Panthers, and the Black Muslims. Their political heroes included George Jackson, Angela Davis, Muhammad Ali, Eldridge Cleaver, and Malcolm X, as well as Martin Luther King, Jr. Although their education was in French, the official language of Mali, Diawara and his peers sought to escape the hegemony of French cultural domination and identify with the vibrant American youth culture. In solidarity with their American heroes of the 1960s, they wore their hair in Afros, "wore shorts with peace signs and flowers on them, . . . smoked marijuana, [and opposed] the war in Vietnam and apartheid in South Africa."

Diawara recalls attending a concert in Bamako in 1965 by the Chicago-based blues singer Junior Wells and his All Stars that was sponsored by Radio Mali. During a break, Diawara bypassed the USIA translator and used his elementary English to engage one of the American musicians in simple exchanges. "The next day," he recalls, "the word spread all over Bamako that I spoke English like an American," making him a cultural celebrity among the city's youth. After the 1969 rock festival in Woodstock, New York, Diawara helped organize "Woodstock-in-Bamako," at which they played recordings of some of the festival's top rock groups and the Bamako youth who attended did their best to dress as their African American rock idols. That concert helped inspire the formation of many Afro-rock groups in Mali.[47]

A bit later and on the other side of the continent, another African engagement with Anglophone African diaspora music is described by Philippe Wamba. The son of a Congolese father and an African American mother, Wamba grew up in two worlds: born in California, living for much of his youth in Dar es Salaam, Tanzania, and receiving his higher education in the United States. He observes that although the vibrant music scene in Dar drew on many African traditions, "West Indian and African American popular music always occupied a privileged position."

Tanzanian youth revered the Jamaican reggae singer Bob Marley (known locally as "Babu") as a prophet and a musical genius. Marley's passionate songs about African unity struck a responsive chord among the youth of the Tanzanian capital, and some of them wore their hair in dreadlocks in appreciation. Michael Jackson ("Maiko") and other African American pop singers became similarly popular, aided by bootlegged music videos. Although English is an official language in Tanzania (along with Swahili), Wamba interestingly points out that even in the capital most found the lyrics of their diaspora heroes hard to understand and devised clever Swahili lyrics that mimicked the sound of the original lyrics. In Brazil, American hip-hop has similarly gained popularity among the urban youth, who likewise substitute Portuguese homophones that approximate English phrases, for example "you talk too much" as "*taca tomate*" (throw tomatoes). Like the youth of Bamako, Dar youth adopted some of the clothing styles of the diaspora, including Malcolm X T-shirts and pan-African red, black, and green colors. His experiences in Dar were intensely local, and Wamba points out that he "came to appreciate the existence of a global cultural network" only when he left for study in the United States in 1985.[48]

Other cultural networks linked Africans and people of African descent. Senegalese poet, philosopher, and president Leopold Senghor celebrated in French the existence of a *negritude* that linked all of Africa's children, but even he acknowledged the importance of Harlem in generating such sentiments. A Lusophone network also connected the inhabitants of Portugal's former colonies on both sides of the Atlantic. But the Anglophone links were much larger. Outside of Africa and the Americas identification based on a common physiology and ancestry was less intense, but Anglo-American cultural influences were still influential in popular cultural.

American pop culture took longer to reach East Asia, but it has put down roots. According to Jeff Chang:

> Today, the message of hip-hop is even transcending borders. From *xi ha* in China to "hip-life" in Ghana, hip-hop is a lingua franca that binds young people all around the world, all while giving them the chance to alter it with their own national flavor. It is the

foundation for global dance competitions, the meeting ground for local progressive activism, even the subject of study at Harvard and the London School of Economics.

Like Africans and African Americans, Asians embraced the hip-hop style as an exercise in liberation communication. Hip-hop (along with rap and break dancing) reached China in the late 1980s through pirated videos. By 2007, the annual rap battle ("Iron Mik") took place in Shanghai, to the delight of a field of Chinese rappers.[49]

As hip-hop has spread around the planet, it has generally found expression in local languages, large and small. But, if hip-hop has spread beyond its English-language origins, it has not broken with other cultural roots, especially as a medium of assertion and protest by minorities, whether ethnic, class, or generational. In some cases, exceptionally, the use of English has enhanced this. Thus, K'naan, a Somali refugee who grew up in Canada, raps mostly in English, not only to reach other expatriate Somali, but also because he finds English a pithier medium than Somali for expressing certain sentiments. As a medium of protest, the Aboriginal Australian artist, MC Wire, embraces hip-hop's black American origins and its American language, although he also favors English because he did not grow up speaking an Aboriginal language.[50] The local is global and the global local (or "glocal").

The spread of American or Anglophone popular culture illustrates three important themes. First, while it is obviously a by-product of economic and political hegemony and privileged access to media, in many cases its spread has been less a product of cultural imperialism than of what might be called cultural anti-imperialism. African American jazz, protest songs, and hip-hop were embraced precisely because they challenged the hegemonic nature of American society and by extension, of hegemonies elsewhere. Second, the English language may initially have been the medium of this transmission but it did not need to remain part of the message. Rock and hip-hop in English might be embraced and appreciated without a firm grasp of the literal meaning of the original words. In some cases, such genres could be imitated using English lyrics, but in other cases local languages could be substituted for English or mixed with English words. A "Big Mac" may be ordered in those English words, but a McDonalds in a non-English-speaking country is not usually an oasis of the English language. As in many other aspects of cultural globalization, music might spread internationally while being transformed by the local culture. Finally, it is necessary to observe that the malleability of cultural globalization has been balanced by the reality of the ascendance of English-speaking societies. More and more popular music is sung in English. As in Japan and elsewhere, eating American fast food may be perceived as participating in a modern global culture. Speaking English is certainly at times being a part of the culturally ascendant community.

In conclusion, English rose to power in international relations, science, and business, as well as in literature and popular culture under circumstances that were largely separate from its rise in colonial and postcolonial societies. Some of these international worlds were quite exclusive. It has become increasingly difficult for a scientist or anyone engaging in international business to escape the predominance of English, whereas the fact that Nigeria and Ghana chose to make English their national languages did not preclude neighboring West African states that had been French colonies from making French their national languages.

Literature is more inclusive. World literature in English doesn't much impede the production of literary works in other languages. Writers in other languages reach substantial audiences. Individual writers, of course, make their choice of language. Translation from English and to English makes for a large crossover market. Still, the numbers of Anglophone readers is very large and book publication in English is very dominant globally. In the early 1990s, almost 30 percent of all books were published in English at presses in over 60 different countries. The Chinese and German languages had about an eighth each of the world share. Japanese, Spanish, and French accounted for between 5 and 8 percent each. No other language accounted for as much as 5 percent of the world total.[51]

Global pop culture is hybrid. The upper stratum is often dominated by Anglophone music, marketing, and production. At other levels this Anglophone warp is interwoven with threads from other linguistic traditions. Trends and music expand out from

Anglophone centers, but fashions and music also move from the edges inward.

In science fiction writing the importance of English in literature and science overlap. In other cases the specialized worlds of English usage can stay quite separate. However, as the next chapter recounts, the cumulative effects of English becoming so important is so many places and spheres built toward a massive tipping point that has made English the global language.

Chapter 6

Tipping Points

In 1998, the South Korean novelist Pok Ko-il proposed that his country make English its new mother tongue and that the Korean language be moved to a museum case where it belongs. Having provoked the uproar he must have intended, he relented a bit, suggesting that English should be the country's second official language, something that many South Korean educators already support. In 2000, the Prime Minister's Commission on Japan's Goals for the 21st Century unleashed a similar storm by advocating that English be made a working language alongside Japanese or even the second official language. In 2003, the Chilean Ministry of Education set in motion a program known as English Opens Doors (*Inglés Abre Puertas*), to make all students proficient in English in a decade and to make all Chileans bilingual (in Spanish and English) in a generation. In 2009, the Swiss National Science Foundation in Berne suggested that the time had come to make English an official language in Switzerland, along with French, German, and Italian.[1] None of these daring proposals has yet become a reality, but they are all signs of the frenzy in the past two decades to meet the challenges of a rapidly globalizing world in which knowing English is a major asset.

As earlier chapters have demonstrated, the English language has established itself around the world, slowly at first and then, especially after 1800, with growing speed. The pace picked up again after 1945 as the use of English accelerated in Europe, in East Asia, and in former British and American colonies. By the 1980s, English had become one of the most important international languages, but it was not yet *the* global language. Scholars differ in the criteria they use for ranking the international languages, though most put English at the top of the list. Arabic, Chinese, French, German, Japanese, Portuguese, Russian, and Spanish (in alphabetical order) are also major international languages, and the stature they have accumulated over many centuries is not slipping.[2]

However, since about 1990, English has moved from being in the forefront of international languages to a special new category, the world's first global language. As the previous chapter argued, English had already become the second language of economic, political, and cultural elites in many parts of the world. What was new was its spread outward to new places and downward to new classes. At the same time English was greatly expanding its global reach, it was also becoming the ladder of upward mobility. So pervasive has English become that in many contexts "international" or "global" have become synonyms for "English-speaking."

It is tempting to see the movement of English to greater global importance as the culmination of a gradual and perhaps inevitable process, but it is more accurate and more insightful to stress the surprising nature of English's final rush to globalism. In the language popularized by Malcolm Gladwell, the "tipping point" for global English that occurred about 1990 was not the direct result of any single event but the cumulative and often indirect result of a series of separate events and circumstances in different parts of the world.[3] Some societies have been strongly pushed by external factors; other responses have had more to do with internal pressures. Some have moved decisively, others have hesitated, and in many places the embrace of English has a long way to go.

Since European and Asian countries get most of the attention below, some examples from Africa may serve here to illustrate the range of particular circumstances surrounding the most recent movements to English. Like many former French colonies where the French language is widely used, Algeria felt the need to address the changing global situation. In 1996, it seriously considered displacing French with English as the major foreign language taught in schools but put off the transition. The Central African country of Rwanda took a more decisive step in 2000 by adding English to French and Rwandan as an official language. The change followed the overthrow of the genocidal government by Rwandans who had been spend a long time in exile in Uganda where English had become their main second language. When Namibia achieved majority rule in 1990, the ruling party, the Southwest African Peoples Organization (SWAPO), made English the country's official language, displacing German (associated with German colonial rule 1885–1919) and Afrikaans (South African administration 1920–90). This action began with SWAPO's decision to use English as its official language in 1981, as a way of easing communication among nationalist leaders and international supporters.

The populous country of South Africa (over 50 million in 2011) is an interesting example of unintended consequences. When majority rule there ended a long period of white settler dominance, the new 1994 Constitution of South Africa added nine African languages to the country's former official languages, Afrikaans and English. However, it quickly became apparent that, while people were pleased to use their home languages in many contexts, when it came to higher education, they preferred the advantages offered by English. Universities scrambled to keep up with the demand for English-medium courses, and the English language was an essential subject in the lower grades. The traditionally Afrikaans-medium universities were particularly affected, first offering alternative courses in English and then having to offer more and more courses only in English. Under such pressures the once primarily Afrikaans-medium Rand Afrikaans University in 2005 became the core of a new University of Johannesburg, which is primarily English medium.

Taken singly such events in Africa appear due to local circumstances, but they are also part of much broader trends. Beyond the particular details in different countries, four major events proved most important in tipping English into its unique global status: (1) the rise of the Internet; (2) the fall of the Soviet Bloc; (3) the economic ascendancy of Asia; and (4) the creation of an international educational marketplace. All four can be subsumed under the convenient rubric of "globalization," so long as that grab-bag term isn't allowed to conceal some surprising and important differences.

The World Wide Web

The creation of the World Wide Web in 1990 made the networks of data transmission now known as the Internet widely accessible at virtually no cost. As the Web was gaining popularity, computers were also becoming cheaper, faster, and more powerful. The cost of web connections and transmissions tumbled, first as telephone rates plummeted and then as the faster cable and satellite systems created for television were adapted to Internet usage. Early web browsers, such as Mosaic (1993) and Netscape Navigator (1994), made browsing the web a breeze. The two Stanford University students who created Google.com in 1998 made searching even faster and easier. As a result, Google became the most visited site on the Internet. The second most visited site is Facebook, started in Harvard dorm room in 2004 as a way of posting personal information. Facebook has greatly broadened its original appeal from American youth to older folks and businesses around the world. It has acquired half a billion registered users. The result of the growth of these new electronic connections, as Tom Friedman put it, "is that never before in the history of the world have so many people been able to learn about so many other people's lives, products, and ideas."[4]

As computer prices fell and their speed rose, the quantity of information available via the Internet was growing rapidly. Businesses, governments, and information-based institutions, such as universities, libraries, archives, and research facilities, all posted a wealth of information. Financial markets and international businesses used the Web to outsource data processing to cheaper lands; scholars gained instant access to the latest research and discoveries—and what is even more important, to each other. All of this was occurring worldwide and in real time.

In theory none of these changes privileged one user language over another. In practice communication was mostly in English for many years. The reasons for English's dominance were both technical and historical. In the early days keyboards could input only the Roman and Cyrillic alphabets that had originated in Europe. Until later developments democratized Internet communication, users of Arabic, Hebrew, Chinese, or other mostly Asian alphabets either had to transform their languages into one of the available keyboard systems or use a Western language. An even larger factor favoring the use of English was that English-speaking states, especially the United States, were the forefront of Internet technology and thus of Internet posting and usage. A third factor was that, as was seen in chapter 4, all sorts of international communication in transportation, business, and scientific and technological writing were already taking place largely or exclusively in English. The growth of web usage accelerated this trend. One widely quoted estimate (at EnglishEnglish.com) is that 80 percent of all home pages are in English.

Even as the Web became more democratic, the dominance of the English language in electronic communication persisted. Much more is now posted in Chinese characters, but China has also established a new English-language website and launched an all-news English-language television channel in July 2010. Those Chinese moves followed similar actions elsewhere. In 1996, the Emir of Qatar funded the launch of a successful Arabic-language all-news channel, Al Jazeera. In 2003, Al Jazeera opened an English-language website to reach a larger audience, and in 2005, launched a new English-language channel, Al Jazeera English, broadcasting round the clock to an international audience. Even the terrorist organization Al-Qaeda posts an online English-language magazine, *Insight*.

Soviet Disintegration

Something else was tipping world relations in new directions: the disintegration of the Soviet Union and the ending of the Cold War. In the late 1980s, Mikhail Gorbachev, the new general secretary of the Soviet Communist Party, pushed through radical changes in the Soviet systems through *perestroika* ("restructuring" the centralized Soviet economy to allow greater competition and efficiency) and *glasnost* (greater "openness" to the outside world with a view to ending the arms race and Cold War). As part of these reforms free elections were allowed in the Eastern European satellites countries in 1989, which resulted in electoral victories by reformist parties in Poland, Hungary, Bulgaria, Czechoslovakia, and Romania. The next year saw the election in East Germany of reformers pledged to union with West Germany, leading to German reunification six months later. Gorbachev agreed to withdraw Soviet troops from the former satellites, and 1991 saw the dissolution of both the Comecon economic union and the Warsaw Pact military alliance. In the second half of 1991, Gorbachev resigned as party head; the party surrendered its monopoly of political power; and the Soviet Union disintegrated into its component parts (and in cases smaller units).

The collapse of the Soviet system was a mammoth global watershed. It left the United States as the lone superpower. For the moment, the global economic, military, and cultural hegemony of the world's largest English-speaking nation was unchallenged. NATO expanded to include Eastern European countries. However, a more subtle and far-reaching change was propelling English forward as the pan-European language of choice. In Europe in the 1980s many languages had vied for prominence. German had the largest number of native speakers. It was the official language of Germany and Austria and had official status in Switzerland as well. Because of the strength of the German economy, many other Europeans studied German as a second language. French was the spoken language of France as well as an official language in Belgium, Luxemburg, and Switzerland and was a favorite second language, especially among speakers of other Romance languages, who could master it without too much difficulty. Decades of compulsory instruction in the schools of the Soviet Union and of Soviet satellite countries had made Russian widely known, even if enthusiasm for it was often muted. English, too, commanded a large following because of its official status in the United Kingdom and the Irish Republic, augmented by the tremendous political, military, economic, and cultural weight of the American colossus.

Eastern Europeans rejection of Soviet hegemony included the rejection of the Russian language. As part of their liberation, students quite literally threw away their Russian grammars and dictionaries. National languages regained prominence, but English became their language of choice for international communication. By the end of the 1990s, 80 percent or more of secondary students in Estonia, Poland, Romania, and Slovenia were studying English, along with over 60 percent of those in Bulgaria and the Czech Republic.[5] The admission of eight former Soviet Bloc countries to the European Union in 2004 and two more in 2007 transformed the linguistic face of Europe. Officially each country's language was equal in the European Union, but amid the babel of 20-plus tongues it was impossible for all to be equal in practice. The arrival of Eastern European observers and members, tipped the linguistic balance in the European Union in favor of English. Even though the key EU institutions are headquartered in non-Anglophone cities (Brussels, Luxembourg, Strasbourg), English began edging out German and French as the common tongue for private conversations, draft documents, and conference presentations at the European Union. One highly placed francophone EU bureaucrat estimated that in 1995, 70 percent of the documents that crossed his desk were in French; by 2003, 70 percent were in English.[6] In March 2006, French president Jacques Chirac stormed out of an EU meeting when a Frenchman began speaking in English. Such displays of pique did not alter the new reality. In the European Parliament in Strasbourg, France, elected delegates may make a formal presentation in any member languages, but when they converse with each other in the hallways, 80 percent of the conversations are in English. All official communication at the European Central Bank in Frankfort, Germany, takes place in English.[7]

English has also become the most popular second language in schools across the face of Europe. In EU schools these days nearly 90 percent of non-English-speaking students study English (compared to 32% for French). In most of Western Europe and Scandinavia, the percentage is over 90 percent. A poll late in 2005 found that more than half of the citizens of EU countries could speak English, only a quarter of whom were native speakers. The poll's results also suggest the proportion of Europeans who will be fluent in English will rise further in the near future: half agreed with the idea that everyone in the European Union needed to speak two foreign languages (beyond the mother tongue) and 77 percent agreed that English should be the first foreign language taught to children. The later figure rises to 92 percent if respondents in English-speaking countries are excluded.[8] When a language becomes that entrenched, it is unlikely to be displaced in any foreseeable timeframe.

In some parts of Europe the percentage of people who can speak English as a second language is already much higher than the EU average. In Denmark, Sweden, and the Netherlands three people out of every four can speak English and the percentage is rising. So widespread has the use of English become in Denmark and Sweden, where it is promoted as the countries' second language, that there is now concern that Danish and Swedish may be losing ground in scientific research, higher education, and business, and language planning measures are being put forward to strengthen national language usage—though without impairing the use of English.[9] In European countries like Switzerland and Belgium that have more than one official language, many young adults prefer to learn and use English rather than mastering the second or third national languages. In advertising and business English often functions as an unofficial national language. Until its demise in 2001, Sabena, the Belgian national airline, used only English signage in its planes. This has largely been continued by its successor Brussels Airlines (SN), whose name employs the English version of Belgium's capital city rather than the French (*Bruxelles*) or Flemish (*Brussel*).

China Tips Asia

Asian countries' policies toward the use of English reflected their different political and economic circumstances. In some democratic countries, cultural and economic nationalists have challenged or derailed policies that promote globalization. In contrast, the Chinese government has aggressively expanded both global trade and teaching English.

As was the case with the Internet and the spread of English in Europe, the key tipping point for global English in Asia occurred recently. In December 1978 in advance of the Third Plenum of the Eleventh Central Committee, the new Chinese Communist Party chairman Deng Xiaoping gave a remarkable speech advocating greater openness internally to private enterprise and competition and externally to foreign trade. In advocating a shift to economic pragmatism, Chairman Deng used a homey image. "It does not matter if a cat is black or white; so long as it can catch mice, it is a good cat."[10] These new policies have transformed China and are transforming the world. Restoring China's long-faltering economy necessitated engagement with the global economy, and that, in turn, required efficient communication. Recognizing the international importance of the English language, Chinese leaders have undertaken the daunting task of teaching English to a very large number of people. Government policy has been matched and exceeded by popular demand, as the parents and grandparents of a single child have seen the mastery of English as a necessary ingredient for success in the globalized world.

Fed by burgeoning foreign exports, China's economy grew more than tenfold between 1980 and 2000. In August 2010, China's economy passed Japan's to become the second largest in the world (after that of the United States). The percentage of China's population living in cities doubled and the percentage of Chinese enrolled in high school tripled. Government policies have expanded higher education at an even faster rate. Between 1998 and 2010, university graduates increased fivefold, while enrollments grew at a similar rate and advances were made in educational quality.[11] These changes were accompanied by a huge demand to learn English. As businesses, teachers, and government bureaus have all clamored for English speakers, the grade in which Chinese students begin to study English in Chinese schools has moved ever downward. By 2006, as much as a fifth of the population was studying English and the quality of the results was increasing.

To meet the demand, massive efforts have been undertaken to recruit native speakers of English as teachers. China has become the largest market for English-language services in the world, worth an estimated US$60 billion a year. Publishers of English-language textbooks and dictionaries have expanded licensing agreements to sell their wares in China, as have the makers of high-tech language-learning devices. Running English-language schools has also become a big business. New Oriental, a Chinese company listed on the New York Stock Exchange, claims to be the largest provider of private educational services in China, serving 2.4 million students in hundreds of schools and centers. A sign of the global times is the fact that another hundred schools in China are run by English First—originally a Swedish company.[12]

However, there are simply not enough native speakers of English available to satisfy the demand for English-language learning in China—not to mention the rest of the world. Other companies have targeted the Chinese market with low-cost English-language learning products. Prominent among these is the Toronto-based Lingo Media Company, which has developed a web-based site for Chinese learning English known as speak2me.cn that provides a virtual teacher, speaking like a native speaker, and an avatar who drills students in oral English, correcting their pronunciation. With over a million registered users in China, speak2me is growing fast.[13] New Oriental reported 7.8 million online students in 2012.

If the expanded learning of English in China seems a product of both public policy push and a strong popular response to learning, in India popular demand to learn English seems to be the dominant force. India's growing prominence in global trade and information processing has led to a huge increase in the demand for people proficient in standard English. Despite the election of an avowedly Hindu nationalist government in 1998, the proliferation of teaching and study of English has grown at a rapid rate. A 2003 story in the *New York Times* reported, "In the past decade, English has moved from being the gatekeeper of the elite to being a ladder up for the masses." This has put great pressure on Indian public schools that teach in Hindi and regional languages. After an exodus of 30,000 students from Mumbai (Bombay) schools during the first three years of the twenty-first century, officials substituted English-medium instruction in about 40 public schools in an effort to hold on to students.

The craze to learn English reaches ever deeper in Indian society. In the poor state of Bihar, where 150 English-medium private schools opened between 1994 and 2003, the government now begins the study of English in the third grade instead of the sixth. According to British linguist David Graddol, among the long-repressed Dalits ("Untouchables") English is regarded as "a mass movement against the caste order" and the way out of poverty. Those sentiments are pervasive among much of the rest of Indian society; a poll in 2009 reported that 87 percent of its respondents agreed that English was "important to success in life." Such attitudes explain the proliferation of schools in India promising proficiency in English. Under such popular pressures and the needs of business, Indian nationalists have muted their criticism of English as a colonial language of oppression. It is now the global language, of course.[14] As elsewhere in South Asia, proficiency in English remains a hallmark of the elite. Better able than the struggling masses to pay for private schools and tutors, middle- and upper-class families are able to ensure that the next generation will get privileged positions in business, the military, and government.[15]

Eagerness to learn English is sweeping through most of the rest of Asia, producing both policy changes and significant resistance in places. The policy of displacing English with indigenous languages adopted in many former British or American colonies in Asia has been profoundly altered in recent years by the dual need to deal with the requirements of globalization and to meet internal demands for social mobility. As a Pakistani scholar noted in 2003, "English is as firmly entrenched in the domains of power in Pakistan as it was in 1947." He also suggested that English was gaining support among nonelite people who are eager to gain entry to high-status employment.[16]

The Sri Lankan government in 1989 altered the policy of promoting Sinhala as the national language that had been followed since 1956. Discontent by Tamil speakers and by parents concerned with their children's ability to compete in the global world crystallized around the revelation that a cabinet minister had enrolled his own children in English-medium schools. Recognizing that the lack of proficiency in English was a root problem of youth violence, the government recalled retired civil servants proficient in English to classroom duty. Education in Tamil was also promoted.[17]

In South Korea, the "fervor" for learning English is so widespread that some educators have advocated making it the country's second official language. Despite some strong nationalist antipathy to growing Western cultural influences, one perceptive observer notes that most Koreans regard such influences as an opportunity for the country to advance itself on the world stage and an expression of Koreans' traditional cleverness and pragmatism. Parents eager for their children to acquire fluency in English sent 27,350 of them abroad for elementary and secondary education in 2009 (up from 1,840 in 1999). To lessen the strains on such young people, the Korean government is developing an English-only island complex where a dozen prestigious British and American private schools will open branch campuses.[18]

In contrast to their Chinese and South Korean neighbors, efforts by the Japanese to master English appear to be lagging. Strong nationalist opposition to a 2000 proposal by Prime Minister Keizo Obuchi to make English universally known in Japan derailed implementation plans and led to what some have called a "lost decade." The fact that English is not introduced until junior high school (later than elsewhere in Asia) adds to the difficulty Japanese students have in speaking the language.[19]

Malaysia faces a similar political quandary. In October 2010, the government ran a full-page ad addressed to the global business community in *The Economist* under the headline, "We speak your language," the language in question being English. The reality is more complex. In 2003, the longtime prime minister of Malaysia, Dr. Mahathir bin Mohammad, succeeded in revising the language policy based on Bahasa Malaysia that his country had adopted after independence. However, the decision to reintroduce English as the language of instruction for math and science in primary schools produced what the *Economist* called "a first-class inter-racial row." The Chinese community won an exemption to continue to teach math and science in Chinese. Opposition from the majority Malay population took longer to organize but has now produced a pledge to rescind the English-medium instruction at that level in 2012. The English language continues to be taught as a subject at every level and receives strong emphasis because of its global and regional importance.[20]

The Global Academic Language

English is the new Latin in much of Europe. In parts of the Middle East it is challenging Arabic as the language for advanced study. Across Asia English has become the academic lingua franca. The phenomenal changes in global higher education have made English "*the* language of higher education" and the "international academic language."[21] Regional academic languages existed in medieval Europe and the Islamic world, but with the rise of nation-states national languages became the medium for instruction, except for foreign language courses. As was recounted earlier, higher education in English became common in some former colonies in Asia and Africa. In modern Europe, some countries composed of small languages groups, such as in the Netherlands and in the Scandinavian countries, have been somewhat exceptional in their early promotion of English-medium courses. In the last 20 years, however, that trickle has become a flood, in Europe, Africa, the Middle East, and parts of Asia where English is not an official language. English is not just a useful language to know; it has become *the* language in which to acquire advanced training in disciplines ranging from diplomacy and economics to science, technology, and business.

Two phenomena are associated with the rise of English-medium instruction: (1) the growing number of students studying outside their home country; (2) new programs and entirely new universities that target upwardly mobile students. As with most other aspects of globalization, there are significant local variations, but the spread of global English is also embedded in remarkable new global systems.

Student mobility has become a major force for standardizing international higher education. Since the late 1990s, the number of students engaged in higher education outside their home countries has been growing by 7 percent a year. In 2003, there were 2.1 million such students, the number in 2010 is thought to have been 5.8 million.[22] By 2004, the majority of such international students (53 percent) were enrolled in English-language programs, most of these in the major English-speaking countries. The number of European students studying outside their home countries (2.5 million in 2009) is expected to rise to 8 million by 2020.[23] Asian students are also increasingly mobile. In recent years, India and China have each been sending 100,000 students a year to study abroad in the United States.[24] While English-language study is expanding, the proportion of international students studying in the major English-speaking countries seems to be declining. That is, growing numbers are studying in English-medium programs in countries where English is not a majority language.

Figure 6.1 shows the sources of international students at the three largest Anglophone destinations: the United States, the United Kingdom, and Australia in 2009. The United States is the largest destination overall, although Australia receives the most overseas students per capita. Asian countries are the principal source of students in each case, accounting for a third of the

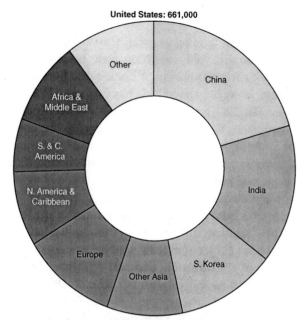

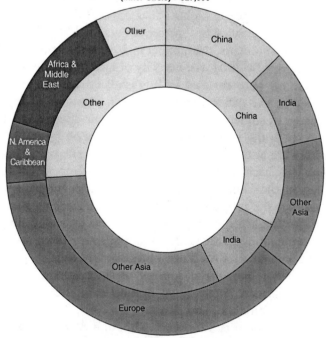

Figure 6.1 University students going abroad for study, 2009, by destination.
Source: UNESCO, Institute for Statistics, Higher Education.

students in the United Kingdom, over half in the United States, and three-quarters in Australia. China is the single greatest source of students for each country, with India coming in second. In addition to the common importance of Asian students, the distribution of international students at each destination is influenced by geographic factors. The United States draws heavily from other parts of the Americas, along with Europe, Turkey, and Saudi Arabia. The United Kingdom receives the greatest number of its international students from other parts of Europe, while Australia's geographical location helps account for the fact that it draws nearly a fifth of its overseas students from Southeast Asia. The remaining part of this chapter looks at other regions and themes.

In Europe, there has been a tremendous shift in favor of Anglophone higher education due to both intra-European and extra-European factors. Within the European Union Germany, France, and the United Kingdom, began encouraging student exchanges in 1981 as a way of promoting intercultural understanding and cooperation. By a simple majority vote in June 1987, the European Commission expanded and consolidated the existing exchanges into the Erasmus Program, which guaranteed that students registering for courses in other EU countries would incur no additional tuition charges and would receive full credit from their home universities. The Erasmus Program proved immensely popular. By 2008, some 183,000 students were taking part. It is estimated that 4 percent of EU students participate in the Erasmus Program at some point in their university studies.[25] Initially, learning each other's languages and cultures was the fundamental goal of the program, which was captured in the title of a popular EU booklet, *Many Tongues, One Family*, published in 2004.[26] However, improving one's grasp of the host-country's language became less central as the program and the European Union expanded. By 2007, the European Union had 23 official languages and 5 others were semiofficial. As a practical matter, most students were interested in learning only a handful of these. To attract students, states using other languages needed to offer courses in a common language. English quickly filled the bill, since so many European students were learning English as a second language in primary and secondary education. English also became the language for communication among European students outside the classroom, as was illustrated in the 2002 film "L'Auberge Espagnol," a joint French-Spanish production, in which a group of Erasmus students from across Europe come to Barcelona to learn Spanish and choose to use English as their common language in the large apartment they share.

A study of European higher education in 1999/2000 found that English-medium courses and programs were a common response to efforts at internationalization, including student and staff recruitment, and the need for graduates to be fluent in English. In Finland, all 55 universities had English-medium programs, as did both universities in Slovenia. A majority of higher-education institutions in six other countries offered English-medium programs, while only five EU countries had none (Croatia, Greece, Italy, Spain, and Switzerland).[27] Since then the trend has accelerated. In a five-year period in the mid-2000s, the number of courses taught in English at European universities tripled. Teaching in English was particularly common in the Netherlands, Germany, and Scandinavia, and was especially strong in graduate programs in engineering, business, and management.

English-medium courses and programs in Europe have also been attractive to non-European students. Asians and Africans made up nearly half of the foreign students in English-medium programs in Europe in 2008. For Europe's cash-strapped public institutions of higher education such tuition-paying foreign students are a major source of revenue, and English is the key to attracting them. Because only 3.3 percent of university students in Italy are from outside the country, the Ministry of Education took two new measures in 2012. The first was to launch a new website, UniversItaly, in English and Italian, which lists all university courses in the country, including those taught in English (especially common in medicine). The second was to start administering the medical school admissions test in English as well as in Italian.[28]

The spread of English in European higher education has come at the expense of other foreign languages, but the larger phenomenon is that Europeans are becoming trilingual. Fully 93 percent of EU students who are not native speakers of English learn English as their second language and most then add a third language. This policy of having every EU citizen fluent in two foreign languages was formalized in a White paper of the European Commission in 1995 and polls indicate that the European public has embraced that goal.

Although studying foreign languages thus continues to be an important part of the Erasmus Program, there is one place in Europe where the spread of English has diminished the study of foreign languages: the British Isles. In the United Kingdom and Ireland, reluctance to study any foreign language has been accompanied by a declining interest in studying in any foreign country other than the United States. Two factors are involved. First, English's international popularity makes learning foreign languages seem unnecessary to native speakers. As one researcher puts it: "The increasing adoption of English-medium teaching in European HE [Higher Education] will arguably reduce the attraction…of study-abroad for native English-speaking students."[29] Second, efforts to revive Celtic languages require teaching time that might otherwise have been devoted to foreign language study. Though bilingualism in Ireland and Wales is increasing, the second language is considered a national not a foreign language. Indeed, Irish is an official EU language.

Anglophone North America exhibits many trends similar to those in the European Union. In the first place, the proportion of American university students studying abroad has grown rapidly since the mid-1980s, although most study abroad for a semester or less. During the two decades ending in 2007–2008, the number of such students grew fourfold to 262,400. Over 50,000 went to other English-speaking countries. Western Europe was the most popular destination, but there has been significant growth in the numbers going to Asia, Latin America, and Africa. Waves of English-speaking Americans studying abroad have fed the demand for English-medium higher education at their destinations. To accommodate them American universities have rapidly expanded the number of satellite campuses and programs overseas. Such programs include foreign language study, but they also have significant English-medium instruction.

Second, spending time abroad has helped stem the decline in foreign language study underway in the United States since the 1960s. Enrollment in foreign language programs has increased sharply since 2000. Some of the increase is due to new interest in languages such as Arabic and Mandarin, but half of American "foreign" language enrollment is in Spanish, which is becoming the second national language.[30] Except among the children of recent immigrants there is little evidence of trilingualism in the United States. A final comparison with Europe is that the number of foreign students studying in the United States has also doubled in the past two decades, in part reflecting the importance of English as the international language of education. Some 671,600 international students enrolled in American colleges and universities in 2008–9, 57 percent of whom came from Asia.[31]

These transformations in Europe and North America are associated with a remarkable increase on the use of English in higher education around the world. This has taken three different forms. First has been the establishment of satellite English-medium universities abroad by American and British universities. The first British university to do so was the University of Nottingham, which opened a campus in Malaysia in 2000 that now enrolls 3,500 students. Nottingham also opened the first foreign campus in China, at Ningbo, which has 4,300 students. The United Kingdom's Middlesex University has a satellite campus in Dubai, a second in Mauritius, a third in India, and plans to open a branch in China.[32] The Middle East has also become a popular destination. New York University opened a campus in Abu Dhabi in September 2010, which will grow to 2,000 students by 2014 when its new campus is completed on an artificial island. The elite members of first class came from 43 countries with a third from the United States, and important contingents from the United Arab Emirates, China, Hungary, and Russia. Not to be outdone another Arab emirate, Dubai, has opened an International Academic City, where, at last count, 27 institutions from 11 countries have opened campuses. Not all teach just in English, but most do.[33]

A second strategy has been the decision of non-English-medium universities to offer some courses in English, either as a way to attract foreign students or to strengthen the language skills of students in fields where English has become the dominant language, such as science, business, and international relations. In Europe this included some 1,500 master's-degree programs in 2003–4.[34]

Before 2002, it was mandatory for German universities to teach doctoral studies in German; by 2006, the German government had funded 50 international postdoctoral programs at German universities using English to make them more attractive to international researchers.[35] In the Netherlands, Sweden, and Finland many or most advanced programs, especially in science and technology are taught exclusively in English. For example, Finland's Aalto University, with a combined enrollment of 17,000 students, was created in 2010 by merging Helsinki University of Technology, Helsinki School of Economics, and the University of Art and Design, Helsinki. The economics school, the best in the country, offers four undergraduate majors and eight masters degrees in English. As is common in other Finnish technological universities, the Aalto University School of Science and Technology offers many of its masters programs exclusively in English.

France has not been in the forefront of moving to English, but some of its top schools have joined the trend. A striking example is the prestigious Institut d'Études Politiques de Paris (better known as "Sciences Po"), which now teaches many courses in English. The elite business school outside Paris, École Supérieure des Sciences Économiques et Commerciales (ESSEC), has increased the number of courses offered in English in its MBA program from 25 percent to 50 percent and has opened a campus in Singapore, where instruction is exclusively in English. At the Lille School of Management more than half of the courses are offered in English. English-medium courses have even appeared at the super-prestigious École Normale Supérieure.[36]

While the trend has moved quickly in Europe, English-medium programs are also prominent in the Middle East and in East Asia, as an effective way to attract international students. In a departure from the country's strict Hebrew-language policy in higher education, Israel's Interdisciplinary Center (founded 1994) offers masters degree programs in English for its students from 63 countries. Singapore and Malaysia have become "education hubs" for Asian students by using English. Beginning at Waseda University in 1963, English-medium programs became commonplace in Japan. In 2007, 65 universities in Japan offered English-medium programs and there were 81 such graduate-level programs at 42 universities.[37]

The study of medicine is also increasingly in English. St. Petersburg State Medical Academy, for example, offers an English-medium curriculum for foreign students that parallels its Russian-medium instruction. To accommodate North American students a number of medical schools using English have opened in the West Indies in English-speaking as well as non-English-speaking lands, such as the Netherlands Antilles. China has English-medium medical training at several universities, including Zhejiang Medical University, Fudan University Medical Center, Tongji Medical College of Huazhong University, China Medical University, and Zhenzhou Medical University. China has also established English-medium programs in engineering (Qingdao Technological University), business (Nanjing University, South China University of Technology), and at the China Studies Institute of Peking University.

One of the most striking developments of recent decades has been the result of a third strategy toward global English: the founding of autonomous English-medium universities in non-English-speaking countries (see table 6.1). The earliest such institutions were founded as missionary enterprises in the Middle East in the 1800s and early 1900s (the American University of Beirut, the American University in Cairo, Bogazici University in Istanbul). Others followed after the Second World War, but the big boom has come since 1990. Many of these institutions are American-style, usually with American accreditation. Most are private and many have agreements with universities in the United States and elsewhere to send students for short-term study, but they also cater to local demand for this type of education. Al Akhawayn, Morocco's only English-medium university, caters to students from several Muslim countries as well as from other lands. In Italy, Venice International University combines a fairly traditional graduate program with a unique undergraduate study-abroad program featuring students and professors from its dozen international partners. In Hungary, Central European University in Budapest, founded in 1991, offers graduate degrees in the humanities, social sciences, law, and management. The newly established (1991) Hong Kong University of Science and Technology is another notable example. As table 6.1, shows, the Middle East (especially Kuwait and the Arab Emirates) has seen the foundation of many new English-medium universities.

Table 6.1 English-medium higher education where English is not an official language

	Location	Founded	Status
Bogazici University	Istanbul, Turkey	1863	public
American U. of Beirut	Beirut, Lebanon	1866	private
American Col. of Greece	Aghia Paraskevi, Greece	1875	private
American U. in Cairo	Cairo, Egypt	1919	private
Middle East Technical U.	Ankara and Erdemli, Turkey; Northern Cyprus	1956	public
American U. of Paris	Paris, France	1962	private
American U. of Rome	Rome, Italy	1969	private
United Arab Emirates U.	Al Ain, UAE	1976	private
American U. of the Caribbean	St. Maarten, NA	1978	private
American Col. of Thessaloniki	Thessaloniki, Greece	1981	private
Aga Khan U.	Karachi, Pakistan, et al.	1983	private
Int'l Islamic U. of Malaysia	Kuala Lumpur, Malaysia	1983	public
Central European U.	Budapest, Hungary	1991	private
American U. in Bulgaria	Blagoevgrad, Bulg.	1991	private
Al Akhawayn U.	Ifrane, Morocco	1993	public
Duxx Graduate School of Business Leadership	Monterrey, Mexico	1993	private
Khazar U.	Baku, Azerbaijan	1993	private
Saba U. School of Medicine	Saba, NA	1993	private
Venice International U.	Venice, Italy	1995	public
American U. in Dubai	Dubai, UAE	1995	private
American U. of Central Asia	Bishkek, Kyrgyzustan	1997	private
American U. of Sharjah	Sharjah, UAE	1997	private
Jacobs U. Bremen	Bremen, Germany	1999	private
Prince Sultan U.	Riyadh, Saudi Arabia	1999	private
Gulf U. for Science and Technology	Kuwait	2002	private
German U. in Cairo	New Cairo, Egypt	2002	private
American U. of Kuwait	Salmiya, Kuwait	2003	private
Abu Dhabi U.	Abu Dhabi, UAE	2003	private
Alfaisal U.	Riyadh, Saudi Arabia	2007	private
American U. in the Emirates	Dubai, UAE	2007	private
American U. of the Middle East	Dasman, Kuwait	2008	private
Vietnamese-German U.	Ho Chi Minh City, Vietnam	2008	private
Tan Tao U.	Near Ho Chi Minh City, Vietnam	2011	private

Note: As in English-speaking countries, some language and literature courses are taught in languages other than English.

Conclusion

By 2010, one could drop the qualifiers: English was *the* global language. Although many languages retained regional strength, no other language was close in its global reach. English was dominant in business, science, technology, diplomacy, and education. It was the language to know in every continent, possibly excepting South America.

Nothing in linguistics is ever permanent, but with such a commanding position English seems likely to remain the global language for the foreseeable future. Latin survived the fall of the Western Roman Empire and the importance of English increased even as the British Empire declined, so there is no reason to believe that English would lose support if American hegemony should slip. Despite China's continued rapid return to global economic and military preeminence, the likelihood of Mandarin becoming a global language seems small. Mandarin is increasing its importance nationally within China, regionally in East Asia, and among overseas Chinese communities, but a leap to international status seems unlikely. In the first place, it will take some time for China to become as preeminent as the United States at its peak. Even when China becomes the world's largest economy, its economic wealth will rank much lower than the United States and the European Union on a per capita basis for some time to come. As China becomes a military superpower, the world is returning to the once-familiar balance-of-power framework, with the United States retaining its superpower status. Moreover, China has powerful Asian competitors. Japan's giant economy may well regain its momentum, and many believe that by about 2050 India will challenge China's economic (and perhaps military) position.

None of these geopolitical and economic changes seems likely to alter the importance of the English language globally. In becoming the global language, English has moved beyond the control of Britain, the United States, and other English-speaking countries. The fate of English as the global language does not depend on those who speak it as their home language; it depends on those who speak it as a second or third language. This includes growing numbers of Chinese and other Asians, Europeans, Africans, and others. Even as the relative importance of native English speakers declines in the twenty-first century, the rest of the world will still needs a common language to communicate with each other. English may not be a permanent feature of the global order, but it is a feature that cannot be changed easily or quickly.

One of the great strengths of global English is its appeal to the young. In much of the world, learning and using English is a new phenomenon. Those now under 25 are much more likely to have a command of English than any other age group. These young English speakers will have a vested interest in English for the rest of their lives; almost certainly they will want their children to know it even better. Even as developments in electronic translation facilitate oral and written communication across languages, English is still likely to remain central to many forms of global communication. Global business, global technologies, and global science all seem impossible without a common language and no other is in sight.

Global English is a product of the complex process called "globalization." It is a commonplace that globalization produces winners and losers; so too does the emergence of global English. It does not, however, seem helpful to judge globalization or global language as though they were moral processes rather than historical products. The world in the early twenty-first century is no utopia. Those born with advantages have a tremendous head start. However, many observers argue that the barriers to social and economic mobility are now lower than in earlier ages. If the world is not yet "flat" in Tom Friedman's pithy description, it does seem to be flattening for many. The appeal of learning English is that it lowers the barriers to advancement for those from less privileged backgrounds. It is they who have turned the spread of English from an imperialist plot to a more nuanced and more complex narrative.

Does English invariably give people a leg up? Clearly not or there would not be so many disadvantaged native speakers of English in places like the United States nor so many speakers of English as a second language in places like Nigeria. Knowing English can confer an advantage, but other circumstances matter, too. One of the arenas where knowing English has been advantageous has been in the recent migrations from lands with few opportunities to those with many more.

The once-poor countries that have managed to greatly improve their economic conditions (the so-called tigers, whether Asian, Irish, or something else) illustrate that dramatic change is possible. English played minor roles in many of these transformations, though it was central in Ireland and in the development of Bangalore, India, as a communication hub. In the future, a knowledge of English will be essential for these tigers and all those who hope to emulate them.

Notes

1 Introduction: Disciplines, Perspectives, Debates, and Overview

1. The evolution of approaches can be comparing earlier editions of the classic guides with their most recent ones: Dominic Head, ed., *The Cambridge Guide to Literature in English,* 3rd ed. (Cambridge: Cambridge University Press, 2006); Dinah Birch, ed., *The Oxford Companion to English Literature,* 7th ed. (Oxford: Oxford University Press, 2009). Alternative approaches that have influenced the revisions of the standard guides are highlighted in Virginia Blain, Patricia Clements, and Isobel Grundy, eds., *The Feminist Companion to Literature in English* (New Haven: Yale University Press, 1990); and Catherine Lynette Innes, *The Cambridge Introduction to Postcolonial Literatures in English* (New York: Cambridge University Press, 2007); George R. Bozzini and Cynthia A. Leenerts, *Literature Without Borders: International Literature in English For Student Writers* (Prentice Hall, 2000). Guides to national literature are too numerous to mention here.
2. Rani Rubdi and Mario Saraceni, eds., *English in the World: Global Rules, Global Roles* (London: Continuum, 2006), 17.
3. Jan Svartvik and Geoff Leech, *English—One Tongue, Many Voices* (New York, Palgrave Macmillian, 2006). Svartvik is a Swedish and an academic specialist in the English language; Leech is a British academic specialist in linguistics.
4. Lawrence D. Carrington, "Caribbean English," *The Oxford Companion to the English Language,* ed. Tom McArthur (hereafter *OCEL*) (Oxford: Oxford University Press, 1992), 191–92.
5. For example, David Crystal (*English as a Global Language* [Cambridge: CUP, 1977, 2003]) and Tom McArthur (editor of *OCEL* and author of *The English Languages* [Cambridge: Cambridge University Press 1998]) are both academic specialists in English language and literature; Robert McCrum (*Globish: How the English Language Became the World's Language* [London: Viking Penguin, 2010]) is a journalist.
6. My thinking about contemporary globalization has been shaped by Thomas L. Friedman's *The Lexus and the Olive Tree: Understanding*

Globalization (New York: Anchor Books, 2000); *The World Is Flat: A Brief History of the Twenty-First Century*, 2nd ed. (New York: Picador, 2006); *Hot Flat, and Crowded: Why We Need a Green Revolution—and How It Can Renew America*, 2nd ed. (New York: Picador, 2009), as well as the authors in *Many Globalizations: Cultural Diversity in the Contemporary World*, ed. Peter Berger and Samuel Huntington (New York: Oxford University Press, 2002).

7. Colin Renfrew, *Archaeology and Language* (New York: Cambridge University Press, 1988), compares the spread of the Bantu, Indo-European, and other language families. A delightful and learned survey down to the present is Nicholas Ostler, *Empires of the Word: A Language History of the World* (New York: HarperCollins, 2005). For Jesuit interest in Chinese as the parent language, see David E. Mungello, *The Great Encounter of China and the West, 1500–1800*, 3rd ed. (Rothman & Littlefield, 2009), 85–86; for Ge'ez, see David Northrup, *Africa's Discovery of Europe, 1450–1850*, 2nd ed. (New York: Oxford University Press, 2009), 140.

8. For estimates of the numbers of languages past and present, see M. Paul Lewis, ed., *Ethnologue: Languages of the World*, 16th ed. (Dallas, TX: SIL International, 2009). Online version: http://www.ethnologue.com/.

9. The theme of divergent/convergent eras is explored in David Northrup, "Globalization and the Great Convergence: Rethinking World History in the Long Term," *Journal of World History* 16 (2005): 249–67; and David Northrup, "Globalization in Historical Perspective," World System History Series, ed. George Modelski, *Encyclopedia of Life Support Systems*. Developed under the Auspices of the UNESCO (Oxford: Eolss'Publishers, 2010).

10. For the expansion of Islam, see Ira M. Lapidus, *A History of Islamic Societies*, 2nd ed. (Cambridge: Cambridge University Press, 2002), 31–111, 197–449; Richard W. Bulliet, *Conversion to Islam in the Medieval Period: an Essay in a Quantitative History* (Cambridge, MA: Harvard University Press, 1979); Ibn Battuta, *Travels, A.D. 1325–1354*, trans H. A. R. Gibb (Cambridge: Hakluyt Society, 1958), retold by Ross E. Dunn, *The Adventures of Ibn Battuta: A Muslim Traveler of the 14th Century*, rev. ed. (Berkeley, CA: University of California Press, 2005).

11. For Polo and the Mongols' language use, see Laurence Bergreen, *Marco Polo: From Venice to Xanadu* (New York: Alfred A. Knopf, 2007), 135–37. Stewart Gordon, *When Asia Was the World* (Philadelphia: Da Capo Press, 2008), 97–136, introduces Battuta and the Ming expeditions.

12. Tomé Pires, *Summa Oriental of Tomé Pires: An Account of the East, from the Red Sea to Japan, Written in Malacca and India in 1512–1515*, trans. Armando Cortesão (London: Hakluyt Society, 1944).

13. Ostler, *Empires of the Word*, 373–79.

14. David Eltis, "Free and Coerced Migration from the Old World to the New," in *Coerced and Free Migration: Global Perspectives,* ed. David Eltis (Stanford, CA: Stanford University Press, 2002), 33–74.

15. S. W. Koelle, *Polyglotta Africana, or a Comparative Vocabulary of Nearly 300 Words and Phrases in More than 100 Distinct African Languages* (London: Church Missionary House, 1854).

16. See James H. Sweet, *Recreating Africa: Culture, Kinship, and Religion in the African-Portuguese World, 1441–1770* (Chapel Hill, NC: University of North Carolina, 2003); Linda Heywood, ed., *Central Africans and Cultural Transformations in the American Diaspora* (Cambridge: Cambridge University Press, 2002); Joel E. Tishken, Toyin Falola, and Akintune Akinyemu, eds., *Sàngó in Africa and the African Disapora* (Bloomington, IN: Indiana University Press, 2009).

17. Pidgin and creole are often used interchangeably, but the technical distinction is that a pidgin is a hybrid language used for cross-cultural communication that is not the mother tongue of either party, whereas a creole is such a language that has become the principal language of a group, themselves often called Creoles.

18. Salikoko S. Mufwene, "West African Pidgin English," in *OCEL,* 1111.

19. Carrington, "Caribbean English Creole," 193.

20. Salikoko S. Mufwene, "Gullah," in *OCEL,* 456–57.

21. For the statistics of the slave trade, see David Eltis, *Voyages: The Trans-Atlantic Slave Trade Database* (http://www.slavevoyages.org). Slavery in North American is discussed in more detail in chapter 3.

22. Sidney W. Mintz and Richard Price, *The Birth of African-American Culture: An Anthropological Perspective,* new ed. (Boston, MA: Beacon Press, 1992), 47.

23. R. K. Kent, "Palmares: An African State in Brazil," *Journal of African History* 6 (1965): 161–75. This and several other case studies are anthologized in Richard Price, ed., *Maroon Societies: Rebel Slave Communities in the Americas,* 2nd ed. (Baltimore, MD: Johns Hopkins University Press, 1979).

24. David Northrup, "Becoming African: Identity Formation among Liberated Slaves in Nineteenth-Century Sierra Leone," *Slavery and Abolition* 27 (April 2006): 1–21.

25. David S. Landes, *The Wealth and Poverty of Nations* (New York: Norton, 1998); and Niall Ferguson, *Empire: The Rise and Demise of the British World Order* (New York: Basic Books, 2002). Their efforts are smart and probing even if their conclusions are not fully satisfactory.

26. See Kenneth Pomeranz, *The Great Divergence: China, Europe, and the Making of the Modern World Economy* (Princeton, NJ: Princeton University Press, 2002); C. A. Bayly, *The Birth of the Modern World, 1780–1914* (Oxford: Blackwell Publishing, 2004); Seguta Bose, *A Hundred Horizons: The Indian Ocean in the Age of Global Empire*

(Cambridge, MA: Harvard University Press, 2006); Northrup, *Africa's Discovery of Europe.*

27. My reading of these debates is much influenced by Ronald Takaki, "Teaching American History through a Different Mirror" American Historical Association's *Perspectives* (October 1994), here applied more broadly that he intended.

28. First published in 1978, Edward Said, *Orientalism: Western Conceptions of the Orient* (Hammondsworth: Penguin, 2003). For a telling critique, see David Scott, "Kipling, the Orient, and Orientals: "Orientalism" Reoriented?' *Journal of World History* 22.2 (2011): 299–328. For other critiques, see Robert Irwin, *Dangerous Knowledge: Orientalism and Its Discontents* (Woodstock: Overlook Press, 2006); Daniel Varisco, *Reading Orientalism: Said and the Unsaid* (Seattle, WA: University of Washington Press, 2007); Ibn Warraq, *Defending the West: A Critique of Edward Said's Orientalism* (New York: Prometheus Books, 2007).

29. Harold Haarmann and Eugene Holman, "The Impact of English as a Language of Science in Finland and Its Role for the Transition to Network Society," in *The Dominance of English as a Language of Science,* ed. Ulrich Ammon (Berlin: Mouton de Gruyter, 2001), 256.

30. Robert Phillipson, *Linguistic Imperialism* (Oxford: Oxford University Press, 1992), 301, 306, and passim.

31. English has been termed a "killer language" and the cause of language suicide ("linguicide") by Daniel Nettle and Suzanne Romaine, *Vanishing Voices: The Extinction of the World's Languages* (Oxford: Oxford University Press, 2000), 5. See also Yukio Tsuda, "Speaking Against the Hegemony of English," Chapter 15 in *The Handbook of Critical Intercultural Communication,* ed. Thomas K. Nakayama and Rona Tamiko Halualani (Oxford: Wiley-Blackwell 2010).

32. Robert Phillipson, *English only Europe? Challenging Language Policy.* (London: Routledge, 2003), title and passim; Tove Skutnabb-Kangas and Robert Phillipson, "The Global Politics of Language: Markerts, Maintenance, Marginalization, or Murder," in *The Handbook of Language and Globalization,* ed. Nikolas Coupland (Chichester: Wiley-Blackwell, 2010), 77–100.

33. Robert B. Kaplan, "English—the Accidental Language of Science?" in *The Dominance of English as a Language of Science,* ed. Ulrich Ammon (Berlin: Mouton de Gruyter, 2001), 16, 26. See also Alan Davies, "Review Article: Ironising the Myth of Linguicism," *Journal of Multilingual and Multicultural Development* 17 (1996): 485–596 (for a critique of Phillipson); and Salikoko S. Mufwene, "Colonization, Globalization and the Plight of 'Weak' Languages" (a review of Nettle & Romaine's *Vanishing Voices*) *Journal of Linguistics* 38.2 (2002): 375–95. Mufwene's first quotation is from

his "Colonization, Globalization," 376–77; the second is from Salikoko S. Mufwene, *Language Evolution: Contact, Competition and Change* (London: Continuum, 2008), 244.

34. Ethnologue, "Languages of Nigeria"; *Wikipedia*, "List of Endangered Languages in Africa."

2   The Language of the British Isles

1. Norman Blake, "Introduction," in *The Cambridge History of the English Language* (hereafter *CHEL*), vol. 2, *1066–1476*, ed. Norman Blake (Cambridge: Cambridge University Press, 1992), 9.
2. Richard M. Hogg, "Introduction," *CHEL*, vol. 1, *1066–1476*, ed. Richard M. Hogg (Cambridge: Cambridge University Press, 1992), 2–5.
3. Dieter Kasovsky, "Semantics and Vocabulary," in *CHEL*, 1: 317–20.
4. Venerable Bede, *Ecclesiastical History of the English Nation* (London: J. M. Dent; New York E. P. Dutton, 1910), Book I; Daniel Donoghue, "Early Old English (up to 899)," in *A Companion to the History of the English Language,* ed. Haruko Momma and Michael Matto (Oxford: Wiley-Blackwell. 2008), p. 156; Thomas E. Toon, "Old English Dialects," in *CHEL*, 1:422.
5. Hogg, "Introduction," 6–7.
6. Gregory the Great, "Introduction to *Pastoral Care*," in *Readings for Use of the Students in the Massachusetts Institute of Technology* (Boston, MA: George H. Ellis, 1916), 14–15.
7. For a critical discussion, see Alfred P. Smyth, *King Alfred the Great* (Oxford: Oxford University Press, 1995), 551–66.
8. Dieter Kastovsky, "Semantics and Vocabulary," in *CHEL*, 1:332–36.
9. Thorlac Turville-Petre, "Early Middle English (1066–ca. 1350)," in *Companion*, 184–85.
10. Richard H. Bailey, *Images of English: A Cultural History of the Language* (Ann Arbor, MI: University of Michigan Press, 1991), 21–22; Robert McCrum, Robert McNeil, and William Cran, *The Story of English*, 3rd ed. (New York: Penguin Books, 2003), 75–77 (quotation 77); Christopher Brooke, *A History of England*, vol. 2, *From Alfred to Henry III, 871–1272* (Edinburgh: Thomas Nelson, 1961), 224–36.
11. Jeremy J, Smith, "Varieties of Middle English," in *Companion*, 198–206.
12. John N. King, "Early Modern English Print Culture," in *Companion*, 284–92.
13. John F. Plummer, "'In swich englissh as he kan': Chaucer's Literary Language," in *Companion*, 445–54; McCrum, McNeil, and Cran, *Story of English*, 91; *Wikipedia*, "Geoffrey Chaucer," consulted March 3, 2010.

14. Paula Blank, "Languages of Early Modern Literature in Britain," in *The Cambridge History of Early Modern English Literature,* ed. David Lowenstein and Janet Mueller (Cambridge: Cambridge University Press, 2002), 169.

15. Blank, "Languages," 145–51; McCrum, McNeil, and Cran, *Story of English,* 91.

16. David Cressy, *Literacy and the Social Order: Reading and Writing in Tudor and Stuart England* (Cambridge: Cambridge University Press, 1980), 175–77; cf. Lawrence Stone, "Literacy and Education in England, 1640–1900," *Past and Present,* 42 (1969): 101–12.

17. Cressy, *Literacy,* 183–86.

18. Charlotte Brewer, "Johnson, Webster, and the *Oxford English Dictionary,*" in *Companion,* 113–21; James Boswell, *The Life of Johnson* (Oxford: Clarendon Press, 1799), 300; Jonathan Hope, "Varieties of Early Modern English," in *Companion,* 216–23; Carey McIntosh, "British English in the Long Eighteenth Century (1660–1830)," in *Companion,* 228–34.

19. Tony Crowley, "Class, Ethnicity, and the Formation of 'Standard English,'" in *Companion* 303–12.

20. Blank, "Languages," 143. Tom McArthur, "Cornish," in *The Oxford Companion to the English Language* (hereafter *OCEL*), ed. Tom McArthur (Oxford: Oxford University Press, 1992), 265.

21. A. J. Aitken and Tom McArthur, "Scottish Languages," in *OCEL,* 906.

22. J. Derrick McClure, "English in Scotland," in *Companion,* 358–65.

23. McCrum, McNeill, and Cran, *Story of English,* 146–52.

24. Samuel Johnson, *A Journey to the Western Islands of Scotland* (London: A. Strahen, 1785), 75.

25. Marion Löffler, "English in Wales," in *Companion,* 351–52; Blank, "Languages," 143; Garland Cannon, Tom McArthur, and Jean-Marc Gachelin, "Borrowing," in *OCEL,* 141–45.

26. Gareth Elwyn Jones and Gordon Wynne Roderick, *A History of Education in Wales* (Cardiff: University of Wales Press, 2002), 28–57.

27. Dylan V. Jones and Marilyn Martin-Jones, "Bilingual; Education and Language Revitalization in Wales: Past Achievements and Current Issues," in *Medium of Instruction Policies: Which Agenda? Whose Policies?* ed. James W. Tollefson and Amy B. M. Tsui (Mahwah, NJ: Lawrence Erlbaum, 2004), 44–47; Löffler, "English in Wales," 351–52.

28. "Welsh Language," *Wikipedia,* consulted September 19, 2011; United Kingdom, Office of National Statistics, online; BBC News Wales, "Report Says Welsh Language 'Losing 3,000 People a Year,'" accessed February 14, 2012.

29. Terence Patrick Dolan, "English in Ireland," in *Companion,* 367–68; Blank, "Languages," 169; Sir John Davies, *A Discovery of the True Causes Why Ireland Was Entirely Subdued and Brought*

under Obedience of the Crown of England until the Beginning of His Majesty's Happy Reign (1612), reprinted in *Historical Tracts by Sir John Davies* (Dublin: William Porter, 1787), 202; "John Davies (poet)," *Wikipedia,* accessed July 19, 2010.

30. Jane H. Ohlmeyer, "A Laboratory of Empire?: Early Modern Ireland and English Imperialism," in *Ireland and the British Empire,* ed. Kevin Kenny (Oxford: Oxford University Press, 2004), 26–51; Dolan, "English in Ireland," 368; McCrum, et al., *Story of English,* 195; Bailey, *Images of English,* 159–61, quoting Joseph Lee, *The Modernization of Irish Society, 1848–1918* (Dublin: Gill and Macmillan, 1973), 28.

31. Bailey, *Images of English,* 158,

3   The Language of North America

1. J. H. Elliott, "The Iberian Atlantic and Virginia," in *The Atlantic World and Virginia, 1550–1624,* ed. Peter C. Mancall (Chapel Hill, NC: University of North Carolina Press, 2007), 541–57.

2. James Axtell, *The Invasion Within: The Contest of Cultures in Colonial North America* (New York: Oxford University Press, 1985), 179–217; Clyde A. Milner, "National Initiatives," in *The Oxford History of the American West,* ed. Clyde A. Milner, II, Carol A. O'Connor, and Martha A. Sandweiss (New York: Oxford University Press, 1994), 173.

3. Estimates Database, 2009, in David Eltis, *Voyages: The Trans-Atlantic Slave Trade Database,* http://www.slavevoyages.org/tast/assessment/estimates.faces, accessed August 25, 2010.

4. Philip D. Morgan, *Slave Counterpoint: Black Culture in the Eighteenth-Century Chesapeake and Lowcountry* (Chapel Hill, NC: University of North Carolina Press, 1998), 59, 61, 63, 559–80, quotation 573.

5. Ira Berlin, *Many Thousands Gone: The First Two Centuries of Slavery in North America* (Cambridge, MA: Harvard University Press, 1998), 126, 128–29, 138–40.

6. Tom Paine, *Common Sense* (New York: New American Library, 1969), 39.

7. Benjamin Franklin to Peter Collinson, MP, May 9, 1753, in James Crawford, ed. *Language Loyalties: A Source Book on the Official English Controversy* (Chicago, IL: University of Chicago Press, 1992), 18–19; Benjamin Rush, "An Account of the Manners of the German Inhabitants of Pennsylvania," *Proceedings and Addresses of the Pennsylvania-German Society* 19 (1789): 104–5; Edith Abbott, ed., *Historical Aspects of the Immigration Problem* (New York: Arno Press and The New York Times, 1969), 423.

8. John Adams to President of Congress, Amsterdam, September 5, 1780, in *Revolutionary Diplomatic Correspondence of the United*

States (Washington: United States Government Printing Office, 1889), vol. 4.

9. Theodore Roosevelt, *The Winning of the West* (New York: G. P. Putnam's Sons, 1889), 1:17.

10. Marc Shell, "Babel in America; or, The Politics of Language Diversity on the United States," *Critical Inquiry* 20.1 (Autumn 1993): 10–18.

11. Noah Webster, *Dissertations on the English Language: With Notes, Historical and Critical* (Boston, MA: Isaiah Thomas, 1789), 18–23; excerpted in Crawford, *Language Loyalties*, 34–35.

12. In the first edition of his encyclopedic *The American Language* (1919) H. L. Mencken asserted the inevitability of the divergence of British and American English, but by the fourth edition in 1936 he had come to believe that the two languages were actually converging, with American English incorporating the best of British speech and predicted that British English would be swallowed by American, something not a few in England now suspect is true. See Dennis E. Baron, "The American Language," in *OCEL*, 47–48.

13. Timothy Dwight, *Travels in New England and New York* (Cambridge, MA: Belknap Press of Harvard University Press, 1969), 4: 195–96.

14. James Fenimore Cooper, *Notions of the Americans Picked Up by a Tavelling Bachelor* (Philadelphia, PA: Lea and Blanchard, 1848), 2: 125–26 I; Robert McCrum, *Globish: How the English Language Became the World's Language* (London: Viking Penguin, 2010), 261.

15. Isaac Candler, *A Summary View of America…by an Englishman* (London: T. Cadell 1824), 327; cited by Albert C. Baugh and Thomas Cable, *A History of the English Language,* 5th ed. (Upper Saddle River, NJ: Prentice Hall, 2002), 357.

16. John Hart Fischer, "British and American, Continuity and Divergence" in John Algeo, ed., *English in North America*, vol. 6 of *CHEL*, 59–61; David Hackett Fischer, *Albion's Seed: Four British Folkways in America* (New York: Oxford University Press, 1989); Joey Lee Dillard, *Toward a Social History of American English* (Berlin: Mouton, 1985), 4; Joey Lee Dillard, *A History of American English* (New York: Longman, 1992), 34, 45; Baugh and Cable, *History of the English Language,* 359. For the larger debate about continuity and change in American immigrant history, see David Eltis, Philip Morgan, and David Richardson, "Agency and Diaspora in Atlantic History: Reassessing the African Contribution to Rice Cultivation in the Americas," *American Historical Review* 112.5 (2007): 1329–58.

17. Walter Nugent, *Crossings: The Great Transatlantic Migrations, 1870–1914* (Bloomington, IN: Indiana University Press, 1992), 154.

18. John Swett, *American Public Schools: History and Pedagogics* (New York: American Book Company, 1900), 12–16.

19. Arthur Schlesinger, Sr., "The Rise of the City," in Mark C. Carnes and Arthur Schlesinger, Jr. eds. *A History of American Life.* Revised and Abridged (New York: Scribner, 1996), 928–29.

20. Diane Ravitsh, *The Great Schools War: A History of the New York City Public Schools* (Baltimore, MD: Johns Hopkins University Press, 2000), 111–14,
21. In Alejandro Portes and Ruben G. Rumbaut, *Immigrant America: A Portrait*, 2nd ed. (Berkeley, CA: University of California Press, 1996), 196.
22. John Algeo, "American Publishing"; and Benjamin Lease, "American Literature," in *OCEL*, 48–53, 58–60,
23. John Algeo, "American Broadcasting," in *OCEL*, 35–37.
24. Nancy C. Carnevale, *A New Language, a New World: Italian Immigrants in the United States, 1890–1945* (Urbana and Chicago: University of Illinois Press, 2009), 46–48.
25. Ernest Ludwig Brauns (1829) translated and excerpted in *Historical Aspects of the Immigration Problem*, ed. Edith Abbott (New York: Arno Press and The New York Times, 1969), 430–36; Thomas J. Archdeacon, *Becoming American: An Ethnic History* (New York: Free Press, 1983), 62–63; Karl Büchele (1856) in Abbott, *Historical Aspects*, 484–92.
26. Nugent, *Crossings*, 65, 151.
27. Andrew R. Heinze, "The Critical Period: Ethnic Emergence and Reaction, 1901–1929," in *The Columbia Documentary History of Race and Ethnicity in America*, ed. Ronald H. Bayor (New York: Columbia University Press, 2004), 425.
28. Roosevelt, *Winning of the West*, 1:33.
29. Quoted in "Spoken Languages of Canada," *Wikipedia*, accessed July 2010.
30. US Census Bureau, American Community Survey, New Mexico, data set 2005–9, accessed September 27, 2011.
31. Native input had much to do with the naming of the National Museum of the American Indian in Washington, DC, and New York. See also the Indian (Pueblo) Cultural Center in Albuquerque, NM.
32. Francis Paul Prucha, *The Great Father: The United States Government and the American Indians* (Lincoln, NE: University of Nebraska Press, 1984), 2:609–10.
33. Prucha, *Great Father*, 2:689–93, 821n.
34. James Crawford, "Seven Hypotheses on Language Loss: Causes and Issues," in *Stabilizing Indigenous Languages*, ed. G. Cantoni (Flagstaff, AZ: Arizona State University, 1996).
35. The statistics on population size and language speakers are primarily derived from United States and Canadian census figures that are conveniently summarized in numerous *Wikipedia* articles that try hard to erase the distortions imposed by national boundaries. The *Wikipedia* statistics have been checked against those in online version of *Ethnologue*.
36. Salikoko S. Mufwene, "Globalization and the Myth of Killer Languages: What's Really Going on?" in *Perspectives on Endangerment*,

ed. by Graham Huggan and Stephan Klasen, (Hildesheim/New York: Georg Olms Verlag, 2005), 19–48; Nicholas Ostler, *Empires of the World: A Language History of the World* (New York: HarperCollins, 2005), 489–90.

37. Carnevale, *New Language*, 50.

38. Thomas J. Meagher, "Racial and Ethnic Relations in America, 1965–2000," in Bayor, *Columbia Documentary History*, 690.

39. For a brief overview, see Scott F. Kiesling, "English in Australia and New Zealand," and Nkonko M. Kamwangamalu, "South African Englishes," in *The Handbook of World Englishes*, ed. Kachru, Braj B., Yamuna Kachru and Cecil L. Nelson (Oxford: Blackwell Publishing, 2006).

4   English in Imperial Asia and Africa

1. Roy's remarks are in James W. Massie, *Continental India: Travelling Sketches and Historical Recollections* (London: Thomas Ward, 1840), II: 439; Gandhi's speech is quoted in Raymond Leslie Buell, *The Native Problem in Africa* (New York: Macmillan, 1928), 2:60; Edward Wilmot Blyden, *Christianity, Islam and the Negro Race,* 2nd ed. (London: W. B. Wittingham, 1888), 243–44; Chinua Achebe, "The African Writer and the English Language" (1964), in Chinua Achebe, *Morning Yet on Creation Day* (Garden City, NY: Anchor Press, 1975), 95; Ali A. Mazrui, *The Political Sociology of the English Language: An African Perspective* (The Hague: Mouton, 1975), 9–11.

2. Thomas Jesse Jones, *Education in East Africa* (New York: Phelps-Stokes Fund, 1925), 20.

3. Poromesh Acharya, "Education in Old Calcutta," in *Calcutta: The Living City,* ed. Sukanta Chaudhuri (Calcutta: Oxford University Press, 1990), 1:85–94; Rajat Kanta Roy, "Indian Society and the Establishment of British Supremacy, 1765–1818," in *The Oxford History of the British Empire,* vol. 2, *The Eighteenth Century,* ed. P. J. Marshall (Oxford and New York: Oxford University Press, 1998), 526–27.

4. Stephen Evans, "Macaulay's Minute Revisited: Colonial Language Policy in Nineteenth-Century India," *Journal of Multilingual and Multicultural Development* 23.4 (2002): 262–70; Roy, "Indian Society," 526–27; Suresh C. Ghosh, *History of Education in India* (Jaipur: Rawat Publications, 2007), 303–4.

5. Ghosh, *History of Education*, 301–3; "Scottish Church College, Calcutta," *Wikipedia*, accessed January 24, 2010.

6. Evans, "Macaulay's Minute," 271–76.

7. Ghosh, *Education in India*, 342–67; Evans, "Macaulay's Minute," 276–77.

8. Ghosh, *Education in India*, 368–434.

9. Quoted in Buell, *Native Problem*, II:60.
10. Syama Prasad Mookerjee, "Schools in British India," *Annals of the American Academy of Political and Social Science*, 233 (May 1944): 30–38.
11. Mookerjee, "Schools in British India," 34.
12. R. K. Agnihotri, "Identity and Multilinguality: The Case of India," in *Language Policy, Culture, and Identity in Asian Contexts*, ed. A. B. M. Tsui and J. W. Tollefson (Mahwah, NJ: Lawrence Erlbaum Associates, 2007), 194–95.
13. Paul R. Brass, *The Politics of India since Independence*. New Cambridge History of India, part 4, vol. 1 (Cambridge: Cambridge University Press, 1990), 140.
14. Ryhana Raheem and Hemamala Ratwatte, "Invisible Strategies, Visible Results: Investigating Language Policy in Sri Lanka," in *Language Policy, Planning, & Practice: A South Asian Perspective*, ed. Sabiha Mansoor, Shaheen Meraj, Aliya Tahir (Oxford: Oxford University Press, 2004), 93–98.
15. Brass, *Politics of India*, 145.
16. E. Annamalai, "Medium of Power: The Question of English in Education in India," in Tollefson and Tsui, *Medium of Instruction Politics*, 177–79.
17. Stephen Evans, "Language Policy in British Colonial Education: Evidence from Nineteenth-Century Hong Kong," *Journal of Educational Administration and History* 38. 3 (December 2006): 293–312; Stephen Evans, "The Making of a Colonial School: A Study of Language Policies and Practices in Nineteenth-Century Hong Kong," *Language and Education*, 22.6 (2008): 346–47.
18. Cheng Ngai-Lai, "Hong Kong: Special Administrative Region," in *Language Policies and Language Education: The Impact in East Asian Countries in the Next Decade*, ed. Ho Wah Kam and Ruth Y. L. Wong (Singapore: Times Academic Press, 2000), 97–111; Amy B. M. Tsui, "Language Policy and the Construction of Identity: The Case of Hong Kong," in Tsui and Tollefson, *Language Policy*, 121–41.
19. Maya Khemlani David, "Language Policy in Malaysia—Empowerment of Disenfranchisement," in Tsui and Tollefson, *Language Policy*, 55–72.
20. Dr. Tony Tan Keng Yam, quoted in Ruth Y. L. Wong and Joyce E. James, "Malaysia," in Kam and Wong, *Language Policies*, 261.
21. Alastair Pennycook, *The Cultural Politics of English as an International Language* (London: Longman, 1994), 223–34; Anne Pakir, "Singapore," in Ho and Wong, *Language Policies*, 259–84; Phyllis Ghim-Lian Chew, "Remaking Singapore: Language, Culture, and Identity in a Globalized World," in Ho and Wong, *Language Policies*, 73–93; Government of Singapore, *Census of Population 2010. Statistical Release 1: Demographic Characteristics, Education, Language and Religion.*

22. David Northrup, *Africa's Discovery of Europe, 1450–1850,* 2nd ed. (New York: Oxford University Press, 2009), 64–69; Stephen D. Behrendt, A. J. H. Latham, and David Northrup, *The Diary of Antera Duke: An Eighteenth-Century Slave Trader* (New York: Oxford University Press, 2010).

23. Northrup, *Africa's Discovery,* 65–66; Leonard Thompson, *A History of South Africa,* 3rd ed. (New Haven, CT: Yale University Press, 2000), 172–73.

24. Northrup, *Africa's Discovery,* 173–85.

25. Lugard and Burns cited in Michael Crowder, *The Story of Nigeria,* 4th ed. (London: Farber and Farber, 1978), 219–20.

26. Marjory Perham, *Lugard: The Years of Authority, 1899–1945* (London: Collins, 1960).

27. Kevin Ward, "Christianity, Colonialism and Missions," in *The Cambridge History of Christianity,* vol. 9, *World Christianities c.1914–c.2000* (Cambridge: Cambridge University Press, 2000), 77–78.

28. Adrian Hastings, *The Church in Africa, 1450–1950* (Oxford: Clarendon Press, 1994), 449–51.

29. Richard Gray, "Christianity," in *The Cambridge History of Africa,* vol. 8, *c. 1940–c. 1975.* (Cambridge: Cambridge University Press, 1984), 184; Frederick G. Guggisberg, *The Keystone* (London: Simpkin, Marshall, Hamilton and Ken, 1924), 5–12.

30. Michael Crowder, "The White Chiefs of Tropical Africa," in *Colonialism in Africa, 1870–1960,* ed. L. H. Gann and Peter Duignan (Cambridge: Cambridge University Press, 1970), II: 321; Thomas Jesse Jones, *Education in Africa* (New York: Phelps-Stokes Fund, 1922), 156; Melville J. Herskovits, *The Human Factor in Changing Africa* (New York: Vintage Books, 1962), 237.

31. David B. Abernathy, "Education and Integration," in *Nigeria: Modernization and the Politics of Communalism,* ed. Robert Melson and Howard Wolpe (East Lansing, MI: Michigan State University Press, 1971), 404.

32. Achebe, "African Writer," 92–95, quote 95.

33. Sir Harry Johnston, "Report by His Majesty's Special Commissioner on the Protectorate of Uganda," *Parliamentary Papers: Africa, No. 7* (1901).

34. Blyden, *Christianity, Islam and the Negro Race,* 416.

35. Buell, *Native Problem,* II: 760–62; "Liberia—History Background, Constitutional, Legal Foundations, Educational System," Education Encyclopedia, "Liberia – History Background, Constitutional Legal Foundations, Educational System," http://education.stateuniversity. com/pages/854/Liberia.html, accessed August 2010.

36. Cecil K. Dotts and Mildred Sikkema, *Challenging the Status Quo: Public Education in Hawaii, 1840–1980* (Honolulu, HI: Hawaii Education Association, 1994), 19–25.

37. United States, Bureau of the Census, census data, 1900; Maenette K. P. Benham and Ronald H. Heck, *Culture and Educational Policy in Hawai'i: The Silencing of Native Voices* (Mahwah, NJ: Lawrence Erlbaum Associates, 1998), 102–7, 148–49, 158–60.
38. David P. Barrows, "Report of the Director of Education, 1908" in *Report of the Philippine Commission, 1908* (Washington: Government Printing Office, 1909), 815–17, 853, 855–56.
39. Arthur L. Carson, *The Story of Philippine Education* (Quezon City: New Day Publishers, 1978), 6, 36–37; Iluminado Nical, Jerzy J. Smolicz, and Margaret J. Secombe, "Rural Students and the Philippine Bilingual Program on the Island of Leyte," in Tollefson and Tsui, *Medium of Instruction*, 155–59.
40. Roland Oliver, *Sir Harry Johnston and the Scramble for Africa* (London: Chatto and Windus, 1959), 182.
41. English-Speaking Union, www.esu.ca/aboutgen.cfm.

5 Cultural Worlds

1. "L. L. Zamenhof" and "Esperanto," in *Wikipedia*, accessed September 2010. Esperanto is one of the languages in which *Wikipedia* is posted.
2. "Britain: Foreign University Students: Will They Still Come," *Economist*, August 7, 2010, 55. For an analysis of some of the same categories see Peter L. Berger, "Four Faces of Global Culture," *The National Interest* 49 (1997): 23–29.
3. James B. Russell, *German Higher Schools: The History, Organization and Methods of Secondary Education in Germany* (New York: Longmans, Green, 1899), 266–67; James C. Albisetti, *Secondary School Reform in Imperial Germany* (Princeton, NJ: Princeton, University Press, 1983), 282, 285; N. S. Seif, "The Teaching of Modern Languages in Belgium, England, Holland, and Germany," *Comparative Education Review* 9 (June 1965): 163–69.
4. Robert K. Hanks, "Georges Clemenceau and the English," *The Historical Journal* 45 (2002): 53–77.
5. Five of the other member countries had English an official language: Australia, Canada, Liberia, New Zealand, and South Africa. David Robin Watson, *Georges Clemenceau: France: The Peace Conferences of 1919–23 and Their Aftermath* (London: Haus Publishing, 2008), 70–75.
6. China long supported Esperanto training. Following government efforts in the 1970s, China in the 1980s had the largest network of Esperanto training in the world. Gerald Chan, "China and the Esperanto Movement," *Australian Journal of Chinese Affairs* 15 (1986): 1–18; Jonathan Clements, *Makers of the Modern World: Wellington Koo* (London: Haus Publishing, 2008).
7. Robert Phillipson, *Linguistic Imperialism* (Oxford: Oxford University Press, 1992), 223–70.

8. Barbara Crossette, "At the UN French Slips and English Stands Tall," *New York Times*, March 23, 2001; *Boston Globe*, June 16, 2002.

9. Ulrich Ammon, ed., *The Dominance of English as a Language of Science* (Berlin: Mouton de Gruyter, 2001), v.

10. For the Islamic learning, see Dimitri Gutas, *Greek Thought, Arabic Culture* (New York: Routledge, 1998).

11. Daniel R. Headrick, *When Information Came of Age: Technologies of Knowledge in the Age of Reason and Revolution, 1700–1850* (New York: Oxford University Press, 2000), 18–19, 36–38.

12. Robert B. Kaplan, "English—the Accidental Language of Science?" in Ammon, *Dominance of English*, 20, note 9.

13. Kaplan, "English—the Accidental Language," 3–13; W. W. Gibbs, "Lost Science in the Third World," *Scientific American* 273.2 (August 1995): 92–99; David Graddol, *The Future of English?* (London: British Council, 1997), 9.

14. Harold Haarmann and Eugene Holman, "The Impact of English as a Language of Science in Finland and Its Role for the Transition to Network Society," in *Dominance of English as a Language of Science,* ed. Ammon Ulrich (Berlin: Mouton de Gruyter, 2001), 248; Bernard Spolsky and Elana Shohamy, "The Penetration of English as Language of Science and Technology in the Israeli Linguistic Repertoire: A Preliminary Enquiry," in Ammon, *Dominance of English*, 171; Péter Medgyes and Mónika László, "The Foreign Language Competence of Hungarian Scholars: Ten Years Later," in Ammon, *Dominance of English*, 274–75.

15. Tom McArthur, "Science Fiction," in *OCEL*, 891–92; Charlie Jane Anders, "Why is English the Language of Science Fiction?" io9.com/5441825.

16. Anthony DeParma, "Border Crossing: Where Language Isn't a Barrier," *New York Times*, March 21, 2001.

17. Laurence Bergreen, *Marco Polo: From Venice to Xanadu* (New York: Alfred A. Knopf, 2007), 135–37.

18. Pierre Labarthe, *Voyage à la côte de Guinée* (Paris: Debray, 1803), 70.

19. David Northrup, *Africa's Discovery of Europe, 1450–1850,* 2nd ed (New York: Oxford University Press, 2009), 67.

20. Tom McArthur, "Business English," in *OCEL*, 169. Cf. Philip D. Curtin, *Cross-Cultural Trade in World History* (Cambridge: Cambridge University Press, 1984), 250.

21. Geoffrey Jones and Tarun Khanna, "Bringing History (Back) into International Business," *Journal of International Business Studies* 37.4 (2006): 457.

22. Rebecca Marschan-Piekkari, Denice Welch, and Lawrence Welch, "Adopting a Common Corporate Language: IHRM Implications," *International Journal of Human Resource Management* 10.3 (June 1999): 377–80. Haarmann and Holman, "Impact of English," 232.

23. "The European Union: After Babel, a New Common Tongue," *Economist,* August 7, 2004, 41.
24. "The World This Week: Business," *Economist,* July 30, 2011, 7.
25. Jason Dean and Christopher Lawton. "Acer Buys Gateway, Bulks Up for Global Fight." *Wall Street Journal Eastern Edition,* August 28, 2007: B1, B4.
26. Suzanne Romaine, "Global English: From Island Tongue to World Language," in *The Handbook of the History of English,* ed. Ans van Kemenade and Bettelou Los (Oxford: Blackwell Publishing, 2006), 592.
27. Schumpeter, "A Post-Crisis Case Study," *Economist,* July 31, 2010, 55.
28. Susanne Ehrenreich, "English as Lingua Franca in Multinational Corporations—Exploring Business Communities of Practice," in *English as Lingua Franca: Studies and Findings,* ed. Anna Mauranen and Elina Ranta (Newcastle upon Tyne: Cambridge Scholars Publishing, 2009), 138.
29. Thomas L. Friedman, *The World Is Flat: A Brief History of the Twenty-First Century,* 2nd ed. (New York: Picador, 2006), 21–29.
30. Loreto Todd, "Anglo-Irish Literature, " in *OCEL,* 69.
31. Vera Kreilkamp, "Fiction and Empire: The Irish Novel, " in *Ireland and the British Empire,* ed. Kevin Kenny (Oxford: Oxford University Press, 2004), 154–55.
32. Raymond Chapman, "Conrad, Joseph," in *OCEL,* 257.
33. Alan Richardson and Debbie Lee, eds., *Early Black British Writing: Selected Texts* (Boston, MA: Houghton Mifflin, 2004); Olaudah Equiano, *The Interesting Narrative and Other Writings,* ed. Vincent Carretta (New York: Penguin Books, 1995); Stephen D. Behrendt, A. J. H. Latham, and David Northrup, *Diary of Antera Duke* (New York: Oxford University Press, 2010); Paul E. Lovejoy and David Richardson, eds., "Letters of the Old Calabar Slave Trade, 1760–1789," in *Genius in Bondage: Literature of the Early Black Atlantic,* ed. Vincent Carretta and Philip Gould (Louisville, KY: University Press of Kentucky, 2001), 89–115.
34. J. F. Ade Ajayi, "Samuel Ajayi Crowther of Oyo," in *Africa Remembered: Narratives by West Africans from the Era of the Slave Trade,* ed. Philip D. Curtin (Madison, WI: University of Wisconsin Press, 1967), 289–316; Christopher Fyfe, *Africanus Horton, 1835–1883: West African Scientist and Patriot* (New York: Oxford University Press, 1972); Africanus Horton, *The Dawn of Nationalism in Modern Africa,* ed. Davidson Nicol (London: Longman, 1969).
35. Ngugi wa Thiong'o, *Decolonizing the Mind: The Politics of Language in African Literature* (London: Heinemann, 1986), 15–16.
36. See Sartre's "Orphée Noir" in *Anthologie de la nouvelle poésie nègre et malgache,* ed. Léopold Senghor (Paris: Presses Universitaires de France, 1948), xiv, and Franz Fanon, "The Negro and Language" in

Black Skins, White Masks, trans. Charles L. Markmann (New York: Grove Press, 1968), 17–40.

37. The essay is reprinted as "The African Writer and the English Language" in Achebe, *Morning Yet,* 95, 103. See also his 1989 essay, "Politics and Politicians of Language in African Literature, in Chinua Achebe, *The Education of a British Protected Child: Essays* (New York: Alfred A. Knopf, 2009), 96–106.

38. Ali A. Mazrui, *The Political Sociology of the English Language: An African Perspective* (The Hague: Mouton, 1975), 43–44, 48.

39. Braj B. Kachru and Tom McArthur, "Indian English Literature," *OCEL,* 508; Barbara Crossette, "R. K. Narayan, India's Prolific Storyteller, Dies at 94," *The New York Times,* May 14, 2001.

40. There is such a list in Kachru and McArthur, "Indian English Literature," 508.

41. Salman Rushdie, "Damme, This is the Oriental Scene for You!" *New Yorker* 73.17 (June 23, 1997): 50ff.

42. Shashi Tharoor, "A Bedeviling Question in the Cadence of English," *New York Times,* July 30, 2001.

43. V. S. Naipaul, "Our Universal Civilization," the Walter B. Wriston lecture delivered on November 5, 1990 at the Manhattan Institute, *New York Review of Books,* October 30, 1990.

44. "Johnny Hallyday," *Wikipedia,* accessed August 16, 2012.

45. I witnessed this phenomenon in 1965–66 while teaching in the rainforest of southeastern Nigeria. The secondary school had a generator that extended daylight by two hours, but other devices, from refrigerators to radios had to depend on alternative power sources.

46. *Wikipedia* has an excellent account of the "Transistor Radio."

47. Manthia Diawara, *In Search of Africa* (Cambridge, MA: Harvard University Press, 1998), 99–104.

48. Philippe Wamba, *Kinship: A Family's Journey in Africa and America* (New York: Penguin Putnam, 2000), 250–58; Vera Lúcia Menezes de Oliveira e Paiva and Adriana Silvina Pagano, "English in Brazil with an Outlook on Its Function as a Language of Science," in Ammon, *Dominance of English,* 433–44.

49. Jeff Chang, "It's a Hip-Hop World," *Foreign Policy* 163 (Nov/Dec 2007): 58–63, quotation 60.

50. Alastair Pennycook and Tony Mitchell, "Hip Hop as Dusty Foot Philosophy: Engaging Locality," in *Global Linguistic Flows,* ed. H. Samy Alim, Awad Ibrahim, and Alastair Pennycook (New York: Routledge, 2009), 36–39.

51. Graddol, *Future of English,* 9.

6 Tipping Points

1. Yim Sungwon, "Globalization and the Korean Language," in *Language Policy, Culture, and Identity in Asian Contexts,* ed. Amy

B. M. Tsui and James Tollefson (Mahwah, NJ: Lawrence Erlbawm Associates, 2007) 41; Kayoko Hashimoto, "Japan's Language Policy and the 'Lost Decade,'" in Tsui and Tollefson, *Language Policy*, 31–32; Larry Rohter, "Letter from the Americas: Learn English, Says Chile, Thinking Upwardly Global," *New York Times*, December 29, 2004; Keith Davidson, "Language and Identity in Switzerland," *English Today* 102, vol. 26.1 (March 2010): 15–17.

2. For example, see the list in David Graddol, *The Future of English?* (London: The British Council, 2000), 59, which is weighted by economic, demographic, and human development factors.

3. Malcolm Gladwell, *The Tipping Point: How Little Things Can Make a Difference* (New York: Little Brown, 2002), 7–9.

4. David Pogue, "Humanity's Database," *New York Tomes Book Review*, July 4, 2010, 11; Thomas L. Friedman, *The Lexus and the Olive Tree: Understanding Globalization*, rev. ed. (New York: Anchor Books, 2000), 61–67, quotation 67.

5. Europa.eu.int; European Commission, "Key Data on Education by Country," 2002, cited in "After Babel, a New Common Tongue: The European Union," *Economist*, August 7, 2004, 41.

6. Charlemagne, "The Galling Rise of English," *Economist*, March 1, 2003.

7. T. R. Reid, *The United States of Europe: The New Superpower and the End of American Supremacy* (New York: Penguin Books, 2004), 213.

8. European Commission, "Europeans and Their Languages: Summary," e-published February 2006, ec.europa.eu/education/languages/pdf/doc629_en.pdf.

9. Niels Davidsen-Nielsen, "Language Policy in Denmark—with Special Reference to Functional Domains," European Federation of National Institutions for Language, http://www.efnil.org/conferences/archives/stockholm-2003/speeches/davidsen-nielsen-english, accessed August 2010.

10. Robert McCrum, *Globish: How the English Language Became the World's Language* (New York: Viking Penguin, 2010), 231–37.

11. Philipp Ivanov, "China's Higher Education Revolution," AustraliaPolicy Online, July 25, 2011. <apo.org.au/commentary/chinas-higher-education-revolution>; Philip G. Altbach, Liz Reisberg, and Laura E. Rimbly, *Trends in Global Higher Education: Tracking an Academic Revolution* (Chestnut Hill. MA: Center for International Higher Education, Boston College, 2009), 195–207.

12. "English Beginning to Be Spoken Here: The Language Business in China," *The Economist*, April 15, 2006, 61–62. New Oriental Educational and Technology Group has a very full website (english.neworiental.org) including financial reports. English First, which also calls itself EF and Education First, says it "is the world's largest privately-owned education organization"; its website, www.englishfirst.com, is concentrated on recruiting teachers.

13. "The Largest English-Speaking Country? China, Of Course," *Irish Times,* June 6, 2009.

14. Amy Waldman, "India's Poor Bet Precious Sums on Private Schools," *New York Times,* November 15, 2003. Amy Waldman, "In India, a Heyday for English (the Language)," *New York Times,* December 14, 2003. David Graddol, "Thoughts from Kolkata on English in India," *English Today,* 25.4 (2009): 21–23.

15. Tariq Rahman, "The Role of English in Pakistan with Special Reference to Tolerance and Militancy," in Tsui and Tollefson, *Language Policy,* 219–27; Tania Hossain and James W. Tollefson, in Tsui and Tollefson, *Language Policy,* 252–55.

16. Tariq Rahman, "Language Policy, Multilingualism and Language Vitality in Pakistan," 2003, accessed January 18, 2006.

17. Barbara Crossette, "English Is Making a Comeback in Sri Lanka," *New York Times,* January 7, 1990.

18. Yim Sungwon, "Globalization and the Korean Language," 41, 51; Choe Sang-Hun, "Western Schools Sprout in South Korea," *New York Times,* September 2, 2010.

19. Kayoko Hashimoto, "Japan's Language Policy", 25–36.

20. "Survey of Malaysia," *The Economist,* April 5, 2003, 11; Maya Khemlani David, "Language Policy in Malaysia–Empowerment of Disenfranchisement," in Tsui and Tollefson, *Language Policy,* 55–72; "English in Schools: Policy Reversed but English Hours Extended," *New Strait Times,* July 9, 2009, cited in *Wikipedia,* "Education in Malaysia."

21. Doreen Carvajal, "English as Language of Global Education," *New York Times,* April 11, 2007; Philip G. Altbach, "Globalization and the University: Realities in an Unequal World," in *International Handbook of Higher Education,* ed. James J. F. Forest and Philip G. Altbach (Dordrecht, NL: Springer, 2006), I: 127; James A. Coleman, "The Language of Higher Education," paper read at the conference Language and the Future of Europe, University of Southampton, July 2004; Altbach, Reisberg, and Rimbly, *Trends in Global Higher Education,* 19.

22. James A. Coleman, "English-Medium Teaching in European Higher Education," *Language Teaching* 39 (2006): 4.

23. David Graddol, *English Next: Why Global English May Mean the End of English as a Foreign Language* (London: British Consul, 2006), 76. The United Kingdom received 25 percent, the United States and Canada 47 percent, Australia and New Zealand 15 percent. Altbach, Reisberg, and Rimbly, *Trends in Global Higher Education,* 7–11.

24. Tamar Lewin, "China Is Sending More Students to U.S.," *New York Times,* November 16, 2009, A13.

25. European Commission, "Statistical Overview of the Implementation of the Decentralized Actions in the Erasmus Program in 2007/2008." ec.europa.eu/education/erasmus/doc/stat/0708/report.pdf.

26. *Many Tongues, One Family,* ec.europa.eu/publications/booklets/ move/45/en.doc
27. U. Ammon and G. McConnell, *English as an Academic Language in Europe: A Survey of Its Use in Teaching* (Bern: Peter Lang, 2002), cited in Coleman, "English-Medium Teaching," 11.
28. Diane Spencer, "Europe: Huge Increase in English-Medium Courses," *University World News,* 22 (April 2008), www.universityworld news. com; Gaia Pianigiani, "Italy Has New Bilingual Education Site," *New York Times,* July 15, 2012.
29. Coleman, "English-Medium Teaching," 9.
30. Modern Language Association, *Enrollments in Languages Other Than English in United States Institutions of Higher Education,* Fall 2009, www.mla.org. Overall enrollment in foreign language majors grew 250 percent between 1960 and 2006, but this still represented a relative decline when compared to overall college enrollment, which increased by 467 percent.
31. Institute of International Education, *Open Doors 2009: Report on International Educational Exchange,* www.iie.org.
32. "Foreign University Students: Will They Still Come?" *Economist,* August 7, 2010, 57.
33. Lisa W. Foderaro, "Talented Students Are Sought Worldwide for N.Y.U.'s Mideast Campus," *The New York Times,* June 21, 2010; Dubai International Academic City (DIAC) has an informative website, www.diacedu.ae, accessed August 18, 2012.
34. Graddol, *English Next,* 74.
35. Anna Fazackerley, "In Line for a Licking from Our Mother Tongue," *Times Higher Education Supplement,* September 29, 2006.
36. www.essec.edu; sciences-po.eu.
37. www.idc.ac.il; Coleman, "Language of Higher Education"; Foreign Desk, "Asian Universities Court Students Nearby," *The New York Times,* September 23, 2009; Akira Kuwamura, "The Challenges of Increasing Capacity and Diversity in Japanese Higher Education through Proactive Recruitment Strategies," *Journal of Studies in International Education* 13 (2009): 195.

Bibliography

Abbott, Edith, ed. *Historical Aspects of the Immigration Problem*. New York: Arno Press and The New York Times, 1969.

Abernathy, David B. "Education and Integration." In *Nigeria: Modernization and the Politics of Communalism*. Edited by Robert Melson and Howard Wolpe. East Lansing, MI: Michigan State University Press, 1971.

Acharya, Poromesh. "Education in Old Calcutta." In *Calcutta: The Living City*. Edited by Sukanta Chaudhuri. Calcutta: Oxford University Press, 1990.

Achebe, Chinua. *The Education of a British Protected Child: Essays*. New York: Alfred A. Knopf, 2009.

————. "The African Writer and the English Language." In *Morning Yet on Creation Day*. Edited by Chinua Achebe. Garden City, NY: Anchor Press, 1975.

Adams, John, to President of Congress, Amsterdam, September 5, 1780. In *Revolutionary Diplomatic Correspondence of the United States*, Volume 4. Washington: United States Government Printing Office, 1889.

Adams, John Truslow. "Provincial Society, 1690–1793." In *A History of American Life*. Edited by Mark C. Carnes and Arthur M. Schlesinger, Jr. New York: Scribner, 1996.

Agnihotri, R. K. "Identity and Multilinguality: The Case of India." In *Language Policy, Culture, and Identity in Asian Contexts*. Edited by Amy Tsui and J. W. Tollefson. Mahwah, NJ: Lawrence Erlbaum Associates, 2007.

Aitken, A. J. and Tom McArthur, "Scottish Languages." In *OCEL*, 906–7.

Ajayi, J. F. Ade. "Samuel Ajayi Crowther of Oyo." In *Africa Remembered: Narratives by West Africans from the Era of the Slave Trade*. Edited by Philip D. Curtin. Madison, WI: University of Wisconsin Press, 1967.

Albisetti, James C. *Secondary School Reform in Imperial Germany*. Princeton, NJ: Princeton, University Press, 1983.

Algeo, John. "American Broadcasting," in *OCEL*, 35–37.

————. "American English," in *OCEL*, 37–41.

————, ed. *CHEL*, volume 6, *English in North America*. Cambridge: Cambridge University Press, 2001.

Altbach, Philip G. "Globalization and the University: Realities in an Unequal World." In *International Handbook of Higher Education,* ed. James J. F. Forest and Philip G. Altbach. Dordrecht, NL: Springer, 2006.

Altbach, Philip G., Liz Reisberg, and Laura E. Rimbly, *Trends in Global Higher Education: Tracking an Academic Revolution.* Chestnut Hill. MA: Center for International Higher Education, Boston College, 2009.

Ammon, Ulrich, ed. *The Dominance of English as a Language of Science.* Berlin: Mouton de Gruyter, 2001.

Ammon, Ulrich and G. McConnell. *English as an Academic Language in Europe: A Survey of Its Use in Teaching.* Bern: Peter Lang, 2002.

Annamalai, E. "Medium of Power: The Question of English in Education in India." In *Medium of Instruction Policies. Which Agenda? Whose Policies?* Edited by J. W. Tollefson and Amy Tsui. Mahwah, NJ: Lawrence Erlbaum Associates, 2004.

Archdeacon, Thomas J. *Becoming American: An Ethnic History.* New York: Free Press, 1983.

Axtell, James. *The Invasion Within: The Contest of Cultures in Colonial North America.* New York: Oxford University Press, 1985.

Bailey, Richard H. *Images of English: A Cultural History of the Language.* Ann Arbor, MI: University of Michigan Press, 1991.

Baron, Dennis E. "*The American Language.*" In *OCEL,* 47–48.

Barrows, David P. "Report of the Director of Education, 1908." In *Report of the Philippine Commission,* 1908. Washington, DC: Government Printing Office, 1909.

Baugh, Albert C. and Thomas Cable. *A History of the English Language,* 5th ed. Upper Saddle River, NJ: Prentice Hall, 2002.

Bayly, C. A. *The Birth of the Modern World, 1780*–1914. Oxford: Blackwell Publishing, 2004.

Bayor, Ronald H., ed. *The Columbia Documentary History of Race and Ethnicity in America.* New York: Columbia University Press, 2004.

Bede, Venerable, *Ecclesiastical History of the English Nation.* London: J. M. Dent; New York: E. P. Dutton, 1910.

Behrendt, Stephen D., A. J. H. Latham, and David Northrup, *The Diary of Antera Duke: An Eighteenth-Century African Slave Trader.* New York: Oxford University Press, 2010.

Benham, Maenette K. P. and Ronald H. Heck. *Culture and Educational Policy in Hawai'i: The Silencing of Native Voices.* Mahwah, NJ: Lawrence Erlbaum Associates, 1998.

Berlin, Ira. *Many Thousands Gone: The First Two Centuries of Slavery in North America.* Cambridge, MA: Harvard University Press, 1998.

Berger, Peter L. "Four Faces of Global Culture." *National Interest* 49 (1997): 23–29.

Berger, Peter L. and Samuel Huntington, eds. *Many Globalizations: Cultural Diversity in the Contemporary World.* New York: Oxford University Press, 2002.

Bergreen, Laurence. *Marco Polo: From Venice to Xanadu*. New York: Alfred A. Knopf, 2007.

Birch, Dinah, ed. *The Oxford Companion to English Literature*, 7th ed. Oxford: Oxford University Press, 2009.

Blain, Virginia, Patricia Clements, and Isobel Grundy, eds. *The Feminist Companion to Literature in English*. New Haven, CT: Yale University Press, 1990.

Blake, Norman, ed. *CHEL*, volume 2, *1066–1476*. Cambridge: Cambridge University Press, 1992.

Blank, Paula. "Languages of Early Modern Literature in Britain." In *The Cambridge History of Early Modern English Literature*. Edited by David Lowenstein and Janet Mueller. Cambridge: Cambridge University Press, 2002.

Blyden, Edward Wilmot. *Christianity, Islam and the Negro Race*, 2nd ed. London: W. B. Wittingham, 1888.

Bose, Seguta. *A Hundred Horizons: The Indian Ocean in the Age of Global Empire*. Cambridge, MA: Harvard University Press, 2006.

Boswell, James. *The Life of Johnson*. Oxford: Clarendon Press, 1799.

Bozzini, George R. and Cynthia A. Leenerts. *Literature without Borders: International Literature in English For Student Writers*. Upper Saddle River, NJ: Prentice Hall, 2000.

Brewer, Charlotte. "Johnson, Webster, and the *Oxford English Dictionary*." In *A Companion to the History of the English Language*. Edited by H. Momma and M. Matto. Oxford: Wiley-Blackwell Publishing, 2008.

"Britain: Foreign University Students: Will They Still Come," *Economist*, August 7, 2010, 55.

Brooke, Christopher. *From Alfred to Henry III, 871–1272. Volume 2: A History of England*. Edinburgh: Thomas Nelson, 1961.

Brass, Paul R. *The Politics of India since Independence*. New Cambridge History of India, part 4, volume 1. Cambridge: Cambridge University Press, 1990.

Buell, Raymond Leslie. *The Native Problem in Africa*, 2 vols. New York: Macmillan, 1928.

Bulliet, Richard W. *Conversion to Islam in the Medieval Period: An Essay in a Quantitative History*. Cambridge, MA: Harvard University Press, 1979.

Candler, Isaac. *A Summary View of America...by an Englishman*. London: T. Cadell 1824.

Cannon, Garland, Tom McArthur, and Jean-Marc Gachelin, "Borrowing." In *OCEL*, 141–45.

Carnes, Mark C. and Arthur Schlesinger, Jr., eds. *A History of American Life*. Revised and Abridged. New York: Scribner, 1996.

Carnevale, Nancy C. *A New Language, A New World: Italian Immigrants in the United States, 1890–1945*. Urbana and Chicago: University of Illinois Press, 2009.

Carrington, Lawrence D. "Caribbean English." In *OCEL*, 191–92.

Carson, Arthur L. *The Story of Philippine Education*. Quezon City: New Day Publishers, 1978.

Carvajal, Doreen. "English as Language of Global Education," *New York Times*, April 11, 2007.

Chan, Gerald. "China and the Esperanto Movement." *The Australian Journal of Chinese Affairs* 15 (1986): 1–18.

Chang, Jeff. "It's a Hip-Hop World." *Foreign Policy* 163 (Nov/Dec 2007): 58–63.

Chapman, Raymond. "Conrad, Joseph." In *OCEL*, 257.

Charlemagne (pseudo.) "The Galling Rise of English," *Economist*, March 1, 2003.

Cheng, Ngai-Lai. "Hong Kong: Special Administrative Region." In *Language Policies and Language Education: The Impact in East Asian Countries in the Next Decade*. Edited by Ho Wah Kam and Ruth Y. L. Wong. Singapore: Times Academic Press, 2000.

Chew, Phyllis Ghim-Lian. "Remaking Singapore: Language, Culture, and Identity in a Globalized World." In *Language Policies and Language Education: The Impact in East Asian Countries in the Next Decade*. Edited by Ho Wah Kam and Ruth Y. L. Wong. Singapore: Times Academic Press, 2000.

Clements, Jonathan. *Makers of the Modern World: Wellington Koo*. London: Haus Publishing, 2008.

Coleman, James A. "English-Medium Teaching in European Higher Education." *Language Teaching* 39 (2006): 1–14.

———. "The Language of Higher Education." Paper read at the conference Language and the Future of Europe, University of Southampton, July 2004.

Cooper, James Fenimore. *Notions of the Americans: Picked Up by a Tavelling Bachelor*. Philadelphia, PA: Lea and Blanchard, 1848.

Crawford, James. "Seven Hypotheses on Language Loss: Causes and Issues." In *Stabilizing Indigenous Languages*. Edited by G. Cantoni. Flagstaff, AZ: Arizona State University, 1996.

——— *Language Loyalties: A Source Book on the Official English Controversy*. Chicago, IL: University of Chicago Press, 1992.

Cressy, David. *Literacy and the Social Order: Reading and Writing in Tudor and Stuart England*. Cambridge: Cambridge University Press, 1980.

Crossette, Barbara. "R. K. Narayan, India's Prolific Storyteller, Dies at 94." *New York Times*, May 14, 2001.

———. "At the UN French Slips and English Stands Tall." *New York Times*, March 23, 2001.

———. "English Is Making a Comeback in Sri Lanka," *New York Times*, January 7, 1990.

Crowder, Michael. *The Story of Nigeria*, 4th ed. London: Farber and Farber, 1978.

————. "The White Chiefs of Tropical Africa." In *Colonialism in Africa, 1870–1960*, Volume 2. Edited by L. H. Gann and Peter Duignan. Cambridge: Cambridge University Press, 1970, 320–50.

Crowley, Tony. "Class, Ethnicity, and the Formation of 'Standard English.'" In *A Companion to the History of the English Language*. Edited by H. Momma and M. Matto. Oxford: Wiley-Blackwell Publishing, 2008.

Crystal, David. *English as a Global Language*. 2nd ed. Cambridge: Cambridge University Press, 2003.

Curtin, Philip D. *Cross-Cultural Trade in World History*. Cambridge: Cambridge University Press, 1984.

David, Maya Khemlani. "Language Policy in Malaysia–Empowerment of Disenfranchisement." In *Language Policy, Culture, and Identity in Asian Contexts*. Edited by Amy Tsui and J. W. Tollefson. Mahwah, NJ: Lawrence Erlbaum Associates, 2007.

Davidsen-Nielsen, Niels. "Language Policy in Denmark–with Special Reference to Functional Domains." European Federation of National Institutions for Language, http://www.efnil.org/conferences/archives/stockholm-2003/speeches/davidsen-nielsen-english (accessed August 2010).

Davidson, Keith. "Language and Identity in Switzerland." *English Today* 102, 26.1 (March 2010): 15–17.

Davies, Alan. "Review Article: Ironising the Myth of Linguicism." *Journal of Multilingual and Multicultural Development* 17 (1996): 485–596.

Davies, John. *A Discovery of the True Causes Why Ireland Was Entirely Subdued and Brought under Obedience of the Crown of England until the Beginning of His Majesty's Happy Reign* (1612). Reprinted in *Historical Tracts by Sir John Davies*. Dublin: William Porter, 1787.

Dean, Jason and Christopher Lawton. "Acer Buys Gateway, Bulks up for Global Fight." *Wall Street Journal Eastern Edition*, August 28, 2007, B1, B4.

DeParma, Anthony. "Border Crossing: Where Language Isn't a Barrier." *New York Times*, March 21, 2001.

Diawara, Manthia. *In Search of Africa*. Cambridge, MA: Harvard University Press, 1998.

Dillard, Joey Lee. *A History of American English*. New York: Longman, 1992.

————. *Toward a Social History of American English*. Berlin: Mouton, 1985.

Dolan, Terence Patrick. "English in Ireland." In *A Companion to the History of the English Language*. Edited by H. Momma and M. Matto. Oxford: Wiley-Blackwell Publishing, 2008.

Donoghue, Daniel. "Early Old English (up to 899)." In *A Companion to the History of the English Language*. Edited by H. Momma and M. Matto. Oxford: Wiley-Blackwell Publishing, 2008.

Dotts, Cecil K. and Mildred Sikkema. *Challenging the Status Quo: Public Education in Hawaii, 1840–1980*. Honolulu, HI: Hawaii Education Association, 1994.

Dunn, Ross E. *The Adventures of Ibn Battuta: A Muslim Traveler of the 14th Century,* rev. ed. Berkeley, CA: University of California Press, 2005.

Dwight, Timothy. *Travels in New England and New York.* 4 vols. Cambridge, MA: Belknap Press of Harvard University Press, 1969.

Education Encyclopedia. "Liberia—History Background, Constitutional Legal Foundations, Educational System," http://education.stateuniversity.com/pages/854/Liberia.html (accessed August 2010).

Ehrenreich, Susanne. "English as Lingua Franca in Multinational Corporations—Exploring Business Communities of Practice." In *English as Lingua Franca: Studies and Findings.* Edited by Anna Mauranen and Elina Ranta. Newcastle upon Tyne: Cambridge Scholars Publishing, 2009.

Elliott, J. H. "The Iberian Atlantic and Virginia." In *The Atlantic World and Virginia, 1550–1624.* Edited by Peter C. Mancall. Chapel Hill, NC: University of North Carolina Press, 2007.

Eltis, David. "Free and Coerced Migration from the Old World to the New" In *Coerced and Free Migration: Global Perspectives.* Edited by David Eltis. Stanford, CA: Stanford University Press, 2002.

Eltis, David, et al. *Voyages: The Trans-Atlantic Slave Trade Database.* http://www.slavevoyages.org.

Eltis, David, Philip Morgan, and David Richardson, "Agency and Diaspora in Atlantic History: Reassessing the African Contribution to Rice Cultivation in the Americas," *American Historical Review* 112.5 (2007): 1329–58.

"English Beginning to Be Spoken Here: The Language Business in China." *Economist* April 15, 2006, 61–62.

Equiano, Olaudah. *The Interesting Narrative and Other Writings.* Edited by Vincent Carretta. New York: Penguin Books, 1995.

European Commission, "Many Voices, One Family." ec.europa.eu/publications/booklets/move/45/en.doc.

———. "Key Data on Education by Country." 2002. ec. europa.eu.int.

———. "Europeans and Their Languages: Summary," e-published February 2006, ec.europa.eu/education/languages/pdf/doc629_en.pdf.

———. "Statistical Overview of the Implementation of the Decentralized Actions in the Erasmus Program in 2007/2008." ec.europa.eu/education/erasmus/doc/stat/0708/report.pdf.

"The European Union: After Babel, a New Common Tongue," *Economist* August 7, 2004, 41.

Evans, Stephen. "Macaulay's Minute Revisited: Colonial Language Policy in Nineteenth-Century India." *Journal of Multilingual and Multicultural Development* 23.4 (2002): 262–70.

———. "Language Policy in British Colonial Education: Evidence from Nineteenth-Century Hong Kong." *Journal of Educational Administration and History* 38.3 (December 2006): 293–312.

———. "The Making of a Colonial School: A Study of Language Policies and Practices in Nineteenth-Century Hong Kong." *Language and Education* 22.6 (2008): 346–47.

Fanon, Franz. "The Negro and Language" In *Black Skins, White Masks.* Translated by Charles L. Markmann. New York: Grove Press, 1968.

Fazackerley, Anna. "In Line for a Licking from Our Mother Tongue." *Times Higher Education Supplement,* September 29, 2006.

Ferguson, Niall. *Empire: The Rise and Demise of the British World Order.* New York: Basic Books, 2002.

Fischer, David Hackett. *Albion's Seed: Four British Folkways in America.* New York: Oxford University Press, 1989.

Fischer, John Hart. "British and American, Continuity and Divergence." In *CHEL,* 6: 59–85.

Foderaro, Lisa W. "Talented Students Are Sought Worldwide for N.Y.U.'s Mideast Campus," *New York Times,* June 21, 2010.

Foreign Desk. "Asian Universities Court Students Nearby." *New York Times,* September 23, 2009.

"Foreign University Students: Will They Still Come?" *Economist,* August 7, 2010, 57.

Franklin, Benjamin, to Peter Collinson, MP, May 9, 1753. In *Language Loyalties: A Source Book on the Official English Controversy.* Edited by James Crowford. Chicago, IL: University of Chicago Press, 1992.

Friedman, Thomas L. *The Lexus and the Olive Tree: Understanding Globalization.* New York: Anchor Books, 2000.

———. *The World Is Flat: A Brief History of the Twenty-First Century,* 2nd ed. New York: Picador, 2006.

———. *Hot Flat, and Crowded: Why We Need a Green Revolution—and How It Can Renew America,* 2nd ed. New York: Picador, 2009.

Fyfe, Christopher. *Africanus Horton, 1835–1883: West African Scientist and Patriot.* New York: Oxford University Press, 1972.

Ghosh, Suresh C. *History of Education in India.* Jaipur: Rawat Publications, 2007.

Gibbs, W. W. "Lost Science in the Third World." *Scientific American* 273.2 (August 1995): 92–99.

Gordon, Stewart. *When Asia Was the World.* Philadelphia, PA: Da Capo Press, 2008.

Gladwell, Malcolm. *The Tipping Point: How Little Things Can Make a Difference.* New York: Little Brown, 2002.

Graddol, David. "Thoughts from Kolkata on English in India." *English Today* 25.4 (2009): 21–23.

———. *English Next: Why Global English May Mean the End of English as a Foreign Language.* London: British Consul, 2006.

———. *The Future of English?* London: The British Council, 1997.

Gray, Richard. "Christianity." In *The Cambridge History of Africa, volume 8, c. 1940–c. 1975.* Cambridge: Cambridge University Press, 1984.

Gregory the Great. "Introduction to *Pastoral Care.*" In *Readings for the Use of the Students in the Massachusetts Institute of Technology.* Boston, MA: George H. Ellis, 1916.

Guggisberg, Frederick G. *The Keystone.* London: Simpkin, Marshall, Hamilton and Ken, 1924.

Gutas, Dimitri. *Greek Thought, Arabic Culture*. New York: Routledge, 1998.

Haarmann, Harold and Eugene Holman. "The Impact of English as a Language of Science in Finland and Its Role for the Transition to Network Society." In *Dominance of English as a Language of Science*. Edited by Ulrich Ammon. Berlin: Mouton de Gruyter, 2001.

Hanks, Robert K. "Georges Clemenceau and the English." *Historical Journal* 45 (2002): 53–77.

Hashimoto, Kayoko. "Japan's Language Policy and the 'Lost Decade'." In *Language Policy, Culture, and Identity in Asian Contexts*. Edited by Amy Tsui and J. W. Tollefson. Mahwah, NJ: Lawrence Erlbaum Associates, 2007.

Hastings, Adrian. *The Church in Africa, 1450–1950*. Oxford History of the Christian Church. Oxford: Clarendon Press, 1994.

Head, Dominic, ed. *The Cambridge Guide to Literature in English*, 3rd ed. Cambridge: Cambridge University Press, 2006.

Headrick, Daniel R. *When Information Came of Age: Technologies of Knowledge in the Age of Reason and Revolution, 1700–1850*. New York: Oxford University Press, 2000.

Herskovits, Melville J. *The Human Factor in Changing Africa*. New York: Vintage Books, 1962.

Heinze, Andrew R. "The Critical Period: Ethnic Emergence and Reaction, 1901–1929." In *The Columbia Documentary History of Race and Ethnicity in America*. Edited by Ronald H. Bayor. New York: Columbia University Press, 2004.

Heywood, Linda, ed. *Central Africans and Cultural Transformations in the American Diaspora*. Cambridge: Cambridge University Press, 2002.

Ho, Wah Kam and Ruth Y. L. Wong, eds. *Language Policies and Language Education: The Impact in East Asian Countries in the Next Decade*. Singapore: Times Academic Press, 2000.

Hogg, Richard M., gen ed., *CHEL*, 6 vols. Cambridge: Cambridge University Press, 1992–2001.

———, ed. *CHEL*, volume 1, *Beginnings to 1066*. Cambridge: Cambridge University Press, 1992.

Hope, Jonathan. "Varieties of Early Modern English." In *A Companion to the History of the English Language*. Edited by H. Momma and M. Matto. Oxford: Wiley-Blackwell Publishing, 2008.

Horton, James B. Africanus. *The Dawn of Nationalism in Modern Africa*. Compiled by Davidson Nicol. London: Longman, 1969.

Hossain, Tania and James W. Tollefson. "Issues in Language Policy, Culture, and Identity." In *Language Policy, Culture, and Identity in Asian Contexts*. Edited by Amy Tsui and J. W. Tollefson. Mahwah, NJ: Lawrence Erlbaum Associates, 2007.

Ibn Battuta. *Travels, A.D. 1325–1354*. Translated by H. A. R. Gibb. Cambridge: Hakluyt Society, 1958.

Ibn Warraq. *Defending the West: A Critique of Edward Said's Orientalism*. New York: Prometheus Books, 2007.

Innes, Catherine Lynette. *The Cambridge Introduction to Postcolonial Literatures in English*. New York: Cambridge University Press, 2007.

Institute of International Education. *Open Doors 2009: Report on International Educational Exchange*. www.iie.org.

Irwin, Robert. *Dangerous Knowledge: Orientalism and Its Discontents*. Woodstock, NY: Overlook Press, 2006.

Ivanov, Philipp. "China's Higher Education Revolution." AustraliaPolicy Online, July 25, 2011. apo.org.au/commentary/chinas-higher-education-revolution.

Johnson, Samuel. *A Journey to the Western Islands of Scotland*. London: A. Strahen, 1785.

Johnston, Sir Harry. "Report by His Majesty's Special Commissioner on the Protectorate of Uganda." Great Britain, *Parliamentary Papers: Africa, No. 7* (1901).

Jones, Dylan V. and Marilyn Martin-Jones. "Bilingual Education and Language Revitalization in Wales: Past Achievements and Current Issues." In *Medium of Instruction Policies. Which Agenda? Whose Policies?* Edited by J. W. Tollefson and A. B. M. Tsui. Mahwah, NJ: Lawrence Erlbaum Associates, 2004.

Jones, Gareth Elwyn and Gordon Wynne Roderick. *A History of Education in Wales*. Cardiff: University of Wales Press, 2002.

Jones, Geoffrey and Tarun Khanna, "Bringing History (Back) into International Business." *Journal of International Business Studies* 37.4 (2006): 453–68.

Jones, Thomas Jesse. *Education in Africa*. New York: Phelps-Stokes Fund, 1922.

———. *Education in East Africa*. New York: Phelps-Stokes Fund, 1925.

Kachru, Braj B. and Tom McArthur. "Indian English Literature." *OCEL*, 508–9.

Kachru, Braj B., Yamuna Kachru, and Cecil L. Nelson, eds. *The Handbook of World Englishes*. Oxford: Blackwell Publishing, 2006.

Kamwangamalu, Nkonko M. "South African Englishes," In *The Handbook of World Englishes*. Edited by Braj B. Kachru, et al. Oxford: Blackwell Publishing, 2006.

Kaplan, Robert B. "English—the Accidental Language of Science?" In *Dominance of English as a Language of Science*. Edited by Ulrich Ammon. Berlin: Mouton de Gruyter, 2001.

Kasovsky, Dieter. "Semantics and Vocabulary." In *CHEL*, 1: 317–20.

Kent, R. K. "Palmares: An African State in Brazil." *Journal of African History* 6 (1965): 161–75.

Kiesling, Scott F. "English in Australia and New Zealand." In *Handbook of World Englishes*. Edited by Braj B. Kachru, et al. Oxford: Blackwell Publishing, 2006.

King, John N. "Early Modern English Print Culture." In *A Companion to the History of the English Language*. Edited by H. Momma and M. Matto. Oxford: Wiley-Blackwell Publishing, 2008.

Kreilkamp, Vera. "Fiction and Empire: The Irish Novel." In *Ireland and the British Empire*. Edited by Kevin Kenny. Oxford: Oxford University Press, 2004.

Koelle, S. W. *Polyglotta Africana, or a Comparative Vocabulary of Nearly 300 Words and Phrases in More than 100 Distinct African Languages*. London: Church Missionary House, 1854.

Kuwamura, Akira. "The Challenges of Increasing Capacity and Diversity in Japanese Higher Education through Proactive Recruitment Strategies." *Journal of Studies in International Education*, 13 (2009): 189–202.

Labarthe, Pierre. *Voyage à la côte de Guinée*. Paris: Debray, 1803.

Landes, David S. *The Wealth and Poverty of Nations*. New York: Norton, 1998.

Lapidus, Ira M. *A History of Islamic Societies*, 2nd ed. Cambridge: Cambridge University Press, 2002.

Lease, Benjamin. "American Literature." In *OCEL*, 48–53.

Lewin, Tamar. "China Is Sending More Students to U.S." *New York Times*, November 16, 2009.

Lewis, M. Paul, ed., *Ethnologue: Languages of the World*, 16th ed. Dallas, TX: SIL International, 2009. http://www.ethnologue.com.

"The Largest English-speaking Country? China, of Course." *Irish Times*, June 6, 2009.

Löffler, Marion. "English in Wales." In *A Companion to the History of the English Language*. Edited by H. Momma and M. Matto. Oxford: Wiley-Blackwell Publishing, 2008.

Lovejoy, Paul E. and David Richardson, eds. "Letters of the Old Calabar Slave Trade, 1760–1789." In *Genius in Bondage: Literature of the Early Black Atlantic*. Edited by Vincent Carretta and Philip Gould. Louisville, KY: University Press of Kentucky, 2001.

Marschan-Piekkari, Rebecca, Denice Welch, and Lawrence Welch. "Adopting a Common Corporate Language: IHRM Implications." *International Journal of Human Resource Management* 10.3 (June 1999): 377–80.

Massie, James W. *Continental India: Travelling Sketches and Historical Recollections*, 2 vols. London: Thomas Ward, 1840.

Mazrui, Ali A. *The Political Sociology of the English Language: An African Perspective*. The Hague: Mouton, 1975.

McArthur, Tom, ed. *OCEL*. Oxford: Oxford University Press, 1992

———. "Business English," "Cornish," and "Science Fiction." In *OCEL*, 169, 265, 891–92.

———. *The English Languages*. Cambridge: Cambridge University Press 1998.

McClure, J. Derrick. "English in Scotland." In *A Companion to the History of the English Language*. Edited by H. Momma and M. Matto. Oxford: Wiley-Blackwell Publishing, 2008.

McCrum, Robert. *Globish: How the English Language Became the World's Language*. London: Viking Penguin, 2010.

McCrum, Robert, Robert McNeil, and William Cran. *The Story of English*, 3rd ed. New York: Penguin Books, 2003.

McIntosh, Carey. "British English in the Long Eighteenth Century (1660–1830)." In *A Companion to the History of the English Language*. Edited by H. Momma and M. Matto. Oxford: Wiley-Blackwell Publishing, 2008.

Meagher, Thomas J. "Racial and Ethnic Relations in America, 1965–2000." In *Columbia Documentary History of Race and Ethnicity in America*. Edited by Ronald H. Bayor. New York: Columbia University Press, 2004.

Medgyes, Péter and Mónika László. "The Foreign Language Competence of Hungarian Scholars: Ten Years Later." In *Dominance of English as a Language of Science*. Edited by Ammon Ulrich. Berlin: Mouton de Gruyter, 2001.

Menezes de Oliveira e Paiva, Vera Lúcia, and Adriana Silvina Pagano. "English in Brazil with an Outlook on Its Function as a Language of Science." In *Dominance of English as a Language of Science*. Edited by Ammon Ulrich. Berlin: Mouton de Gruyter, 2001.

Milner, Clyde A. "National Initiatives." In *The Oxford History of the American West*. Edited by Clyde A. Milner, II, Carol A. O'Connor, and Martha A. Sandweiss. New York: Oxford University Press, 1994.

Mintz, Sidney W. and Richard Price. *The Birth of African-American Culture: An Anthropological Perspective*, new ed. Boston, MA: Beacon Press, 1992.

Modern Language Association. *Enrollments in Languages Other Than English in United States Institutions of Higher Education, Fall 2009*, www.mla.org.

Momma, Haruko and Michael Matto, eds. *A Companion to the History of the English Language*. Chichester: Wiley-Blackwell, 2008.

Mookerjee, Syama Prasad. "Schools in British India." *Annals of the American Academy of Political and Social Science* 233 (May 1944): 30–38.

Morgan, Philip D. *Slave Counterpoint: Black Culture in the Eighteenth-Century Chesapeake and Lowcountry*. Chapel Hill, NC: University of North Carolina Press, 1998.

Mufwene, Salikoko S. *Language Evolution: Contact, Competition and Change*. London: Continuum, 2008.

———. "Globalization and the Myth of Killer Languages: What's Really Going on?" In *Perspectives on Endangerment*. Edited by Graham Huggan and Stephan Klasen. Hildesheim/New York: Georg Olms Verlag, 2005.

———. "Colonization, Gobalization and the Plight of 'Weak' Languages." *Journal of Linguistics* 38.2 (2002): 375–95.

———. "Gullah" and "West African Pidgin English." In *OCEL*, 456–57, 1111.

Mungello, David E. *The Great Encounter of China and the West, 1500–1800*, 3rd ed. Lanham, MD: Rowman & Littlefield, 2009.

Naipaul, V. S. "Our Universal Civilization." *New York Review of Books*, October 30, 1990.

Nettle, Daniel and Suzanne Romaine. *Vanishing Voices: The Extinction of the World's Languages*. Oxford: Oxford University Press, 2000.

Ngugi wa Thiong'o, *Decolonizing the Mind: The Politics of Language in African Literature*. London: Heinemann, 1986.

Nical, Iluminado, Jerzy J. Smolicz, and Margaret J. Secombe. "Rural Students and the Philippine Bilingual Program on the Island of Leyte." In *Medium of Instruction Policies. Which Agenda? Whose Policies?* Edited by J. W. Tollefson and Amy Tsui. Mahwah, NJ: Lawrence Erlbaum Associates, 2004.

Northrup, David. "Globalization in Historical Perspective." In *Encyclopedia of Life Support Systems.* World System History Series. Oxford: Eolss Publishers, 2010.

———. *Africa's Discovery of Europe, 1450–1850,* 2nd ed. New York: Oxford University Press, 2009.

———. "Becoming African: Identity Formation among Liberated Slaves in Nineteenth-Century Sierra Leone" *Slavery and Abolition* 27 (April 2006): 1–21.

———. "Globalization and the Great Convergence: Rethinking World History in the Long Term." *Journal of World History* 16 (2005): 249–67.

Nugent, Walter *Crossings: The Great Transatlantic Migrations, 1870–1914.* Bloomington, IN: Indiana University Press, 1992.

Ohlmeyer, Jane H. "A Laboratory of Empire?: Early Modern Ireland and English Imperialism." In *Ireland and the British Empire.* Edited by Kevin Kenny. Oxford: Oxford University Press, 2004.

Oliver, Roland. *Sir Harry Johnston and the Scramble for Africa.* London: Chatto and Windus, 1959.

Ostler, Nicholas. *Empires of the Word: A Language History of the World.* New York: HarperCollins, 2005.

Paine, Tom. *Common Sense.* New York: New American Library, 1969.

Pakir, Anne. "Singapore." In *Language Policies and Language Education: The Impact in East Asian Countries in the Next Decade.* Edited by Ho Wah Kam and Ruth Y. L. Wong. Singapore: Times Academic Press, 2000.

Pennycook, Alastair. *The Cultural Politics of English as an International Language.* London: Longman, 1994.

Pennycook, Alastair and Tony Mitchell. "Hip Hop as Dusty Foot Philosophy: Engaging Locality." In *Global Linguistic Flows.* Edited by H. Samy Alim, Awad Ibrahim, and Alastair Pennycook. New York: Routledge, 2009.

Perham, Marjory. *Lugard: The Years of Authority, 1899–1945.* London: Collins, 1960.

Pianigiani, Gaia. "Italy Has New Bilingual Education Site," *New York Times,* July 15, 2012.

Pires, Tomé. *Summa Oriental of Tomé Pires: An Account of the East, from the Red Sea to Japan, Written in Malacca and India in 1512–*1515. Translated by Armando Cortesão. London: Hakluyt Society, 1944.

Phillipson, Robert. *English Only Europe? Challenging Language Policy.* London: Routledge, 2003.

———. *Linguistic Imperialism.* Oxford: Oxford University Press, 1992.

Plummer, John F. "'In swich englissh as he kan': Chaucer's Literary Language." In *A Companion to the History of the English Language.* Edited by H. Momma and M. Matto. Oxford: Wiley-Blackwell Publishing, 2008.

Pogue, David. "Humanity's Database." *New York Times Book Review*, July 4, 2010.

Pomeranz, Kenneth. *The Great Divergence: China, Europe, and the Making of the Modern World Economy.* Princeton, NJ: Princeton University Press, 2002.

Portes, Alejandro and Ruben G. Rumbaut. *Immigrant America: A Portrait*, 2nd ed. Berkeley, CA: University of California Press, 1996.

Price, Richard, ed. *Maroon Societies: Rebel Slave Communities in the Americas*, 2nd ed. Baltimore, MD: Johns Hopkins University Press, 1979.

Prucha, Francis Paul. *The Great Father: The United States Government and the American Indians.* 2 vols. Lincoln, NE: University of Nebraska Press, 1984.

Rahman, Tariq. "The Role of English in Pakistan with Special Reference to Tolerance and Militancy." In *Language Policy, Culture, and Identity in Asian Contexts.* Edited by Amy B. M. Tsui and J. W. Tollefson. Mahwah, NJ: Lawrence Erlbaum Associates, 2007.

———. "Language Policy, Multilingualism and Language Vitality in Pakistan," 2003. www.tariqrahman.net (accessed January 18, 2006).

Raheem, Ryhana and Hemamala Ratwatte. "Invisible Strategies, Visible Results: Investigating Language Policy in Sri Lanka." In *Language Policy, Planning, & Practice: A South Asian Perspective.* Edited by Sabiha Mansoor, Shaheen Meraj, and Aliya Tahir. Oxford: Oxford University Press, 2004.

Ravitsh, Diane. *The Great Schools War: A History of the New York City Public Schools.* Baltimore, MD: Johns Hopkins University Press, 2000.

Reid, T. R. *The United States of Europe: The New Superpower and the End of American Supremacy.* New York: Penguin Books, 2004.

Renfrew, Colin. *Archaeology and Language.* New York: Cambridge University Press, 1988.

Richardson, Alan and Debbie Lee, eds. *Early Black British Writing: Selected Texts.* Boston, MA: Houghton Mifflin, 2004.

Rohter, Larry. "Letter from the Americas: Learn English, Says Chile, Thinking Upwardly Global." *New York Times*, December 29, 2004.

Romaine, Suzanne. "Global English: From Island Tongue to World Language." In *The Handbook of the History of English.* Edited by Ans van Kemenade and Bettelou Los. Oxford: Blackwell Publishing, 2006.

Roosevelt, Theodore. *The Winning of the West.* 4 vols. New York: G. P. Putnam's Sons, 1889–96.

Roy, Rajat Kanta. "Indian Society and the Establishment of British Supremacy, 1765–1818." In *The Oxford History of the British Empire*, volume 2, *The Eighteenth Century.* Edited by P. J. Marshall. Oxford and New York: Oxford University Press, 1998.

Rubdi, Rani and Mario Saraceni, eds. *English in the World: Global Rules, Global Roles.* London: Continuum, 2006.

Rush, Benjamin. "An Account of the Manners of the German Inhabitants of Pennsylvania," *Proceedings and Addresses of the Pennsylvania-German*

Society (1789). In *Historical Aspects of the Immigration Problem*. Edited by Edith Abbott. New York: Arno Press and The New York Times, 1969.

Rushdie, Salman. "Damme, This is the Oriental Scene for You!" *New Yorker* 73.17 (June 23, 1997): 50ff.

Russell, James B. *German Higher Schools: The History, Organization and Methods of Secondary Education in Germany*. New York: Longmans, Green, 1899.

Said, Edward. *Orientalism: Western Conceptions of the Orient*. Harmondsworth: Penguin, 2003.

Sang-Hun, Choe. "Western Schools Sprout in South Korea." *New York Times*, September 2, 2010.

Sartre, Jean-Paul. "Orphée Noir." In *Anthologie de la nouvelle poésie nègre et malgache*. Edited by Léopold Senghor. Paris: Presses Universitaires de France, 1948.

Schlesinger, Arthur, Sr. "The Rise of the City." In *A History of American Life*. Edited by Mark C. Carnes and Arthur Schlesinger, Jr. Revised and Abridged. New York: Scribner, 1996.

Schumpeter. "A Post-Crisis Case Study," *Economist,* July 31, 2010, 55.

Scott, David. "Kipling, the Orient, and Orientals: 'Orientalism' Reoriented?" *Journal of World History* 22.2 (2011): 299–328.

Seif, N. S. "The Teaching of Modern Languages in Belgium, England, Holland, and Germany." *Comparative Education Review* 9 (June 1965): 163–69.

Shell, Marc. "Babel in America; Or, The Politics of Language Diversity on the United States," *Critical Inquiry* 20.1 (Autumn1993): 10–18.

Singapore, Government of. *Census of Population* 2010. *Statistical Release 1: Demographic Characteristics, Education, Language and Religion*.

Skutnabb-Kangas, Tove and Robert Phillipson, "The Global Politics of Language: Markerts, Maintenance, Marginalization, or Murder." In *The Handbook of Language and Globalization*. Edited by Nikolas Coupland. Chichester: Wiley-Blackwell, 2010.

Smith, Jeremy J. "Varieties of Middle English." In *Blackwell Companion to the History of the English Language*. Edited by H. Momma and M. Matto. Oxford: Wiley-Blackwell Publishing, 2008.

Smyth, Alfred P. *King Alfred the Great*. Oxford: Oxford University Press, 1995.

Spencer, Diane. "Europe: Huge Increase in English-Medium Courses." *University World News* 22 (April 2008), www.universityworld news.com.

Spolsky, Bernard and Elana Shohamy, "The Penetration of English as Language of Science and Technology in the Israeli Linguistic Repertoire: A Preliminary Enquiry." in *The Dominance of English as a Language of Science* . Edited by Ulrich Ammon. Berlin: Mouton de Gruyter, 2001,

Stone, Lawrence. "Literacy and Education in England, 1640–1900." *Past and Present* 42 (1969): 101–12.

Svartvik, Jan and Geoff Leech. *English–One Tongue, Many Voices.* New York: Palgrave Macmillan, 2006.

Sungwon, Yim. 'Globalization and the Korean Language." In *Language Policy, Culture, and Identity in Asian Contexts.* Edited by Amy B. M. Tsui and J. W. Tollefson. Mahwah, NJ: Lawrence Erlbaum Associates, 2007.

"Survey of Malaysia," *The Economist,* April 5, 2003, 11.

Sweet, James H. *Recreating Africa: Culture, Kinship, and Religion in the African-Portuguese World, 1441–1770.* Chapel Hill, NC: University of North Carolina, 2003.

Swett, John. *American Public Schools: History and Pedagogics.* New York: American Book Company, 1900.

Takaki, Ronald. "Teaching American History through a Different Mirror." *American Historical Association's Perspectives.* October 1994.

Tharoor, Shashi. "A Bedeviling Question in the Cadence of English." *New York Times,* July 30, 2001.

Thompson, Leonard. *A History of South Africa,* 3rd ed. New Haven, CT: Yale University Press, 2000.

Tishken, Joel E., Toyin Falola, and Akintune Akinyemu, eds. *Sàngó in Africa and the African Disapora.* Bloomington, IN: Indiana University Press, 2009.

Todd, Loreto. "Anglo-Irish Literature." In *OCEL,* 68–69.

Tollefson, James W. and Amy B. M. Tsui, eds. *Medium of Instruction Policies: Which Agenda? Whose Policies?* Mahwah, NJ: Lawrence Erlbaum, 2004.

Toon, Thomas E. "Old English Dialects." In *CHEL,* 1: 422.

Tsuda, Yukio. "Speaking Against the Hegemony of English." In *The Handbook of Critical Intercultural Communication.* Edited by Thomas K. Nakayama and Rona Tamiko Halualani. Chichester: Wiley-Blackwell 2010.

Tsui, Amy B. M. "Language Policy and the Construction of Identity: The Case of Hong Kong." In *Language Policy, Culture, and Identity in Asian Contexts.* Edited by Amy Tsui and J. W. Tollefson. Mahwah, NJ: Lawrence Erlbaum Associates, 2007.

Tsui, Amy B. M. and James W. Tollefson, eds. *Language Policy, Culture, and Identity in Asian Contexts.* Mahwah, NJ: Lawrence Erlbaum Associates, 2007.

Turville-Petre, Thorlac. "Early Middle English (1066–ca. 1350)." In *A Companion to the History of the English Language.* Edited by H. Momma and M. Matto. Oxford: Wiley-Blackwell Publishing, 2008.

United Kingdom, Office of National Statistics, online; BBC News Wales, "Report Says Welsh Language 'Losing 3,000 People a Year'." (accessed February 14, 2012).

United States. Bureau of the Census. American Community Survey, New Mexico, data set, 2005–9.

———. Bureau of the Census. Census data set, 1900.

Varisco, Daniel. *Reading Orientalism: Said and the Unsaid.* Seattle, WA: University of Washington Press, 2007.

Waldman, Amy. "India's Poor Bet Precious Sums on Private Schools." *New York Times,* November 15, 2003.

———. "In India, a Heyday for English (the Language)." *New York Times,* December 14, 2003.

Wamba, Philippe. *Kinship: A Family's Journey in Africa and America.* New York: Penguin Putnam, 2000.

Ward, Kevin. "Christianity, Colonialism and Missions," In *The Cambridge History of Christianity,* volume 9, *World Christianities c.1914–c.2000.* Cambridge: Cambridge University Press, 2000.

Watson, David Robin. *Georges Clemenceau: France: The Peace Conferences of 1919–23 and Their Aftermath.* London: Haus Publishing, 2008.

Webster, Noah. *Dissertations on the English Language: With Notes, Historical and Critical.* Boston, MA: Isiah Thomas, 1789.

Wong, Ruth Y. L. and Joyce E. James. "Malaysia." In *Language Policies and Language Education: The Impact in East Asian Countries in the Next Decade.* Edited by Ho Wah Kam and Ruth Y. L. Wong. Singapore: Times Academic Press, 2000.

"The World This Week: Business," *Economist,* July 30, 2011, 7.

Index

CPSIA information can be obtained at www.ICGtesting.com
Printed in the USA
LVOW10*0512031213

363621LV00004B/33/P